Labour Law in Italy

Labour Law in Italy

Seventh Edition

T. Treu

This book was originally published as a monograph in the International Encyclopaedia of Laws/Labour Law and Industrial Relations.

Founding Editor: Roger Blanpain
General Editor: Frank Hendrickx
Volume Editor: Roger Blanpain

Wolters Kluwer

Published by:
Kluwer Law International B.V.
PO Box 316
2400 AH Alphen aan den Rijn
The Netherlands
E-mail: lrs-sales@wolterskluwer.com
Website: www.wolterskluwer.com/en/solutions/kluwerlawinternational

Sold and distributed by:
Wolters Kluwer Legal & Regulatory U.S.
920 Links Avenue
Landisville, PA 17538
United States of America
E-mail: customer.service@wolterskluwer.com

ISBN 978-94-035-0487-2

e-Book: ISBN 978-94-035-0497-1
web-PDF: ISBN 978-94-035-0507-7

This title is available on www.kluwerlawonline.com

The Author

Professor Dr T. Treu (born 22 August 1939), graduated from the Catholic University of Milan, Italy, with a degree in Law (November 1961). He was Assistant Professor of Labour Law at the same university until 1968 and Harkness fellow at Cornell University's School of Industrial and Labour Relations, United States, and at the University of Chicago Law School, United States, from 1962 to 1964. He was certified as Professor of Labour Law in 1968 and selected, in the same year, to teach Labour Law at the University of Pavia (Law Department), Italy and the Catholic University of Milan (Economics Department). He has been Tenured Professor of Labour Law from 1971 to 1988 at the University of Pavia (Law Department). From 1988 until 2013, he has been a full professor at the Law Department of the Catholic University of Milan. He is now a professor Emeritus at the Catholic University of Milan. He was a visiting scholar at Sophia University in Tokyo in 1974 and visiting professor at the National University of Mogadishu, Somalia, in 1973, as well as at the Law Department of the University of Lovanio (Belgium), in autumn 1985, and at the Law Department of the University of Paris 5 in 1986.

He was the President of the Italian Association for the Study of Industrial Relations from 1980 to 1991. He was member of the Executive Committee of the Italian Association of Labour Law and Social Security from 1978 to 1988, and from 1991 to 1994, he was the President of the same association.

He also served as President of the International Industrial Relations Association from 1995 to 1998, and President of the International Society for Labour and Social Security Law from 2015 to September 2018.

He was member of the Scientific Committees of the *Journal of Labour Law*, of the New Annotated Civil Laws and of the *Journal of Labour Law and Industrial Relations*. Since 1975, he has been the member of the Bar. He has served as consultant for the CISL labour union, as well as for the International Labour Office of Geneva, regarding labour law, and the Commission of the European Communities, General Directorate.

From July 1990 to July 1992, he was member of the National Guarantee Commission on Strikes affecting Essential Services. From 1989 to 1994 he was President of STOA', a study institute for business management and operations. From 1992 to 1993, he was an outside councilman appointed to Milan's 'civic' municipal council, with responsibility for institutional affairs, education, labour economics and social concerns.

In 1993 he served as Director of ARAN, the Agency for the representation in negotiations of the Public Administration, sponsored by the Italian Prime Minister's Office – Department of Public Services. From January 1995 to October 1998, he was the Minister of Labour and Social Security, and from October 1998 to December 1999 Minister of Transport in the Italian government.

In 2001 he was elected to the Italian Senate. From 2006 to 2008, he was President of the Senate Committee on employment and welfare. From 2008 to March 2013, he was vice president of the same committee, and from 2013 to 2015 a member of National Council for Economy and Labour (CNEL). Since May 2017, he has been the President of CNEL.

He is the author of numerous essays and books on labour law, union law and industrial relations, both Italian and comparative.

Note of the Author

This edition of the Encyclopaedia monograph Italy is updated on 31 December 2022.

This volume has undergone quite a few a major revisions, following the changes in Italian legislation and collective bargaining and systems of replacement.

the Author

Table of Contents

the Author

Table of Contents

List of Abbreviations

ARAN	Agenzia per la rappresentanza Negoziale delle Pubbliche Amministrazioni
CGIL	General Confederation of Italian Workers
CISL	Italian Confederation of Workers' Unions
CNEL	National Council for Economy and Labour
CISNAL	Confederazione Italiana Sindacati Nazionali Lavoratori
ECJ	European Court of Justice
ILO	International Labour Organisation
INAIL	National Institute for Work Accidents Insurance
INAM	National Institution Health Insurance
INPS	National Institution Social Providence
INPDAP	Istituto Nazionale Previdenza Dipendenti Amministrazione Pubblica
ISTAT	The Italian National Institute of Statistics
NGEU	Next Generation EU
UGl	Unione Generale del Lavoro
UIL	Union of Italian Workers

List of Abbreviations

General Introduction

Chapter 1. General Features

§1. Geography and Population

1. Italy is a peninsula covering an area of 301,277 sq. km. In 2022 the country had a resident population of 59.983.122 million (28.747.417 males, 30.235.705 females). The population has been stable in the past decade due to the increased number of immigrants (in 2022 the official number of immigrants having a residence permit is 356,540; the total number of foreigners regularly present in Italy is around 5.2 million). Recently the Italian population has begun to decline and this trend, unless reversed, will have seriously negative consequences on the economic and social future of the country. Density is about 190 inhabitants per square kilometre.

The distribution by age group (2022) is as follows and reflects a considerable ageing of the Italian population:

Age	Total	%
0–14	7.636.545	12.7%
15–64	37.658.137	63.5%
Over65	13.941.531	23.8%

Life expectancy at birth has greatly increased in the recent decades: now it is among the highest in Europe: 80.5 males, 84.8 females (2022).

The vast majority of people speak Italian (or one of its dialects); a German-speaking population is concentrated along the Austrian borders and small French-speaking groups are to be found in the Aosta Valley. The population is relatively homogeneous from an ethnic point of view. Traditionally there have been no racial problems, but recent immigration from Eastern European and African countries is creating new social and ethnic tensions. The population officially is Catholic, with very small religious minorities.

§2. Political System

2. Italy became a centralised unitary state in 1861. It was a kingdom until 2 June 1946, when it became a parliamentary republic as a result of a referendum. The basic features of the Italian political system are set out in the Constitution, promulgated on 27 December 1947. Parliament is entrusted with legislative powers and with control over the main activities and orientation of the government. It is composed of two chambers enjoying the same powers, elected by universal suffrage for five years. The House of Representatives (Deputies) until 2021 had 630 members, the Senate had 315 members elected on a regional basis (+5 nominated for life by the President of the Republic and former Presidents). A recent Act effective after the elections of 2022 has greatly reduced the number of MPs: the Deputies to 400 and the Senators to 200. The voting age is 18 for the House and 25 for the Senate; the age of eligibility is 25 for the former, 40 for the latter.

3. The President of the Republic is elected by a joint sitting of both Houses, supplemented by three delegates for each region, and remains in office for seven years. The executive is composed of a variable number of ministers, and of the President of the Council of Ministers, appointed by the President of the Republic after consultation with the political parties; it is responsible to Parliament.

4. The supreme guarantee of the Constitution of the Republic rests with the Constitutional Court, composed of fifteen judges (five appointed by Parliament, five by the highest jurisdictional authorities, five by the President of the Republic), all remaining in office for nine years. The Court has the power to rule on the constitutionality of Acts passed by the legislature; to judge on the conflicts of competence between the various powers of the state, between the state and the regions, and between the regions; to judge on certain accusations made by Parliament against the President of the Republic or against ministers.

5. The Constitution recognises a number of local entities provided with a defined area of autonomy and which are involved in the administration and government of the country: the communes or municipalities, the provinces (103), the regions (20). These local entities are headed by councils or assemblies elected by universal suffrage and by executive committees (*giunte*) elected by the assemblies and headed by a President or Mayor (in the case of the municipalities). In particular, the regions have important administrative and legislative powers, some of which are directly or indirectly relevant to labour matters, namely professional training and education, regulations in the field of small-size industry and craftsmanship, agriculture, territorial planning and ecology. The administrative functioning of local government has been greatly increased (Act 59/1997) in response to the need for autonomy coming from the regions, particularly those that are more active. Act 3/2001, a constitutional law, has reinforced this trend, and transferred to the regions many legislative competences in labour market matters.

6. The political scene has been traditionally fragmented, with a wide range of political parties contending for the electorate's favours. However, for a long time the politics of the country has been determined by the Christian Democrat Party, in power alone or in coalition with smaller parties for the whole post-war period; opposition has been represented since 1948 mostly by the Communist Party (the strongest communist party in the Western world) and in the 1980s with the socialist party playing a major role. Lately Italian political life has been deeply transformed by major events: the collapse of the communist regimes (after the fall of the Berlin wall in 1989), the transformation of the Communist Party into a political group similar to the social democratic parties of the Western tradition and a wave of very serious cases of corruption, severely prosecuted by the judiciary, which has led to the practical disappearance of the two most important governing parties: the Christian Democrats and the Socialists.

7. After this event Italy has experienced a sequence of different coalition governments, some composed of centre-left parties – like the Cabinet led by Prodi and D'Alema from 1996 to 1999 – and again in 2006–2007; others composed of centre right parties, in particular with Berlusconi premier (2001–2011). The election of 2013 confirmed the political instability of Italy. Since none of the parties obtained a clear majority in Parliament the subsequent government, led by Enrico Letta, was supported by a coalition of the major parties (Partito Democratico, Popolo delle Libertà, UDC, Scelta Civica) of uncertain cohesion. In fact this government was short lived and was substituted by an executive led by Matteo Renzi in March 2014, which lasted until December 2016 and again was substituted by a Cabinet led by Paolo Gentiloni.

The election of 2018 marked another revolution of the political scenario with land slide success of two parties: the 'League' (evolution of Northern League) and the 'Five stars' movement. The two parties have some common populist and Eurosceptic positions but also major political differences. Their coalition government led by Giuseppe Conte lasted until August 2019 when he resigned following a breakdown of the coalition. A new cabinet was formed, supported by a coalition between the five stars and the Democratic Party, still led by Giuseppe Conte which lasted from September 2019 to February 2021. The emergency of the COVID-19 pandemic brought to the formation of a government of national unity led by Mario Draghi, former President of the ECB, but this unity broke down abruptly in October 2022. New elections were called which again presented a different political scenario. A centre right coalition formed a new government led by Giorgia Meloni (Brothers of Italy) which took office on 22 October 2022.

Table 1 Election Results in 2022

Chamber of Deputies Political Parties	*Votes*	*%*
Unione Popolare	402.987	1.4%
Alleanza Sinistra Italiana/Verdi	1.018.669	3.6%
Partito Democratico	5.356.180	19.1%
+Europa	793.961	2.8%

Chamber of Deputies Political Parties	*Votes*	*%*
Impegno Civico	169.165	0.6%
SVT – PATT	117.010	0.4%
Movimento 5 Stelle	4.333.972	15.4%
Azione/Italia Viva	2.186.747	7.8%
Fratelli d'Italia	7.302.517	26.0%
LEGA	2.464.005	8.8%
Forza Italia	2.278.217	8,1%
Altre Liste	874.371	3.1
Totale	28.087.885	100

Table 2 Election Results in 2022

Senate Political Parties	*Votes*	*%*
Alleanza Sinistra Italiana/Verdi	972.316	3,5%
Partito Democratico	5.226.732	18,9%
+Europa	808.676	2,9%
Movimento 5 Stelle	4.285.894	15,5%
Azione/Italia Viva/Calenda	2.131.310	9%
Fratelli d'Italia	7.167.136	26%
LEGA	2.439.200	8,8%
Forza Italia	2.279.802	8,2%
Altre Liste	917.422	3,9%

§3. The Economy

8. The key sector of the economy is still industry, though declining: it contributes to the total gross national product and employees 4,203 million people (2018). The major industries are textiles, clothing, steel, automobile, mechanical and chemicals and construction.

The working population in agriculture has been steadily declining in the post-war period: it was 42.1% of the total in 1951 and is now 0.51 million people. A corresponding rapid shift of employment has taken place towards service industries (other activities): they employ 12,613 million people in the private sector, 3,200 in the public sector, and now accounts for 67.3% of the total working population.

Subordinate workers, according to the last official The Italian National Institute of Statistics (ISTAT 2022) survey, are 18,244 million; independent workers and assistants are 4.987.000. Employment in the public sector has been increasing since the 1970s and 1980s. Recently the trend has been reversed. Publicly controlled enterprises have played a major role, especially in the post-war reconstruction and development of some key sectors of industry (steel, basic chemicals, ship building).

The financial crisis of the state, and the poor performance of the public sector in general, has also spurred in Italy a trend toward privatisation beginning in the early 1990s. This trend has been visible in various changes: the introduction of common labour law rules and of collective bargaining in the public sector (Act 29/1993), a slight decline in its size, and the commercialisation of some entities once belonging to the public sector (ports, postal services and railroads). The public sector in the strict sense is now reduced to 3.2 million people (2018). The state presence in publicly controlled enterprises has been reduced often to a minority position, i.e., in some large banks and insurance companies. The major state enterprises are now privatised while the largest industrial holding, IRI, has been dismantled. The state still keeps a majority position only in the major electrical enterprise ENEL and in ENI.

9. The structure of the Italian economy is rather fragmented, i.e., largely based on small- and medium-size enterprises. In the last few decades there has been a trend on the part of employers to decentralise production from larger to smaller enterprises and to home work, among other reasons, to gain a greater flexibility in manpower employment and to escape the control of the unions. Recent data (2020 ISTAT) are as follows:

(1) Pnl 0 < 50 – 4.226.623.
(2) Pnl X > 250 – 4.055.000.
(3) Pnl 50 < α < 250 – 22.601.000.

The large prevalence of small and smallest enterprises is considered by the Bank of Italy a major element of weakness and dualism of the Italian economy: about 25,000 enterprises (in industry and market services) with more than fifty employees produce almost half of the value added and employ over 5 million people; 4.3 millions of small enterprises employ 6 million employees, 5 million of self-employed, 86% of small enterprises (below ten employees), belong to one family.

10. The official rate of employment in Italy is rather low. It has been slowly growing after 1996. 51.3% in 1996; 57.5 in 2003; 57.7 in 2005; 58.7 in 2008; in 2015 the rate of employment was reduced to 56.3%. Lately the rate has recovered and is 60.5% (October 2022). But the actual amount of hours of work is still lower due to the higher percentage of part-time (often non-voluntary). The real percentage of employment is much higher, taking into account irregular workers.

The population employed officially amounted in 1989 to 23.9 million, in 2003 to 24.31 million; it decreased to 22,443 in 2015. In 2022 (October) it amounts to 23.231 million (18,244, subordinate employees, 4.987 independent). Unemployed in 1996 were officially 2.6 million (11.2%); in 2003 2 million (8.4%). Unemployment has been growing, during the crisis, to 12.9% in 2014, but decreased to 7.8% in October 2022. Young people between the ages of 15 and 29 are most affected: according to official analysis (ISTAT 2022), it is 23.9% of the labour force.

A significant difference remains in the employment of men and women (October 2022): rate of employment Males 69.5%, Females 51.4%; rate of inactivity Males 25.3%, Females 43.3%.

11. The distribution in various areas of the country of unemployment and productive activity is still uneven, reflecting another (geographical) dualism of the Italian economy. The major difference is between the highly industrialised area of the north and the historically underdeveloped south. In the centre-northern areas the rate of employment is 68.2% and in the south the rates are 46.7%. (Source: ISTAT, 2022).

Chapter 2. Definitions and Notions

12. The most comprehensive notion is labour law. In a broad sense it comprises individual labour law or labour law in a strict sense, trade union law (*diritto sindacale*) and social security law.

§1. Individual Labour Law

13. Individual labour law includes the body of rules, whether of legislative or collective origin, which govern the individual relationship between (private) employers and employees who carry out their work in a subordinate position: formation of the individual labour contract, rights and duties of the parties, suspension and termination of employment, etc. (as resulting from Part I of this monograph). It is the core of labour law in a broader sense, and is traditionally very well developed and studied in Italy.

§2. Trade Union Law (*Diritto Sindacale*)

14. Trade union law (the terms 'collective labour law' and 'law of industrial relations' are not generally used in Italy) comprises the body of rules fixed by the state or by the social partners themselves, which regulate the organisation and activities of trade unions' and employers' associations, the relationships between these organisations, internally with their members, with the workers and with the state. The name is taken from the trade unions, which are the vital agents of collective labour relations, but the law also considers other activities of the workers or organisations different from the trade unions (e.g., strike action, *see* below).

15. The social importance of trade union law is widely recognised, but now often with a critical approach. As we shall see, its nature and fundamental principles sharply differ from those of individual labour law and from the Italian legal tradition in general.

16. Industrial relations is a more uncertain notion: indeed, in Italy it has become a subject of academic interest only in the last twenty years. Generally, the scope of the subject is determined empirically: it basically coincides with the object of union law, as indicated above. Industrial relations are studied with an interdisciplinary approach.

§3. Social Insurance and Social Security Law

17. Social insurance and social security law include legislation regulating the compulsory social insurance and social security system (old age and invalidity pensions, unemployment, health, work accidents and occupational diseases, family allowances). This legislation has been traditionally concerned with protecting subordinate workers against some basic risks or needs through a compulsory insurance mechanism, financed by contributions paid by employees and employers (paid by the latter on behalf of the former), and administered by various public bodies. The most important are the Istituto Nazionale Assicurazione Infortuni sul Lavoro (INAIL) for work accidents and occupational diseases; National Institution Social Providence (INPS) for pensions, unemployment, family allowances, of the private sector; National Institution Health Insurance (INAM) for health insurance replaced in 1978 by the National Health Service (Servizio Sanitario Nazionale). Istituto Nazionale Previdenza Dipendenti Amministrazione Pubblica (INPDAP) was created in 1995 to administer pensions in the public service. The two major institutes INPS – INPDAP (and other smaller) have been merged by Act 214/2011. Significant changes have taken place in the legislation concerning pensions. The scope of protection has been extended to categories of workers who are not in a position of subordination (as this will be defined later on): farmers, land tenants, small entrepreneurs, craftsmen, members of work cooperatives, and lately economically dependent or para-subordinate workers, etc. State intervention is more and more needed to finance the mounting costs of the benefits to be paid. But the trend to move from an insurance system paid for by workers and employers, who are the beneficiaries, to a social security system extended to all citizens and paid out of the state budget is also being questioned because of the financial crisis of the state. A major reform of the pension system approved in August 1995 (Act 335/1995) points in this direction, by linking pensions more closely to the contributions paid by the employers and the employees during working life: while the contributions remain fixed, the actual pension will depend on the contributions, the age of retirement and life expectancy and the growth of the GNP. Consequently it is no longer fully secure. The system has been repeatedly revised by subsequent legislation, which has raised progressively the retirement age up to 67 years according to Act 124/ 2012 but with the some major exceptions (e.g., heavy works).

Contrary to the previous trends, Act 26/2019 has reduced the age of retirement. According to this Act which is valid for a period of three years (up to 2021), the possibility to retire is recognised to all those who have a minimum of thirty-eight years of contributions combined with a minimum age of 62 (so-called Quota 100). The budget law, Act no. 197/2022 of 29 December 2022, has raised again the age by setting this quota at level 103.

§4. The Scope of Labour Law

18. The legislation and collective regulations dealing with the settlement of labour grievances fall in part within individual labour law (individual grievances settlement), in part within trade union law (collective grievances and industrial disputes) and in part within civil procedure law. Since the distinction is not always easy, this branch of labour law will be treated separately.

19. Labour law – broadly defined – is basically concerned with work done in a position of subordination, in the sense that only subordinate employees enjoy its full protection. Some of its rules have been, however, extended over time to different categories of non-subordinate workers, who are considered by the legislator to be in a position similar to subordination and deserving of equal protection (sometimes the notion of economic subordination is used as opposed to legal or technical subordination). The process of widening the field of protection is most advanced in social security, but it also concerns some rules of individual labour law (e.g., most of these rules apply to métayers and other agricultural workers who have an associate labour relationship and to commercial agents) and the legislation concerning the settlement of labour disputes. Act No. 533 of 1973 has been declared applicable to commercial agents and to all contractual relations which imply a continuous performance of work, mainly of a personal character, although not in a position of subordination (mainly for these workers, the concept, indeed approximate, of 'para-subordination' or economic dependence has been adopted). The outright extension of labour law to these contracts has been criticised because it imposes excessive rigidity and burdens on these types of activities which need the flexibility of regulation. The possibility of diversifying the scope and content of protective legislation according to the type of work relation has been considered in recent years (for details *see* below).

20. Labour law is concerned only with the private sector and is traditionally well distinguished from the law on public employment. The latter was considered part of administrative law and applied by administrative tribunals, not by ordinary civil courts (as labour law). This traditional demarcation has become, however, less clear. On the one hand publicly owned or controlled enterprises fall under labour legislation and private collective bargaining. On the other hand there has been a growing interchange between the fundamental principles of private labour law and the law of public employment. Act No. 29 of 1993 followed by Act No. 59 of 1997, by Decree 165/2000 and Act 150/2009, have made the former fully applicable to the public service, aiming at the 'privatisation' of the employment relationship in public administration (not of public administration itself) as a way to increase its efficiency; moreover, collective bargaining and trade union rights have been extended to public employees. But quite a few regulations still apply only to public employees and distinguish their contracts from private employment.

Innovations in many aspects of the organisation of public administrations and in the regulations of public employment have been introduced by Act 124/2015 and lately by a series of provisions finalised to improve the efficiency of public administrations and its capacity to implement the various projects of the National Recovery Plan: e.g., simplified procedures for hiring public employees, for promoting labour mobility, increased investments in continuous professional training of the employees (*see* in particular Act. 150/2022).

§5. Legal Nature of Labour Law

21. Labour law is regarded as having in general an 'imperative' nature (of public order) for the main reason that it is aimed at protecting the worker as the weaker part of the labour relationship. This nature implies that private agreements deviating from the law are in principle absolutely null and void: the nullity can be invoked by any of the parties concerned and by the courts ex officio. The declared nullity is ex tunc (retroactive). In many cases, private clauses are automatically substituted by legal terms and conditions of work, safeguarding the validity of the labour relation. Labour regulations in general set minimum standards of treatment which can therefore be improved by private agreement. Another consequence of this imperative nature is that the rights deriving from imperative norms cannot be validly waived or disposed of by individual workers (Article 2113 of the Civil Code, *see* below paragraph 316).

22. In principle, imperative provisions of labour law cannot be modified for the worse (*in pejus*) by collective agreements either. But the relationship between the law and collective bargaining is much more complex than that with individual agreements and cannot be judged by the same rigid standards. The rationale for this legal protection arising from the weakness of the individual worker vis-à-vis the employer cannot be transferred to the field of collective activities whose essential function is to overcome it. That is why the rule of invalidity laid down by Article 2113 of the Civil Code does not apply to waivers or compromises reached between, or with the assistance of, the collective partners. And the comparison between collective agreements and legal regulations to judge what is more 'favourable' to the worker may be very subtle and cannot be made in a mechanical and static way without taking into account the whole context of collective relations, its dynamics and putting possible results in perspective.

Economic difficulties and inflation have in the past induced the legislature to adopt norms setting maximum standards, in particular limits to the wage increases that can be bargained for by social parties (*see* Part II, paragraphs 407, 415, 417, 461). On the other hand, in some areas of the law (labour market) statutory regulations have been made more 'flexible' by allowing collective agreements to adapt and modify them, even for the 'worse'.

23. Many labour law regulations protecting the worker are also sanctioned penally. Being of public order means that most labour legislation also applies to foreigners working in Italy. Other more specific definitions and notions will be examined in the course of the monograph dealing with the relevant subject matter.

Chapter 3. The Historical Background

24. The development of Italian labour law and the attitudes of the public authorities towards industrial relations have been changing with the process of time, corresponding to the different phases of the economic and political history of the country and to general changes in the relations between the social classes. It is impossible to explore this historical development in any depth: we will limit ourselves here and in the course of the monograph to giving only that information about the nature of the history of Italian labour law and industrial relations which is strictly necessary in order to appreciate the major trends which have taken place up to the present day.

§1. The Origins: Liberalism and Repression

25. In Italy, as in most industrial countries, the original attitude of the law and of public authorities towards labour was inspired by the ideologies of liberalism and of individualism. This meant that absolute freedom of competition and of contract was the basic principle governing labour relations. The individual labour relation was governed by the general rules of the law of contract, based on the assumption of the equality of the parties. State intervention in labour matters, in principle, was non-existent. Coalitions and collective action were prohibited as an illegal restraint of the freedom of labour, which could be penalised.

§2. Tolerance and Protection: 1889–1922

26. A more tolerant attitude towards collective action developed in the last part of the nineteenth century, beginning with the new penal code of 1889, which abolished the general criminal prohibition of strikes and lock-outs (industrial conflict still remained punishable in specific cases and illegal under civil law as a contractual violation).

27. The first two decades of the twentieth century were a period of great social and economic change: the launching of Italian industrialisation, the consequent formation of great concentrations of industrial workers, the spread of unionism, the strengthening of the socialist movement in such a way as to exert growing pressure on the ruling class. All these changes deeply affected the development of labour law. The major expression of state interventionism in labour matters was the enactment of a wide range of legislation protecting the individual worker, as the weak party of the labour contract, from the 'negative' consequences of the freedom of contract, still retained as a major tenet of the social and legal system. This legislation, largely advocated by the trade unions and by the labour movement, had a long-lasting influence in shaping the major aspects of the individual labour relationship and remained, up to recent times, the core of the Italian labour law system.

28. Contrary to the considerable development of individual protective legislation, no fundamental change was introduced in collective labour law. Industrial conflict continued to be regulated by the courts' decisions and directly by the executive through the exercise of its police powers.

29. Collective agreements developed outside any precise legal framework. Trade unions also grew without any legal recognition, although they were increasingly called upon to collaborate de facto with the public authorities in the shaping of social measures and coopted into some public bodies with the task of their administration. This informality and low institutionalisation of collective labour relations, which is typical of the Italian system, reflected the unstable balance of our social structure and the low level of consensus on its features. On the one hand, labour was still too weak and divided (the major division being between socialist and communist unionism on the other hand and Catholic unionism on the other) to achieve a more extended and formal recognition of its right to participate collectively in the handling of economic and social matters.

§3. The Fascist Period

30. The major characteristics of the fascist regime, as we shall see further in Part II, were the total suppression of trade union freedom and the creation of a system of industrial relations completely controlled by the state, which was highly centralised and bureaucratic. In keeping with the regime's interventionist policy, the fascist legislator completed the system of widespread protective labour legislation founded by conservative reformism at the beginning of the century. Labour matters ended up being regulated by a very rigid set of rules guaranteeing the workers minimum standards of assistance, but which were largely static, prohibiting any real bargaining and keeping the actual levels of labour treatment substantially low. Collective wages were frozen for long periods and even reduced to correspond to the deflationary policy of the fascist government.

§4. The Reconstruction of Free Unionism in Post-War Italy and the 1950s

31. After the fall of the fascist regime, in the spirit of the partisans' resistance and due to post-war enthusiasm, free unionism was rapidly rebuilt and for the first time in Italian history, it was united and acquired unprecedented strength. The membership of the united General Confederation of Italian Workers (CGIL), although a very loose membership, reached a peak of nearly 6 million workers.

32. The three major parties (the Christian Democrats, the Communists and the Socialists who formed a coalition government until 1947), all pledged to recognise organised labour not only basic collective rights (freedom to organise and to bargain, right to strike) but also its major role in the economic and social life of the country. These principles were solemnly declared, even though they meant subtle and difficult compromises, in the Italian Constitution. For the first time, the state was forced to abandon the traditional attitudes of repression of industrial conflict and/or of non-intervention in industrial relations and to support collective bargaining and the concerted action of the workers as the basic means of guaranteeing their effective participation in the political, economic and social life of the country.

33. But the unity of organised labour was to last a very short time due to growing political tension and then to the open struggle between the three major parties, each one of which closely controlled its component within the united CGIL. In 1948 the CGIL split into three with the separation of the Catholic Christian democratic and the social democratic components, which shortly afterwards formed the two other major confederations still representing Italian workers. The former created the Italian Confederation of Workers' Unions (CISL), the latter the Union of Italian Workers (UIL). The breaking up of this political and labour unity deeply influenced the evolution of Italian industrial relations and labour law. The constitutional model remained frozen for over two decades.

34. The 1950s were characterised by an industrial relations system largely 'blocked' by political tension: centralised and static collective bargaining, weak and divided trade unions, strictly dependent on the major political parties, public control and repression of industrial conflict (using the articles of the fascist criminal code punishing concerted action). Traditional protective labour legislation still played a major role in guaranteeing minimum standards of treatment to workers.

§5. The 1960s and 1970s

35. The 1960s – as we shall see – showed important signs of change: a loosening of political tensions, an initial unity of action between the three major confederations and greater autonomy vis-à-vis the political parties, the first decentralisation of bargaining and a more liberal attitude of the state as regards industrial conflict. Collective labour relations still developed independently of any legal intervention and with a largely shared trust in the capacity of the social parties to govern the industrial relations systems and its relationship with the political system by general consent and to contribute by bargaining to the economic planning of the country. This is the period in which Italy comes close to a pluralist, collective laissez-faire system of industrial relations.

36. The crisis of this model at the end of the 1960s necessitated more decisive intervention in industrial relations by the state and by the legislator – chiefly the Workers' Statute of 1970 – with the objective of promoting the unions as bargaining agents from the enterprise level upwards and as political agents, and with the aim of institutionalising their position indirectly. We shall see later on in detail the characteristics of the system, which is largely different from the constitutional model, and based on a rather complex balance of promotion and institutionalisation of industrial relations. It is sufficient to say here that this balance has proved to be unstable and has faced serious difficulties in meeting the needs of the economic and political crisis of the late 1970s. Economic crisis and high inflation have pushed for greater institutionalisation and for public control of the activity of the social parties. The public authorities and the major political parties have induced them to cooperate and to behave consistently with the broader social and political plans considered necessary for overcoming the impact of the crisis on the economic and social welfare of the country. Experiments of social concertation characterised the period 1977–1984.

§6. The 1980s and 1990s

37. International competition and new technologies have put increasing pressure on traditional models of industrial relations.

Decentralisation and flexibility are keywords of these decades. Indeed they have influenced many traits of the Italian system, though not to the point of introducing the deregulation, individualisation and decline of industrial relations anticipated by some observers. Both flexibility and decentralisation have been basically controlled by the social parties through bargaining and by the state, whose role has become more selective and indirect but not irrelevant. Collective bargaining, too, has become more flexible, being supplemented by some participation practices and, for some employers, by individual bargaining. The 1990s have confirmed that the trends towards deregulation and decentralisation of industrial relations are far from absolute. The period of economic crisis and inflation has been met with renewed experiments of social concertation in 1992 and 1993, with relatively positive results (in fact they were repeated in 1995–1996, and in 1998).

Public powers and the legislators have also shown a considerable activism in labour relations: *see* Act 146/1990 and Act 83/2000 on strikes in essential services, Act 29/1993, Act 59/1997, Decree 165/2000 on the privatisation of the public service, Act 335/1995 Act 449/1997, Act 453/2005 on the reform of the pension system, Act 196/1997 on employment promotion and labour market regulation.

§7. From 2000 to Present: The Impact of Economic Crisis on Labour Law

38. In recent years the labour relations system has presented contradictory traits rather than a clear tendency. This is true in many developed countries but is particularly noticeable in Italy due to both external and internal factors. On the one hand, traditional protections from competitive pressures have been dropped, with a negative impact on the Italian economy and labour market. On the other hand, some traits of labour relations have reduced their resistance to external shocks, namely: the scarce autonomy from the political system whose instability increases the tensions within the labour movement, the dualism of the Italian labour market and the scant cohesion of a society still divided by ideological conflict, the uncertain capacity of self-regulation of the social parties not consistently supported by public legal intervention.

Contradictory trends are visible in key areas of labour law and industrial relations. Social concertation has been practised at intervals and with different approaches according to the government in power. The centre-left coalition (2006–2008) has confirmed the traditional approach, and promoted the agreement of 2007 signed by the united front of Union's and employer's associations. The centre-right government has been inclined to reach an agreement with the unions regardless of their unity and in fact the agreements of 2002 and 2009 have been signed only with some unions, CISL, UIL, Unione Generale del Lavoro (UGL), without the consent of CGIL (*see* below paragraph 417). The approach to flexibility has also been variable: Act 30/2003, while not adopting an outright deregulation of the labour market, has favoured the adoption of flexible labour contracts of different kinds. This trend was (partially) resisted in the short period of centre-left government (2006–2007) but has been confirmed by subsequent legislation: particularly Act 92/2012, Act 76/2013 modified by Act 99/2013 and Act 183/2014 implemented in 2015 by a series of decrees (so-called Jobs Act). These measures have introduced important reforms in the functioning of the labour market in two major directions inspired by the European guidelines on 'flexicurity':

(a) By simplifying and making more flexible the access to employment, the termination and the implementation of the employment contracts.
(b) By reinforcing the protections of employees in case of enterprise crisis and unemployment, reorganizing the placement services and the system of active labour policies.

The increasing fragmentation of the labour market and the individualisation of employment practices and working life have reduced the room for traditional collective bargaining. The bargaining structure has been affected by divergent pressures. The need to resist the economic crisis would favour, as in the past, the trend toward centralisation, but centrifugal pressures and the diversification of the markets require more room for decentralised bargaining (*see* below paragraph 409). In spite of recent interventions of public powers, the Italian labour relations system remains weakly regulated, which accounts for a persistent state of instability.

The economic crises of 2008 and the following of 2020–21 due to the COVID-19 have affected the basic economic and social conditions of all industrialised countries. But even beyond the crisis, major structural factors, in particular, the globalisation of markets and the new pervasive in particular digital technologies, are posing unprecedented challenges to the traditional regulation of employment and labour relations.

The pressure has been growing on the national systems of labour law and industrial relations to adapt in different ways: i.e., to change some traits of their legal and contractual regulations in order to give room to the new needs for flexibility and more in depth to face the new aspect of the digital economy and its impact on the conditions of work (*see* below).

The future prospects are more uncertain than ever, also because the ultimate impact of the global competition is unclear. The pandemic crisis of 2020 has reduced the impetus of global trade showing the fragility of the global supply chains and causing a partial 'regionalisation' of production and commerce. The social parties are directly involved, and their reaction will be decisive if the voluntaristic system of industrial relations is to survive. The public powers, national and supranational, are equally challenged. The economic crisis of 2008 and the impact of the COVID-19 pandemic have confirmed – if it was necessary – that their intervention is necessary to promote a balanced functioning of the markets, particularly of labour markets and to support the initiatives of the parties conducive to economic growth and social welfare.

Chapter 4. Government Institutions and Their Functions

39. The shaping and administration of labour law and of industrial relations are deeply influenced by the public authorities and by the political system as a whole. A series of public institutions – as we shall see – intervenes with a major role in crucial aspects of industrial relations such as labour mobility, distribution of employment opportunities, professional education and training, industrial planning and reorganisation. But industrial relations are indirectly determined by the broader policies of the central and regional government as regards basic social reforms and consumption, economic planning, the use of public expenditure, etc. This wide range of public interventions cannot be explored here in any depth. Our interest will be limited to the government institutions which have direct competence in labour matters.

§1. The National Council for Economy and Labour

40. This is a special constitutional organ regulated by Article 99 of the Constitution and by various Acts (the first was Act No. 33 of 1957, revised by Act No. 936 of 30 December 1986) entrusted by Parliament with consultative functions, with the power to submit Bills to the Chambers and to contribute to the shaping of economic and social legislation. The council is composed of 10 experts and of 54 representatives of the 'productive categories' and the so-called third sector appointed by the government according to proposals made by the most representative organisations. The work of the council has been uneven in the various periods of time, often unsatisfactory also because the social partners have chosen other, more direct and informal ways of contributing to economic and social legislation and decisions. Proposals to abrogate the council have been reiterated. But the constituent organisations, labour unions, employer's associations and the organisations of the third sector have reasserted the importance of the council and have been committed to relaunching its functions.

§2. The Department of Labour and Social Insurance (Since 2001 Department of Labour and Welfare)

41. The department has traditionally carried the main responsibility for administering labour law and industrial relations (mostly mediation and conciliation). Various commissions operate within it with the participation of representatives of the most representative trade unions and employers' associations and have specific tasks: prevention of work accidents and promotion of hygiene, public employment proceedings, cooperatives, industrial statistics, social security contributions, etc. The decentralisation process decided by Act 59/1997 and Decree 469/1997 has transferred most administrative functions in labour market matters and vocational training to the regions and other local entities (provinces in particular). The 'federalist' reform of the Constitution introduced by Act 3/2001 has reinforced this decentralisation and also transferred to the region's legislative powers in the same matters. The Labour Department, which was merged with the Department of Welfare in 2001, retains the tasks of directing labour policies, controlling their implementation and shaping labour legislation, and has a role in mediation and conciliation in major collective disputes and in individual disputes of rights (*see* below paragraph 280).

§3. The Offices of Labour and the Centres for Employment

42. The Department of Labour has been traditionally organised at a regional and provincial level in local offices, with subsections traditionally at a municipal level and after 1987 (Act 86) at the level of *circoscrizione* (a middle level between province and municipality). These offices have been responsible for collecting statistics, for the protection of migrant workers, for labour grievances, conciliation and mediation, and for the public service of manpower employment. Responsibility for the implementation of the two latter tasks rests not only on the officers of the service but also on decentralised tripartite commissions. Now these tasks have been greatly reduced, basically to the conciliation of labour disputes, by Act 59/1997 and Decree 469/1997 because most administrative functions concerning the labour market have been transferred to local entities by Act 30/2003 and Decree 276/2003. The organisation of these functions has been revised by Decree 150/2015 (implementing Act 183/2014). Some recent European provisions have been approved linked to the implementation of the National recovery plan aimed at reorganising the central administration of the ministry of employment and at strengthening both active labour policies and continuous professional training (*see* below).

§4. The Labour Inspectorate

43. The labour inspectorate, the other main branch of the Department of Labour, is composed of a central office, of peripheral branches at a regional, provincial and inter-provincial level, and of a medical inspectorate. Following a general reorganisation of the Department all inspection activities have been rationalised with the aim of reducing overlapping and discrepancies in intervention. The coordination of these activities is entrusted to a national directorate operating within the Department, and at local levels to the regional and provincial directions of employment (Article 8, Act 30/2003 and Decree 110/2004).

The inspectorate is responsible for the general surveillance of the application of labour legislation, social security and generally binding collective agreements. Labour inspectors are judicial police officers, with the power to enter and inspect work premises freely; they cannot, however, enter an employer's domicile without the prior permission of a magistrate's court. Their reports are public acts, provided with the relevant probatory value. When labour inspectors ascertain the violation of protective laws, they may, at their discretion, instead of denouncing the violation, issue an 'intimidation' to the employer to comply with the law fixing the time thereof. Finally, in many cases where the law only prescribes in general terms the standards to be complied with, especially in the field of health and work safety, labour inspectors have the power to specify these standards, by an appropriate 'order', which may be opposed before the superior authorities (*see* now Decree 124/2004).

Decree 149/2015 has reorganised the labour Inspectorate and attributed to it also the inspection activities carried out by the inspectorate of INPS and INAIL. The administration of social security is entrusted to specialised public bodies, according to the aim of insurance and social protection (*see* above paragraph 22).

Chapter 5. Sources of Labour Law

§1. The Constitution

44. The first in the hierarchy of sources, common to other branches of law, is the Constitution, which has been in force since 1 January 1948, and which contains some basic provisions relating specifically to labour matters, both individual and collective: namely Article 3 (equality), Article 4 (right and duty to work), Article 35 (protection of work), Article 36 (right to equitable remuneration, annual vacations and weekly rest), Article 37 (women and young workers), Article 38 (social security and assistance), Article 39 (trade union freedom and collective bargaining), Article 40 (right to strike), Article 46 (workers' participation in the enterprise). The constitutionality of Acts passed by the legislature is decided by the Constitutional Court.

§2. Ordinary Legislation

45. Of major importance are Acts of Parliament and decrees having the force of ordinary legislation: decrees enacted by the government following general principles stated by Parliament (Article 76 of the Constitution) and decree laws enacted by the government in case of necessity and urgency to be ratified within sixty days by Parliament. The government has often made wide use of decree laws, in labour matters as well, due to the need for urgent intervention under the pressure of crisis situations and to the weakness of the governing coalitions themselves. The use of this legislative technique has been widely criticised as being well beyond the limits envisaged by the Constitution. Italy traditionally has an extensive labour legislation, mostly aimed at protecting individual workers as the weaker party to the labour contract, which in recent years was often the result of informal bargaining between the government, trade unions and, sometimes, employers. The Civil Code lays down some fundamental principles regulating individual labour contracts still in force, but it is of less and less importance (Articles 2094–2134).

46. On the other hand, intervention by the legislator in collective labour relations was almost non-existent up to 1970. Since that date the official laissez-faire attitude has given way to a more supportive pro-labour attitude and more recently to interventions directed to guide and control collective agreements. There are also very detailed (and indeed confusing) social security regulations.

47. Limited regulatory powers can also be exercised in the field of labour law by the President of the Republic, the ministers, some public bodies and local authorities in the field of competence. Local government powers have greatly increased since 1997. The regulations and administrative practice of the Ministry of Labour and its peripheral offices and, after 1997, of local government, are of major importance, particularly in some areas of labour law: settlement of industrial conflicts by mediation and conciliation, health and safety, etc.

§3. Court Decisions

48. From a formal point of view court decisions are not considered a source of law because they are supposed to apply the existing law. But it is well known that the application and interpretation of the law always imply a margin of discretion and creativity by judges. In fact jurisprudence has played an important role in shaping Italian labour law, particularly in some important areas of collective labour relations, where legislation has been largely absent in the whole post-war period – such as limits on industrial conflict, effects of collective agreements, and, more recently, in other areas where the legislator has intervened not by means of the traditional defining techniques, but through broad directives of principles: for example, most matters regulated by Act No. 300 of 1970 (workers' and unions' right in the enterprise), individual and collective dismissals.

49. Dealing with collective labour law is a major challenge to Italian courts (and to Italian lawyers), which are accustomed to handling individual and monetary grievances mainly in relation to individual labour contracts. This is hardly an adequate background for coping with the realities of collective bargaining and industrial conflict.

§4. Collective Bargaining Agreements

50. Collective agreements, being private agreements according to current Italian law, are not traditionally considered sources of law either. But their normative effects, inexplicable in civil law, make them in substance, a direct source of the discipline of the individual labour relationship. Their number and scope have increased so much in the last years also with the support of legislation that they have become the most extensive and important source of labour law in many crucial areas of individual and collective labour relations.

51. The set of rules produced through collective bargaining has acquired a definite identity, on the whole different from the rules coming from the state, so that it can be appropriately studied – according to some opinion – as a system of its own, not closed but open to inter-relations with the legal and public labour law system.

§5. Custom

52. Custom, originally very important in shaping the individual labour relationship, has become less important with the development of legislation and collective bargaining. According to general principles, in order to be recognised as a source of law, a practice must be constantly, generally and uniformly repeated in the course of time, with the characteristic of binding behaviour (*opinio juris*). In labour law custom has a different meaning from that stated in Article 8 of the general provisions of the law preceding the Civil Code. According to Article 2078 of the Civil

Code, custom can be applied when legislation and collective agreements are lacking and, if it is more favourable to workers, it can prevail over non-imperative provisions of law (not over provisions of collective agreements). Custom never prevails over the terms of individual labour contracts.

53. Custom and practice can be relevant also as means of interpreting and integrating a labour contract (like any other contract) according to Articles 1368 and 1340 of the Civil Code. Workplace practice, also resulting from informal bargaining, is often recognised de facto by the courts as an important element for interpreting the content and effect of labour relations.

§6. Rules of Work

54. According to past practice and to the inter confederal agreement on works committees (*see* below), these rules were fixed unilaterally by management, after consultation with the work committees. Italian law does not provide for any obligation of the employer to establish or to publish the rules of work. An obligation to publish or communicate is necessary only as regards specific items, e.g., disciplinary procedures by Article 7 of Act No. 300 of 1970 (*see* below paragraph 142). Most subject matters traditionally regulated by work rules are now being handled by formal and informal collective bargaining at the plant or enterprise level, acquiring the binding effect of collective agreements.

55. Unilateral rules of work are not a source of law as such, but may become part of the employment contract according to the ordinary principles of contract law either by express incorporation or more often tacitly, according to Articles 1341–1342 (general conditions of contract laid down unilaterally by one party bind the other if the latter knows them or should know them; need of specific written approval for some restrictive clauses).

§7. International Sources

56. As a member of various international organisations (the United Nations, the International Labour Organisation (ILO), the Council of Europe, the European Union) Italy has a number of international obligations in the labour field.

57. International conventions are not in principle self-executing and therefore do not operate as direct sources of law. In order for labour relations to be affected by them, it is necessary that Italy implements the obligations resulting from ratification and transfers their contents into Italian legislation or adapts the latter to the former.

58. Italy has ratified most of the principal ILO conventions in labour matters, but the adaptation of our legislation to their content is still not complete, as will be seen in the course of this monograph. In some cases the concept of adaptation may in itself be somewhat elastic, because the objectives pursued by international conventions may be stated in general terms and may be implemented (or understood as such) in different ways. For example, Italy ratified the ILO convention on minimum wages law in the 1930s, when this objective could be considered as achieved by the then existing system of generally binding collective agreements. Under the present system of collective agreements, binding only for the members of the stipulating organisations, it is doubtful whether the Italian situation can be considered as consistent with these international obligations even when taking into account the various ways adopted to broaden the limited effects of private collective agreements, in particular the courts' interpretation of Article 36 of the Constitution on minimum wages (*see* below Part II, paragraph 449).

59. The nature of direct source of law can be recognised in some of the measures taken by the European Union authorities, which have binding effects on the citizens of the member countries, without any need for intervention by the national legislator. This is the case with general regulations and decisions on specified subjects, while directives and decisions aimed at Member States are not sources of law for the aforesaid reasons. The aim declared in the 1957 Treaty which established the EEC, of gradually unifying the main rules concerning economic activities, including labour matters, is politically very important. The impact of the European Union on employment relations has grown in the process of time, particularly following the Maastricht Treaty (February 1992), the Amsterdam Treaty (October 1997), and the Lisbon Treaty (December 2009) which emphasise the social role of the Union. But the process has not advanced enough to impinge on the national character of labour law and labour relations. This is also because the Union has often resorted less to binding *regulatory directives and more to broad guidelines for Member State policies (soft law).*

60. The new European commission chaired by Ursula Von der Leyen in response to the challenges of the covid pandemic has inaugurated a new course in the European initiatives, both economic and social.

61. A major set of resources has been approved in 2020 under the title 'Next generation EU' (NGEU) finalised to support the transition of Member States economy towards a more sustainable development. The national recovery plans of the states (including Italy) to be implemented within 2026, include not only investments in the digital and green economy but also major reforms in the areas of labour relations and welfare.

62. In fact the Commission, following the guidelines set by the European Pillar of Social Rights has approved quite a few directives: on European minimum wages, on the promotion of transparency in labour contracts, on better work-life balance (*see* below).

63. These European initiatives will have a significant influence on the economy and social evolution of Italy and of other Member States.

64. An important principle asserted within the European Union is the complete freedom of movement enjoyed by workers of Member States and the equal standing immigrants have with national workers, at least under the law. This is not always true in fact, e.g., as far as priority in collective dismissals, opportunities for employment and professional education are concerned.

Part I. The Individual Employment Relationship

Chapter 1. Definitions and Concepts

§1. The Usual Definition of 'Employee'; The Meaning of Subordination

65. Labour law, both individual and collective, is mainly concerned with work done in a position of subordination, although the tendency to apply particular pieces of legislation to categories of workers different from subordinate employees has already been noted. Recent changes in the labour market have contributed to multiplying the types of employment often called 'atypical' but in fact becoming more and more common. Their legal regulation is also being diversified (*see* below). This growing diversity of work types is a major aspect of the labour market flexibility which has also been introduced in Italy. A major characteristic of the Italian system is that this diversity, like other forms of flexibility (in working time, in work organisation, etc.), has been introduced gradually (the process began over twenty years ago) and with a significant involvement of the social parties in the process of change. Many aspects of flexibility, as we shall see, have been decided by the legislator after consultation and bargaining with the social parties; moreover, the law has delegated many aspects of the regulation and of the administration of flexibility to collective bargaining (*see* below).

66. The criteria used to identify the employee covered by labour law have been discussed for decades by legal commentators and in the courts. The basic definition, laid down in the Civil Code of 1942 (Article 2094), does not refer to a labour contract, but to a 'subordinate employee' as being a worker 'who engaged himself to cooperate for remuneration in an enterprise by working manually or intellectually under the direction of the entrepreneur'. According to the prevailing opinion, subordination is the key element in defining the typical 'labour' relation and the labour contract, and is decisive in distinguishing it from self-employment and from other types of employment (e.g., employment under a partnership). The element of cooperation expressly mentioned by the Civil Code is generally held by legal commentators as lacking legal significance in itself. It is not given real importance even by the courts, who often refer to it verbally. Most probably it is a moderate and innocent homage to the ideology, of German origin, of the 'enterprise community'.

67. The element of remuneration – again often used by the courts – is common to other types of employment and therefore not sufficient. The notion of subordination is, however, rather ambiguous in fact and from a legal point of view; for example, the duty of the employee to obey the employer's orders as to how the work should be done is certainly a necessary ingredient of subordination but it may also be common to some forms of self-employment (Article 2224, Civil Code) and also be imposed on a contractor (Article 1665, Civil Code). On the other hand, the mere fact that the employee has some freedom of action in his work does not, per se, exclude subordination. Usually it is stressed that the subordination of the employee, as required by Article 2094, is qualified by the continuity of the power of the employer and the extent of that power, which comprehends controlling the whole personal activity of the employee as being part of the employer's organisation.

68. Absolute criteria to define subordination and thus qualify the 'labour' relationship probably do not exist (as it is confirmed by notions such as 'para-subordination' or economic dependence; *see* above paragraph 19). In practice the courts use a combination of criteria, relevant de facto for deciding the qualification case by case: a fixed working time to be respected by the worker (probably the most used); the use of control and disciplinary powers by the employer; the continuity of the work – and its tie to the employer's organisation; the possibility or not of the employee risking loss by his investing money in the business. The type of remuneration, e.g., variable or fixed, and the mere conventional qualification of the contract are not conclusive. Traditionally courts have given a rather broad interpretation of the concept of subordination in order to ensure protective labour legislation to a wide range of workers; in recent years, this attitude has been questioned (*see* below paragraphs 94 ff.). The Decree 81/2015 (implementing Act 183/2015) has redefined the concept of subordination and its borders with the so-called autonomous collaborations. Article 2 of the decree provides that labour law regulations apply not only to subordinate employment, but also to those collaborators who perform continuous activities on a personal basis (i.e., without other employees) which are organised by the employer also with respect to the working time and the workplace.

The court implementation of the decree seems to indicate that quite a few cases of collaborators who are closely controlled and organised by the employer will fall under the provision of the decree, and hence be subject to all or most labour legislation.

§2. Platform-Based Work

69. The Italian courts like those of other countries have given different answers to the platform-based workers, in particular to the so-called riders: i.e., workers who deliver goods mainly in cities.

Some decisions consider them as independent workers, mainly because they are usually free to accept or refuse the work. Other decisions hold them to be subordinate employees because they must follow directives more or less stringent by the platform.

Faced with these divergent opinions Decree 101/2019 (transformed into Act 128/2019) has intervened with two sets of norms.

Article 47 gives a general rule providing that the regulation of Act 81/2015 concerning the workers whose activity is organised by others is also applicable when the work is organised through a digital platform. The platform is defined for the purpose of the act as a set of informative programmes or procedures which are instrumental to the activity of goods delivery, fixing the remuneration and the modalities of work execution.

While Act 81/2015 provided that the organisation of workers' activity included the definition of the 'time and place of work', these two specifications have been abolished by the new Act 128. Some interpreters believe that this change has no real implications on the scope and effects of the Act. But the issue is controversial.

A second change introduced by the new Act is that the work must be performed predominantly and not exclusively by the worker.

The second part of the act is devoted to the 'riders', who are defined rather restrictively as those independent workers who perform the activity of goods delivery within cities with cycles or motorcycles.

To these riders the Act provides for some protections. The most relevant are the following: the contractual agreement must be proved in writing and the workers must receive all the information useful for the protection of their interests, rights and personal safety; the collective agreements signed by the most representative unions and employer's associations may determine the criteria for the remuneration of work taking into account the modalities of the activity and the organisation of the work provider; lacking these agreements the worker cannot be paid in accordance to the number of goods deliveries and must be guaranteed a minimum hourly wage not inferior to the minimum standards set by the collective agreements signed by the most representative social parties for similar productive sectors.

Special indemnities are due to the worker not being inferior to 10% of the regular wage for night work, for work performed during the festivities or in unfavourable weather conditions. Furthermore the riders are protected by the anti-discrimination legislation applicable to subordinate employees and must benefit from public insurance against work accidents and professional diseases.

The workers organised by platforms not only the riders fall under the application of the European legislation on personal data protection (Regulation 2016/676).

Finally the act forbids to exclude from the platform workers and to reduce the work opportunities offered to them due to their refusal to accept some work offers.

Some norms of the act have raised various objections. The major platforms which organise the riders have criticised the extension to these autonomous workers of most protective legislation conceived for subordinate employees which considerably increases the costs of this business model.

Many interpreters have criticised the distinction between the general provision for the workers organised through platforms according to which they fall under all or most of the protective legislation applicable to subordinate employees, in spite of the fact that they are considered to be independent by the same legislator, and the regulation of the riders which include only a few protective norms typical of subordinate employment.

§3. Different Categories of Employees

70. Italian labour law distinguishes between different categories of subordinate employees, usually according to the nature of their work. A major distinction laid down by Article 2095 of the Civil Code, but of contractual origin, is between blue-collar, white-collar and leading personnel or management (*dirigenti*).

I. Blue-Collar and White-Collar Workers

71. The distinction between blue-collar and white-collar workers goes back to early Italian labour legislation. While the very first protective measures, for example, on injuries at work, aimed mainly at manual workers, the first comprehensive law on the labour contract was enacted in favour of white-collar employees, granting them a privileged status (more than in other industrial countries) as being the employer's most important collaborators, whose loyalty had to be also guaranteed by way of legislation (Act No. 1825 of 13 November 1924). This Act sets down the basic notion of white-collar workers and, indirectly, the criteria for defining blue-collar workers. A white-collar employee is defined (Article 1) as a worker who undertakes a professional activity with functions of cooperation with the employer and with the exclusion of merely manual labour. The vital part of this distinction, most often used by the courts, although not defined more precisely, is the criterion intellectual/manual. Some legal commentators have attempted to give more relevance to the notion of cooperation with the employer, holding that only white-collar workers contribute to organising productive activity, while blue-collar workers merely carry it out. In fact, this distinction was clear in the simple enterprise organisation at the beginning of the twentieth century, because it was also connected to a clear social status distinction. But it has long ceased to be tenable: even the detailed definitions of collective agreements, to which the courts generally refer, are clearly conventional, and their application has given rise to many controversies, particularly in the case of workers with specific technical skills.

72. In fact, the social legitimacy of this distinction has been heavily questioned and its legal significance has been largely reduced since 1973 through collective bargaining. Most national collective agreements have extended to blue-collar workers the treatment provided by law or by agreement to white-collar workers on the following items: intervals at which salaries are paid (now blue-collar workers also receive monthly salaries), disciplinary procedures, guarantees of salary and job security in case of suspension of the labour relation due to illness, work accidents, maternity, and annual holidays, duties and rights under the labour contract, and in general the system of job classification (the so-called unitary classification).

73. The very traditional division of collective agreements into two parts, one for blue-collar workers and one for white-collar workers has been reduced to a minimum. It has been legally possible to equalise the position of blue- and white-collar workers because the legal distinction of Article 2095 of the Civil Code does not prevent the social parties from granting workers (here blue-collar workers) more favourable conditions than those provided for by imperative norms of law. The distinction is now relevant mostly as regards terms of notice, trial clause, length of job security guarantee in case of suspension of the labour relation (paragraphs 178 ff.) and as regards some provisions of the law on social security. The same process of equalisation has reduced the importance of a special intermediate category between blue-collar and white-collar workers but closer to the latter – the so-called intermediates– traditionally created by collective agreements in most sectors of the economy.

II. Leading Personnel, Management (*Dirigenti*)

74. This category is of more recent origin than the two former ones. Traditionally managers were considered as the highest level of white-collar worker. Their birth dates back to 1926 when the corporative regime decided that managers should be organised in unions apart from those of other workers and connected with the employers' organisations. Even now managers (*dirigenti*) have separate unions (the major confederations are CIDA and Confedir), and conclude separate collective agreements. Their special legal status results mainly from the fact that they are excluded by law from certain provisions applying to other workers, namely norms on work time, overtime limits, limits on the possibility of concluding a contract for a fixed term, norms on dismissal. They also have a separate social security system. However, collective agreements grant them preferential treatment as regards wages, terms of notice, fringe benefits and many other aspects of the labour relationship. The criteria for distinguishing managers from white-collar workers are set by collective agreements and by the courts, who have the last word. The most common definition, shaped by an established jurisprudential tradition, is that a manager is the alter ego of the employer, in charge of the direction of the whole enterprise or of an important and autonomous branch thereof, operating with full autonomy within the general directives of the employer. It is a rather abstract definition contradicted largely by practice and by collective agreements which also include in this category employees lacking any directive powers but having very high technical and professional qualifications. Since the category is expanding far beyond the original concept of alter ego, the unity of the notion itself is under attack. According to a trend of opinion, a distinction should be made between higher managers, for whom the traditional privileges and exemptions from protective labour law can still be justified, and middle and lower-level managers who are in fact nearer to white-collar workers and need the same protection, for example, against dismissal.

75. The Italian Civil Code (Article 2095) does not mention cadres and nor has this category traditionally been considered by collective agreements.

In recent years dissatisfaction among cadres has been growing with respect to bargaining and wage policies adopted by the major confederations, where they are underrepresented.

A few organisations representing this category have consequently appeared or become more active. Some of them are openly advocating a role for occupational labour unions others define themselves as professional associations.

In practice they often act like pressure groups (only lacking the power to strike) and they participate to the tripartite consultations with the government on specific social issues.

The two largest federations are Federmanager *(Federazione Nazionale Dirigenti Aziende Industriali)* declaring 86,560 members in the industrial sector. Manageritalia (*Federazione Nazionale Dirigenti, Quadri* and professional of the tertiary sector) 35015 members. Separate federations represent leading personnel in health services (CIMO), in insurance, agriculture.

The number one claim of these organisations has been that cadres be recognised by law, i.e., by amending Article 2095 of the Civil Code so as to include the fourth category, and through collective agreements. Legally speaking Article 2095 need not be changed: the norm is definitional and not permissive, therefore the fact that only three categories are mentioned does not imply the exclusion of others, as borne out by the traditional presence (up to 1999) of the functionaries in the banking sector. An Act has, however, been passed (190/1985), which modifies Article 2095 including cadres as a fourth category of employees – thereby accepting the request of the organisations. But the definition of the category is vague and substantially left to collective bargainings, like the regulation of other major aspects of the labour relationship. Most definitions include not only the traditional 'directive' employees – line employees exercising directive powers delegated by the employer – but also staff or professional employees with high-standard qualifications. So the category overlaps on the one hand with higher white-collar levels (the so-called employees with a function of direction) and on the other hand with *dirigenti.* The figure is uncertain – like the borderline. According to recent estimates (2020, Manageritalia, INPS) *dirigenti* are 120.000 in the private sector and 263.000 in the public service. The members of CIDA is 133.785 (including retired members).

In recent bargaining rounds the major confederations have tried to respond to the claims of cadres, mostly by introducing one or two special categories and wage increases in the wage scale (10%–15% of the wage scale parameter). This solution is considered insufficient by the employees concerned who are in fact being granted growing merit wage increases by employers. Future developments are uncertain, also due to the ambivalent position of political parties and of the three major confederations. It is probably unrealistic to think that the latter may fully represent the cadres together with all other employees. On the other hand, the attempt of the existing organisations of cadres to acquire an independent role as interlocutors of both the enterprise and labour movement, is not an easy task.

§4. Different Kinds of Individual Labour Contract

I. The Individual Labour Contract for an Indefinite Period

76. A major classification of the individual labour contract can be made from the point of view of the term, i.e., of the duration in time. The distinction is between the labour contract for an indefinite period and the labour contract for a definite period (or for precisely indicated work or for replacement). Italian legislation has been traditionally in favour of the former, originally because of the preoccupation that a fixed-term limits the personal freedom of the employee and above all because the use of a contract for a definite period is believed to go against the employee's interests in having continuous employment – highly rated in a country with traditionally high unemployment – and reduces his job security. More recently, the (presumed) existence of a greater willingness on the part of certain groups of workers to accept even precarious employment, the need to deal with a situation in the labour market characterised by high levels of unemployment (especially affecting the young and women) as well as the need to respond to the pressing demands of firms for greater flexibility, have led to the passing of legislation that is more inclined than in the past to consider fixed-term contracts (*see* below paragraphs 80–81).

77. The contractual job security implied in the term (the worker cannot be dismissed before the end of the term without a just cause) is less significant than the security provided by law in the case of a contract for an indefinite period, due to the development of legal protection against unfair dismissals, which obviously does not apply to contracts for a definite period.

But the protective law of dismissal has been changed several times: by Act 92/2012, And by Decree 23/2015, implementing Act 183/2014, which have reduced the sanctions for unfair dismissals (*see* below), and lately by the dignity decree (Act 96/2018).

According to the basic rule, originally expressed in Article 2097 of the Civil Code and in Act No. 230 of 18 April 1962, a labour contract is assumed to be for an indefinite period; the parties can resort to a contract for a fixed term only in exceptional cases and under conditions strictly determined by the law (seasonal activities, replacement of temporarily absent employees, managerial activities, etc.).

Italian legislation following a formula widely used in Europe has repeatedly stated that the contract for an indefinite period is the common type of employment contract. But in fact this has not always been the case because contracts for a fixed term have been widely used, due to their lower costs and their flexibility greater than that of contracts for an indefinite period.

II. The Individual Labour Contract for a Definite Period

78. The restrictions imposed by traditional legislation on fixed-term contracts have been gradually reduced by subsequent Acts, initially limited to specific sectors (radio-TV: Act 266/1983; air transport: Act 84/1986), to specific activities (seasonal peaks: Act 79/1983) and groups of people (employees laid-off: Act 223/1991) subsequently by an Act (56/1987) which has granted to collective agreements the power to introduce new types of fixed-term contract beyond those provided by the law.

This process of liberalisation has continued in Act 368/2001, which has implemented EU Directive 99/1970 and has regulated the matter until the approval of Decree 81/2015 which has reformed the entire regulation. Act 368/2001 innovated the tradition, insofar as fixed-term contracts were allowed not in a series of legally specified cases, but whenever they are justified by 'technical, organisational or substitutional reasons' (Article 1(1)).

The meaning of these general reasons was determined by the judiciary which has been rather restrictive.

For this reason (Act 92/2012, Act 99/2013 and Act 34/2014, as modified by Decree 81/2015, have again intervened in the matter, pushing toward a further liberalisation, while maintaining some limits of duration and quantity.

According to the first two Acts the possibility to hire without giving any specific reason was limited to a maximum of one year. But Act 34/2014 and Decree 81/2015 have completed the process by abolishing the need to give specific reasons for hiring with fixed-term contracts, whose duration is set at a maximum of thirty-six months.

However the employer hiring for a fixed term has to pay an additional 1.4% of the basic wage. The rationale is to discourage an excessive use of these contracts and to favour contracts for an indefinite period, because they promote stability and firms, investments in employee training.

79. Moreover, the total amount of these contracts concluded by an employer could not exceed the maximum of 20% of the employees having a contract for an indefinite period present in the enterprise at January first of the year of hiring. Administrative monetary sanctions are provided the employers who exceed the limit of 20%.

Other general rules concerning fixed-term contracts are provided by Act 368/2001. The existence of conditions necessary for the use of fixed-term contracts must be proved by the employer. Lacking the formal and substantial requirements, the contract will be regarded as being for an indefinite period. When the employee is rehired within ten or twenty days – according to the duration of the first contract – after the end of this contract, the second contract is considered to be for an indefinite period. When a series of consecutive contracts for a fixed term is included, the contract is considered as for an indefinite period from the beginning.

If employment continues beyond the fixed term the employer must pay a wage supplement for each day of continuation. The contract is considered to be for an indefinite period if employment continues beyond thirty or fifty days, according to the duration of the first contract. Decree 368/2001 has maintained the traditional rule stated by Act 230/1962, whereby temporary agency employees are entitled to the same treatment as workers for an indefinite period as long as this is compatible with the nature of the contract.

Most of these limits do not apply to seasonal industries as identified by decree or by national collective agreements. This exception is due to the fact that seasonal activities typically require temporary employment. Employees working on a fixed term for more than six months in the same firm have priority in future hiring by the employers for an indefinite period (the employees must exercise this right by giving advance notice to the employer).

Same traditional rules protecting this type of employment have been maintained. One is the fixed-term employees are entitled to the same treatment as standard employees, in so far as it is compatible with the nature of the contract.

According to the EU Directive, the law since Decree 368/2001 imposes on the employer duties to inform and to provide specific training to temporary employees. The content of these duties must be determined by collective agreements (Articles

7 and 9). Seasonal workers have the right to priority in the hiring by the same enterprise in the same job position during the year following the end of the contract (Article 10(9)).

The use of fixed-term contracts is prohibited for substituting strikers, in productive units which have resorted in the last six months to collective dismissals and during lay-offs, for firms not abiding by the law on health and safety (Act 626/1994). Specific provisions favouring fixed-term contracts are maintained for management and for some sectors: air transport (Article 2 Act 368), commerce and tourism (Article 10), for the hiring of laid-off workers (Article 8(2) Act. 223/1991), postal service (Act 266/2005), etc. No specific provision exists for public administration, which follows the general rules.

80. The number of fixed-term contracts has been growing in various European countries over the last years, in spite of the fact that the law maintains the concept, shared by the EU directive, that the normal employment contract is for an indefinite period. But the use of fixed-term contracts is one of the most controversial issues in labour market regulation. Its diffusion remains a source of preoccupation because it increases the instability and possibly the precariousness of employment; even more so because in recent years, also due to economic crisis the majority of new hirings are for fixed-term or under atypical contracts.

81. To counteract the increase of fixed-term contracts Act 190/2014 has introduced fiscal incentives to favour hirings for an indefinite period. The first data (January–September 2015) indicate a moderate reversal of a trend. But this effect has not continued after 2017 once the incentives ceased to operate.

82. In this area another reversal of trend has been marked by the so-called Dignity Decree (converted into Act 96/2018) which introduces a series of restrictions to the use of fixed-term contracts.

The first chapter of the 'Dignity Decree' (Articles 1–3) introduces a new regulation aimed at discouraging the use of fixed-term contracts by companies, amending a previous related regulation, under the Job's Act (Legislative Decree No. 81/2015, Articles 19 to 20). Articles 5 and 6 of the second title place restrictions on the ability of companies in receipt of state aid to relocate their business activities and/or dismiss employees.

The new regulation applies to all fixed-term employment contracts signed after the 'Dignity Decree' came into force on 14 July 2018. It also applies to fixed-term employment contracts signed prior to the 'Dignity Decree' coming into force, but which are renewed or extended after 31 October 2018.

Article 1 modifies Articles 19 and 21 of Legislative Decree No. 81/2015 by allowing parties to freely execute fixed-term employment contracts without having to provide a reason for a maximum duration period of twelve months.

According to the new Article 19, paragraph 1, a fixed-term employment contract also has a duration period longer than twelve months (but never more than twenty-four months), provided it can be justified for the following reasons that must be stated in the contract in writing: (i) temporary and objective needs unrelated to the employer's ordinary business such as the need for replacements (e.g., of employees during maternity, paternity or sick leave); (ii) needs relating to temporary, significant and unforeseeable increases in the employer's ordinary business.

Subsequently Act 73/2021 authorizes collective agreements to introduce new reasons justifying fixed-term contracts with the aim of allowing for more flexibility.

Should an employer draft a fixed-term contract for a period longer than twelve months in the absence of one of the above-mentioned conditions, said contract will be automatically transformed by law into an open-ended employment contract from the day after the twelve month-period has elapsed.

Where the fixed-term employment contract has a duration of more than twelve days, the terms of said employment must be fully outlined in writing.

Through this mechanism, an employer has the option to hire an employee for a short period (maximum of twelve months) without specifying any reason for the fixed term. During this period, the employer can assess the benefits of keeping the employee on full-time by: (i) executing a subsequent open-ended employment contract, or (ii) renewing the fixed-term contract for up to twenty-four months on the occurrence of one of the circumstances listed in the Article 19, paragraph 1. At the same time, should an employer fall within one of the above-mentioned categories at the time of signing of a fixed-term employment contract, they can extend said employee's contract for a longer period of up to twenty-four months, specifying the reason in writing as per the new Article 19, paragraph 1.

The difference compared to the previous regulation implemented by the Jobs Act (Legislative Decree No. 81/2015) is clear. According to the latter, the maximum duration of a fixed-term employment contract is thirty-six months with no reason specified. Employers were able to renew fixed-term employment contracts sequentially with the same employee up to a maximum final term of thirty-six months without any reason given.

Regarding extending the duration of fixed-term employment contracts before the expiration of their final term ('proroga'), Article 1 of the 'Dignity Decree' reduces the number of possible extensions to four (five under the Jobs Act). Exceeding the said number of extensions convert fixed-term employment contracts into open-ended ones.

Employers can extend fixed-term employment contracts for a maximum period of twenty-four months, regardless of the number of renewals made with the same employee. Should an extension be applied within the initial twelve months of a contract, the employer is not required any specific reason for doing so. Should an extension be applied following the initial 12-month period, the employer must provide a reason covered under the new Article 19, paragraph 1, of the Legislative Decree No. 81/2015. The only exception relates to seasonal workers. Indeed, fixed-term employment contracts executed for seasonal activities can be extended and renewed without giving any reason.

Article 1 extends the period within which an employee can challenge the lawfulness of a fixed-term employment contract and request its conversion to an open-ended employment contract from 120 to 180 days.

Article 1 *bis* in order to incentivise the use of open-ended employment contracts provide that the employers hiring employees aged 34 or younger with open-ended employment contracts in 2019–2020 will benefit from a 50% reduction in social contributions to be paid in favour of said employees during the first three years of their employment relationship.

Similar reduction in social contributions for the hiring of youngsters have been introduced by subsequent legislations, the last being the budget law of Dec. 29, 2022.

Article 2, amending Article 34, paragraph 2, of the Legislative Decree No. 81/2015, establishes that the above-described rules will also apply to temporary Agency contracts (‘*contratti di somministrazione di mano d’opera*’).

Therefore, fixed-term temporary employment contracts agreed between a supplier agency and an employee will be subject to the same rules as fixed-term employment relationships outlined in Chapter III of the Legislative Decree No. 81/2015, as amended by the new regulations.

Article 3 provides for an increase in the additional contributions payable by employers pursuant to Article 2, paragraph 28, of Law No. 92/2012. This contribution is calculated based on an employees’ taxable salary that their employer pays to social unemployment allowance (NASPI). Prior to the ‘Dignity Decree’ coming into force, this contribution was set at 1.4% of taxable salary for social security purposes and applied to all fixed-term contracts. It is increased by 0.5% on each renewal of a fixed-term employment contract.

The impact of this Act on employment, in particular on the pursued reduction of a fixed-term contract, is uncertain.

In fact the total number of these contracts has continued to increase: according to last data by ISTAT (October 2022) it amounts to 2.980.000.

83. The labour contract for a fixed term must be distinguished from the labour contract with a clause guaranteeing a minimum duration or stability. This contract comes under the discipline of employment for an indefinite period, but an employer is conventionally bound not to dismiss an employee for a definite period of time (this conventional limit is now less important for an employee due to statutory limits on dismissals).

III. Temporary Agency Work

84. Italy has for a long time prohibited temporary work, unlike other European countries. The intermediation of a temporary work firm was forbidden in any form by Act No. 264 of 1949, which entrusted the public employment agency with an exclusive role in the placement of workers if the firm limited itself to a placement activity without engaging the worker directly, and/or by Act No. 1369 of 23 October 1960, which forbade in principle the so-called fraudulent interposition in employment or labour-only subcontracting, i.e., the hiring of a worker by a person different from the employer-user, if a temporary work firm engaged the temporary worker. This discipline was frequently violated. It was also criticised as being too strict and as forbidding, together with serious forms of exploitation of labour, the useful activity of temporary work firms in providing an employer with short-time staff who were actually needed, a practice quite acceptable to many workers.

85. A major innovation was introduced by Act 196/1997 which legalised temporary work.

According to this Act, temporary work implies, as in other countries, a trilateral relation between the agency (which is the employer), the temporary employee, and the enterprise actually using the services of the employee. The original regulation was rather strict as a consequence of the traditional Italian diffidence about this type of relationship. The contracts, both between the agency and the user firm and with the employee, must be in writing and contain the essential elements. The temporary work agency is authorised to operate by the Ministry of Labour only if it meets some requirements consisting in a minimum financial capital of the firm, an operative extent in at least four regions, adequate professional skills and exclusive dedication to this business. According to Act 196 the use of temporary work was limited to types of work which were not normally used in the firm in order to substitute for absent employees of the firm and to cases provided for by collective agreements (in much the same way as for fixed-term contracts). Act 30/2003 implemented by Decree 276/2003, in line with its general aim of liberalisation, allows the use of temporary work whenever it is justified by ‘productive, technical, organisational, substitutional reasons’ (the expression is similar to that used for fixed-term contracts, even though they relate to the ordinary business of the user company).

The use of temporary work is excluded in specific cases: to replace strikers; by firms which have resorted to collective dismissals in the last twelve months; in dangerous works and by firms not complying with the law on safety (Decree 626/1994 and Decree 242/1996) and originally also for unskilled workers (the exclusion was scarcely justified, hardly used and finally abolished by Act 30/2003).

Temporary workers have in principle the same rights, individual and collective, as are recognised by ordinary employees of the utilising firm. This latter is responsible in particular for all obligations concerning health and safety (Decree 626/1994, now Act 81/2008). The temporary worker has the right to economic treatment (wages and accessories, social contributions) not inferior to that pertaining to the employees of the utilising firm. This latter is responsible together with the agency for this treatment.

86. The temporary worker can be hired by the agency for a fixed term, coinciding with the actual employment by the utilising firms, or for an indefinite period: in this latter case he will be entitled, in addition to the wage for the work done, to an indemnity determined by collective agreements (or by decree) in compensation for his being ‘on call’ at the disposal of the agency. No limit can be posed to the right of the utilising firm to hire the worker directly at the end of the temporary work period.

87. A special fund is established (financed with 4% of wages) for vocational training and possibly other services intended to favour the full participation of temporary workers to the labour market. Trade unions have the right to be informed by the utilising firm of the resort to temporary work. A decree implementing Act No. 59/1997 concerning organisation and labour relationships in public administration explicitly made temporary work also available to public employees.

88. Act 30/2003, specified by Decree 276/2003, has given further impulse to this type of employment by rewriting with fewer restrictions the provisions of Act 196/1997 (*see* above) and by enlarging the scope of temporary work agencies. According to Act 196 they could previously operate only as providers of temporary employees. Now, they can perform all kinds of mediation services on the labour market.

89. Moreover, according to Act 30 these agencies can provide to user firms employees not only for a definite period, as under Act 196/1997 but also for an indefinite duration. This kind of employment, called staff leasing, follows basically the same rules as temporary work; it is allowed for 'technical, productive and organisational reasons' and for specific activities fixed by the law (Article 20), e.g., cleaning, custody, construction within the plant, information services, operation of call centres. Other activities can be included by collective agreement. Staff leasing has been initially opposed by the unions, particularly by CGIL, which considered it an abnormal 'separation' between the employee and the actual employer. In fact, it has been abolished by Act 247/2007 (Article 1, co. 46). But it has been reintroduced in the budget law for 2010 (Act 191/2009, Article 2, co. 143) which has also extended its scope and is now more widely accepted.

In fact recent legislation has favoured temporary work. Staff leasing has also been allowed in the wide area of personal services and assistance, and in all cases, provided by national and territorial collective agreements signed by most representative social parties (unions and employers associations).

Temporary work in general, may be used even lacking any specific productive reasons, and without quantitative limits for disadvantaged categories of employees (long-term unemployed, disabled workers etc.) and again in all cases provided by collective agreements of all levels signed by most representative social parties (Act. 24/2012 implementing EU Directive 2008/104).

Similarly, according to Act 92/2012, as modified by Act 99/2013, the first use of temporary work for a period of twelve months by an individual firm does not need any specific reason (this position is similar to that applicable to this first use of fixed-term contracts). The same Act has introduced the possibility of using temporary work, in the form of staff leasing, to hire and train apprentices. The favour towards temporary work is also expressed by the Act that it has been exempted from the payment of the 1.4% extra costs due in case of fixed-term contracts (Act 92/2012).

90. The process of liberalisation of fixed-term contracts (*see* above) has been extended to temporary work by Act 92/2014, and by Decree 81/2015 (Article 30). The latter has abolished the need to give specific reasons also for hiring temporary workers. But the Decree has stated that the number of temporary employees hired for an indefinite period cannot exceed the 20% of the employees having a contract for an indefinite period will the utilising firm (a limit which can however be changed by collective agreements). The same agreements are entitled to determine the maximum number of temporary workers having a fixed-term contract. This limit is lifted for disadvantaged employees and for long-term unemployed, Decree 81 (Article 32) has confirmed some norms provided by previous legislation, on the exclusion of temporary work; on the requisites of form; and on the rights and obligations of temporary employees.

Temporary work has been widely accepted in practice also by the originally diffident unions and has grown in quantity: in 2003, 600,000 employees were hired as temporary workers. The crisis of 2008 has partially reversed the trend and the COVID-19 pandemic has produced the same effect. But growth has restarted after the crisis. According to the last data (2022) these temporary employees amount to 482.000.

IV. The Trial Clause

91. The trial clause included in a labour contract is aimed at verifying the usefulness of the work relationship for both parties before the engagement becomes definitive: mainly the employer verifies the professional attitudes of the worker, but possibly the employee verifies the type of job. Legally it is held to fix a condition to the labour contract. The trial clause must be in writing (Article 2096 of the Civil Code). The courts hold that this form is required only for reasons of proof; many legal commentators, however, consider that it is required *ad substantiam*, if it is not written down, the clause is null and void. The traditional characteristic of the probationary period is that each party can terminate the contract without a term of notice and without any justification. Recently a few court decisions have questioned the absolute validity of this principle, namely the possibility for the employer to escape any judicial control over the reasons for dismissal of a probationary employee (particularly in a case of suspected discrimination). The parties can fix a minimum and a maximum duration of the trial period. A maximum duration of six months is indirectly fixed by Act No. 604 of 1966 on unfair dismissals (after which period the dismissal must be justified and preceded by due notice as in the case of a definitive labour contract).

92. Act 104/29022 has confirmed explicitly the maximum duration of six months (which can be reduced in collective agreements) and has provided that in fixed-term contracts the duration must be in proportion to the length of the contract and the type of job. A shorter maximum duration is fixed by law for apprentices (two months), for domestic servants, and very often by collective agreements; for example, the metalworkers' national agreement set a maximum period of twelve days for blue-collar workers and of three months for most white-collar workers. Collective agreements often provide also that the trial period is prolonged, to various degrees, in cases of illness or of work accident. If the trial period expires without either party terminating it, and if any other general reason for terminating the contract is lacking, the labour relationship between the parties becomes a definitive one, falling therefore under the general discipline of labour contracts, and the trial period is counted for the worker's seniority.

§5. SPECIAL LABOUR CONTRACTS

93. While the three categories of employees described above (blue-collar, white-collar, managers) represent a distinction within the typical individual labour contract regulated by Article 2094 of the Civil Code, a special discipline different from the general regulation of the typical labour contract and consequently a special individual labour contract has been drawn up by the legislator for other categories of employee covering the nature of their work or the employer. The main sorts of special labour contracts refer to the following categories of workers: maritime and airline workers (regulated by Articles 323ff. and 900ff. of the Code of Navigation, 1942); domestic servants (Act No. 339 of 2 April 1958 and Articles 2240–2242 of the Civil Code); apprentices (Act No. 25 of 19 January 1955 and now Act 30/2003); homeworkers (Act No. 877 of 18 December 1973); sportsmen (Act 91/1981).

The recent trend has been to increase the number and cases of the so-called atypical works as a response to the needs of the flexibility of the labour market. Most noticeable examples are temporary workers and staff leasing; so-called project workers (a re-regulation of para-subordinate workers); job on-call or intermittent works and accessory works (*see* below).

I. Work on Projects and Collaborations

94. Article 409(3) of the Code of Civil Procedure (Act 533/1973) regulates a type of work called coordinated and continuous collaboration mainly with the aim of including it within the same jurisdiction and procedures applicable to ordinary subordinate employment. This contract has been regulated more in details by Act 230/2003 and by subsequent Acts, under different names: para-subordinate work and more recently work done by 'economically dependent workers'.

Collaboration differs from subordination insofar as the employee has more autonomy in the organisation of his work and the work itself must be prevalently personal (i.e., the personal activity of the employee must be more relevant than the other productive factors). The legal qualification of this contract has always been controversial: sometimes it has been considered a sub-type of self-employment, sometimes a third type between self-employment and subordinate work. Traditionally the legal protection typical of labour law has not been held applicable to these collaborators, apart from the judicial procedures of Act 533 and the special regulation of waivers stated by Article 2113 Civil Code (*see* below). But this rule has been progressively changed.

Act 335/1995 (law on pensions) extended to the collaboration contract the duty to pay social security contributions, although in a reduced quantity in order to guarantee to these workers, like all others, a future old age pension. The original quantity was limited to 10% of wages, but it has been progressively raised to 27% and lately equalised to that of subordinate workers (*see* below).

In the following years, the number and types of collaboration contracts. have been growing. They included a variety of people: fully autonomous employees (administrators, professionals), workers with a degree of formal autonomy, but economically dependent on one or two employers; really dependent workers who had been hired as 'collaborators' in order to save on the costs of social security (the cost of subordinate employees is 33% of the wages). Act 30/2003 and the following Decree 276 (Article 61) had the purpose of restraining the abuse of these collaborators. They were allowed only if they had to perform a specific work project, to be implemented independently by the collaborator in view of the expected result.

The Act recognised for these workers some minimal rights and protections: the right to be recognised as an author of inventions formulated during the contract, the right not to have the contract terminated before the end of the project, unless for just cause, the suspension of the contract (for some time) in case of illness, work accidents, maternity (but without any indemnity). Act 926/2006 (Article 1, co. 788) granted to these workers a daily indemnity in those events; its duration and amount were lower than the indemnity granted to an ordinary dependent worker.

The Act excluded from the regulation and the relevant requirements so-called occasional works, which were defined as those lasting less than thirty days during the year with the same employer unless they are remunerated with more than EUR 5,000 (Article 61, Decree 276).

95. This regulation has been very controversial. The critics argue that the rights recognised for project workers are insufficient to protect their work, which is economic if not legally similar to that of subordinate workers; moreover, they doubt that the change of definition and the thin regulation of the new contract will be effective in repressing current abuses. One reason for these abuses is that the differentials, particularly in social security costs with subordinate work have been traditionally high. The progressive increase of these contributions however has contributed to reducing the number of these contracts.

The number of these collaborators, after reaching a peak of over 1.6 million in 2008, has been declining also due to the increase of these costs and to legal restrictions aimed at fighting abuses: in 2019, their number was down to 230,000.

96. Act 92/2012 as amended by Act 99/2013 introduced further restrictive regulations in this area with the purpose of avoiding that contracts having the characters of dependent workers shaped as work on projects or independent collaborators. Firstly the Act has raised the social security contributions with the objective to equalise them with those paid by dependent employees (33% of wages). Moreover, it has introduced restrictive requisites for the use of work on projects: a more severe definition of a project which shall include identifiable results; exclusion of low-skilled and repetitive tasks; exclusion of tasks similar to those performed by regular employees. Lacking these requisites, the contracts will be transformed in regular employment relationships from the beginning.

These workers were entitled to be paid a minimum wage fixed by collective agreements or, lacking specific agreements, a wage similar to collective wages paid to comparable dependent employees.

Restrictive requisites were also fixed for the semiautonomous contracts of VAT holders.

97. Decree 81/2015, implementing Act 183/2014, has reregulated the whole matter. Taking into account the critics addressed by many observers, practitioners and social parties to the previous regulation of the work on project, the Decree has abrogated this type of contract (Article 52).

The 'continuous and coordinated' collaborations provided by Article 409, 3°co., remain applicable; but its regulation is limited to procedural rules, as indicated above.

A most important innovation has been introduced by Article 2 of Decree 81, which has redefined the category of collaborations in two subcategories one: the so-called autonomous collaborations, two: the collaborations which are 'organised by the employer also with respect to the working time and to the work place' (*see* above paragraph 68). To the latter Article 2 declares applicable all the protective legislation typical of labour law. Indeed this category becomes equivalent to the contract of subordinate employment.

It remains to be seen which criteria will be used by courts in order to distinguish this type from category of 'autonomous collaboration'.

The new rule of Article 2 might lead the courts to widen the area of subordinate employment, with the consequent application of labour law legislation. As indicated above (§ 63) this trend might be favoured, also by the economic and normative incentives provided by recent legislation, which have made it more convenient for employers to hire with a contract of subordinate employment.

These incentives and the wider notion of subordination introduced by Article 2 could converge in attracting a certain number of semi-autonomous collaborations in the area of labour law.

Recent data seem to confirm this attraction. The number of hirings for an indefinite period has also grown due to the transformation of fixed-term contracts and of the decrease of collaborations (–15% with respect to 2014) (*see* above paragraphs 80–81).

II. Accessory or Occasional Work

98. Accessory works are a subspecies of occasional work. Their discipline has been changed several times and follows different often opposing rationales. The first regulation is Article 70 of the Decree 276/2003 which defines them as some activities, merely occasional, performed by persons at risk of social exclusion, or non-participating in the labour market or about to be expelled: namely small domestic works, including assistance to children, the old aged, disabled and ill people; small activities of cleaning, maintenance, gardening, participation in sporting, cultural, social, charitable activities, collaboration with voluntary associations for emergency works. These accessory works could not be paid more than EUR 5,000. The amount has been increased to EUR 10,000 for work within the family (Act 80/2005 modifying Article 70 of Decree 276).

Accessory works could be performed only by the following categories of people: those unemployed for more than one year, students, housewives, retired people, disabled persons, extra-community workers regularly present in Italy for six months after the loss of a regular job. The scope of accessory works has been extended by subsequent legislation (in particular Act 80/2005, Act. 133/2008, Act 5/2009). A wide range of activities: can be performed domestic work cleaning, maintenance, gardening, private teaching, sporting cultural, social, charitable activities. Pensioners can perform accessory work without limitation of activity and so can students below 25 years during week-ends and vacations. The possibility of accessory works has been extended, for the year 2009, in all activities, to workers laid off and receiving welfare benefits, within the limit of EUR 3,000 of pay.

Act 92/2012 has redefined this type of work confirming the maximum amount of 5,000 of total income perceivable but setting a further limit of 2,000 per purchaser in the commercial and service sector. This work has to be paid not in cash but by special 'vouchers' distributed by authorised agencies, marked with date and time with the present value of 10 per hour.

This remuneration is exempt from tax and is subject to social contributions of reduced amount for work accident insurance and pension; moreover, it is compatible with the status of unemployment for the beneficiary.

Following these provisions accessory works have acquired considerable importance. They are intended to favour the regularisation of many small activities which are performed outside the regular market. But this too is a rather controversial issue: the critics object that the loose regulation and lower costs of these works might instead attract activities which would and should be performed as ordinary dependent work.

Decree 81/2015 (Article 48) has increased to EUR 7,000 the maximum amount of total income perceivable by the employee. But within the limits of EUR 2,000 for one employer (enterprise or professional). This limit does not operate when this work is performed for a private person or family.

In order to prevent abuses the Decree has excluded the use of accessory work in the execution of contract works.

Article 2 bis of the Dignity Decree has modified and restricted the regulation relating to 'occasional work' as per Law No. 96/2017. 'Occasional work' can be used in two different forms, so-called family booklet to be used by a person not in their professional activity and contract of occasional activity for entrepreneurs. It refers to temporary work undertaken by employees on short-term employment contracts valued at no more than EUR 2,500 for each user, 5000 in total. Employers remunerate such work via vouchers provided by the Italian National Social Insurance Institution (INPS). Each voucher is worth EUR 10. The 'Dignity Decree' allows companies in the tourist sector who employ up to eight employees on the open-ended contracts to hire further staff on an occasional basis.

The budget law of Dec. 29, 2022 (Act 197/2022), has reintroduced in a new form the vouchers for occasional activities which were conceded in 2017. The new law reproduces some of the traits of the past regulation if applicable to the new form. The use of voucher is allowed for a defined set of activities: agriculture, domestic work, hotel and catering industry, personal care and assistance activities, etc. It is reserved to specific groups of people: students, retired, workers, unemployed, extra community workers.

The total amount of wages which can be paid to these workers is raised to EUR 10.000. In agriculture a max of forty-five days yearly is allowed for each worker.

III. Contract of Intermittent Work or 'Job on Call'

99. The contract of intermittent work is another 'atypical' contract introduced by Act 30/2003 after bitter controversy. Decree 276 defines (Article 33) it as a contract whereby an employee put himself at the disposal of an employer for the execution of intermittent or discontinuous activities.

Contracts can be stipulated:

- for workers below 25 and over 45 years of age;
- for specific periods of time: week-ends, vacations, etc. (Article 37);
- in other cases determined by collective agreements.

Lacking these agreements a Ministerial decree (23 October 2004) has admitted the use of job on-call for a series of intermittent activities indicated by Act 2657 of 1923. In any case it can be used by a person below the age of 25 and over 45, including pensioners. The use of this contract is prohibited in the same cases as temporary work (substitution of strikers, etc., above paragraph 90). For periods during which the employee agrees to remain at the disposal of the employer and guarantees to respond to a call-out he is entitled to an indemnity determined by collective agreement or in its absence by ministerial decree (now is 20% of contractual wage).

The contract must be in writing in order to prove its essential elements: type of work, duration, location and conditions under which the employee is at disposal, advance notice for calls, remuneration and indemnity, measures necessary to protect the health and safety of the employee (Article 35).

Intermittent workers must receive equal treatment as ordinary employees performing the same or equivalent job (Article 38). The employer must inform the union representatives of the use of this contract yearly.

The criticisms that have been expressed against this contract have led to its abolition by Act 47/2007. But Act 133/2008 has reintroduced it. Act 92/2012 has modified the age bracket of persons who can use intermittent work: it is now 25 and over 55.

100. In order to prevent abuses the employee is obliged to communicate the adoption of this contract, before its beginning, to the labour offices (also via e-mail or SMS). Decree 76/2013, as amended by Act 99/2013, has introduced a further limit, namely that this work cannot be allowed for each worker for more than 400 days in total, during a period of 3 years. Because of this limit this employment is considered to be for an indefinite period and full-time.

Decree 81/2015, has confirmed this type of contract, in spite of many critical opinions. But it has innovated the previous regulation in two mains aspects. This contract is allowed in employment with the same employer for a maximum of 400 days of work in a period of three years: the limit does not apply to the sectors of tourism, entertainment, hotels, bars, etc.

In order to prevent abuses the employer is obliged before the beginning of the work period to notify by electronic mail the duration of the contract to the territorial labour offices.

IV. Part-Time Work

101. According to prevailing opinion, part-time work does not imply a special labour contract: the general principles and regulations of the standard labour contract also apply to part-time workers. But adaptations of the discipline are necessary, plus the fact that the reductions in working time create specific problems for both the status of the individual and for collective representation. Part-time work has been traditionally opposed by trade unions and for some time is has been less used in Italy than in other developed countries. In recent years however it significantly increased.

The unions which opposed part-time for a possible discriminatory use for women and young workers they have become more inclined to accept particularly in cases of mixed study/work relationships, and whenever part-time work can enable a more flexible use of manpower capacities during working life and restore individuals or groups otherwise excluded from the (full-time) labour market to partial activity, at least.

Part-time work has been regulated by a considerable number of collective agreements at the national and enterprise levels. The most common provisions concern wages (they are reduced but not always in strict proportion to the reduction in working time); passage from part-time to full-time and vice versa (sometimes with an option for part-timers to become full-timers in the case of new hirings); sometimes a maximum quota of part-timers with respect to total employment of the firm. A very special use of part-time work has occasionally been worked out in plant bargaining as a way to share scarce employment opportunities in the face of serious productive crises.

A similar formula has been recognised and supported by statutory law: so-called solidarity contracts (*see* paragraph 249). In fact, the legislature too has taken a favourable view towards part-time work, regulating the education contract (*see* paragraphs 99 ff.) on numerous occasions and approving in the last two decades different sets of regulations.

Part-time work is widely defined by Article 1, Act 61/2000, so as to comprise its various possible forms also indicated in the ILO definition: the hours are fewer than those of normal working time and can be distributed throughout the week (horizontal) or concentrated only in certain days or periods of the month or year (vertical) or distributed according to a combination of the two modalities (mixed part-time). The labour contract must be concluded in writing and indicate the job and distribution of working hours.

102. The variation of working time during the contract has always been a critical issue because the conflicting interests of the firm and of the employee to dispose of his free time must be balanced. The strict regulation of Act 61/2000 has been made more adaptable by Act 30/2003.

Decree 81/2015 has introduced further flexibility in the use of part-time. The law allows the provision of so-called flexible clauses empowering the employer to change the distribution of working time from that originally planned (Article 3, Act 61/2000 as modified by Article 46 of Decree 276), and Act 247/2007, Article 1, co.

44. The terms and conditions of these clauses are determined by collective agreements. Lacking these agreements the flexible clauses can be agreed upon individually by the parties to the contract, in front of special certification commissions (Decree 81/2015, Article 6). This is an important exception to the exclusive role so far recognised by Italian law to collective agreements in the regulation of flexibility.

A controversial issue has concerned the possibility of the employee to 'change his mind', i.e., to revoke his consensus to the flexible clauses. Act 276/2003 excluded this possibility, Act 92/2012 has allowed it for personal and family reasons (health, education) and in cases provided by collective agreements. Decree 81/2015 has maintained this possibility only in cases of serious illness of the employee and of family members, and of parents of handicapped children (Article 6, co. 7).

In the case of variation of working time the employee is entitled to advance notice (minimum two days) and to special compensation fixed by collective agreements (Article 46, Decree 276).

Lacking specific provisions of collective agreements the employer can require from the employee an increase in working hours for a maximum of 25% of normal working time (so-called supplementary work) paid by a wage increase of 15% (Article 6).

Overtime is allowed in all cases of part-time according to the general legal and contractual rules (*see* below paragraph 149).

103. Precise formalities are provided for the passage from full-time to part-time work in order to protect employees: a written agreement of the parties and confirmation by the provincial labour office after hearing the interested employee are required. In cases of hiring of new full-time employees the right of precedence is recognised for those employees on part-time contracts, with priority being given to those who were already employed by the firm and had transformed their employment relationship from full-time to part-time (Act 247/2007, Article 1, co. 44 (*e*). According to Decree 81/2015, employees can opt for the transformation of their contract full-time into part-time instead of using their parental leave, for a corresponding period (Article 8).

Employers willing to hire part-timers are obliged to give previous notice in adequate form to full-time workers employed in all productive units located within the same municipality. Collective agreements are the major source of regulation of part-time work, also regarding the ratio of part-timers to regular workers; the jobs in which part-timers may be employed and employment conditions. Part-time workers are counted in proportion to their working time in the number of employees of the firms for various reasons (mainly fiscal).

A basic principle of the law is that part-timers are entitled to treatment not inferior to that granted to a comparable full-time worker (*see* already Act 61/2000 and now Article 7 Decree 81/2015). The provisions of Decree 81 apply in principle also to part-time in the public service (*see also* Article 2.co. 2, Decree 165/2001).

104. Some regulations of the law concern social security. Their aim is to adapt contributions and benefits to the reduction in the amount of time worked. Subsequent periods of part-time and full-time work during the life of the employee are counted separately for social security purposes. The burdens of social security have made part-time work relatively more expensive than full-time work. Act 549/1995 and Decree 61/200 have redressed the balance and adapted the amount of social security contributions to the specificity of part-time – calculating them in proportion to the actual amount of work.

The use of part-time work has been allowed in public service where it has been indirectly favoured. Act 662/1996 provides that only for part-timers their commitment to the public service is compatible with other (part-time) work also in the private sector (apart from specific cases of conflict of interest). The general rule is the non-compatibility and the same Act 662 has tightened the sanctions for public servants who break this rule.

The use of part-time employees over a certain age in order to favour a gradual retirement and possibly the hiring of part-time youngsters has been regulated by the Stability Act for 2016 (Article 1, co. 284, Act 208, 28 December 2015). This norm expired at the end of 2018 and was substituted by the so-called contract of expansion (*see* below).

The use of part-time has progressively increased due to favour of the legislation and to the changing attitude and culture of workers. But this type of work is still mostly for women.

The total number is now (October 2022) 4.205.000 of total employment. The number of involuntary part-timers has been increasing due also to the economic crisis.

105. A specific type of work arrangement similar to part-time is so-called job sharing, whereby two or more persons share the same job. This type of arrangement has been held admissible according to the general principles of labour law, as confirmed by a ministerial regulation of 1998. Act 30/2003 has formally recognised it and determined some basic regulations (Article 41, Decree 276). But this form of contract has been abrogated by Decree 81/2015.

V. Homeworking

106. The regulation and control of homeworking has always been difficult and employers have resorted to this type of work since it is less costly than that done inside the enterprise: it is estimated that there are more than 2 million homeworkers, most of whom are women. Act No. 877 of 1973 is intended, more clearly than the previous law of 1958, to guarantee homeworkers terms and conditions of work as similar as possible to those of regular workers so as to discourage resort to this type of work, considered as socially undesirable.

107. The law adopts a rather precise definition of subordinate homeworkers (Article 1, as modified by Article 1(2) of Act 858/1980) including in it all workers who work at their domicile or in premises of their own only with the help of members of the family (excluding salaried workers) for an entrepreneur, who directs the character of the job to be done and its execution. Autonomous homeworkers – not covered by the law – are those who work directly for the consumer or without a link with an entrepreneur. If the premises are provided by the entrepreneur – although rented – the workers are considered as regular employees of the enterprise. Homeworking is prohibited for activities which require the use of materials that are dangerous to health and safety, and to entrepreneurs who have discharged or laid off workers within the previous year due to reorganisation or restructuring of the enterprise (Article 2). Homeworking is also forbidden, in order to avoid fraud, when it is made possible by the decentralisation, in whatever form, of machinery outside the enterprise to workers.

108. Homeworkers are paid at a piece rate (Article 8), according to tariffs bargained collectively. When there are no collective agreements, as is usually the case, the law empowers a joint (regional) committee (four representatives of the most representative trade unions and four representatives from employers' associations) to fix the piece rate tariff. If this committee does not reach an agreement within a fixed term, the director of the regional labour office has the power to decide and must fix the rate according to the quality of the work done and to the collective tariffs paid by the entrepreneur to regular workers or to collective tariffs for similar jobs (the same criteria as followed by the jurisprudential interpretation of the fair wage, under Article 36 of the Constitution, *see* below paragraph 447). The strict regulation provided for by this Act encounters, however, serious obstacles when it has to be put into practice, due to the difficulty of controlling homeworking, the weakness of public labour inspection and, last but not least, the structural reasons for this phenomenon, which is a major aspect of the dual labour market existing in the Italian economy.

VI. Telework and Smart Work

109. Telework in Italy has not been covered until recently by specific legislation, probably because their number was relatively small. An exception is Article 4 of Act 191/1998 which sets basic rules for telework in the public service (which were implemented by a collective agreement in 2000). An inter confederal collective agreement was signed on 9 June 2004 aimed at promoting telework.

Telework is seen as a significant example of new forms of working activity and defies any easy classification. Telework does not present the characteristics of spatial and temporal subordination that are so important in the legal definition of employee. But on the other hand, the employer has evidently the means to develop a telematic job control. As to the category of homework (Act 877 of 1973), telework does not present the characteristics of physical manufacturing, of low-skilled jobs, and of partial autonomy in working that are typical of this working condition. But on the other hand, teleworkers may display some aspects of economic and technical subordination under the employer (single or multiple) and of technological homogeneity with contractors defined for homeworkers. With respect to self-employment (both as 'autonomous work' and 'semi-subordinated work'), telework does not always present the characteristics of technical autonomy, high-skilled and professional jobs, self-control and self-determination which are provided for these categories by the Civil Code. But, on the other hand, the teleworker has various possibilities for deciding where and when he will work. In summary, telework may assume such different practical forms that it may be classified within a very broad range of legal status, depending on the specifics of the case. However, if we observe social tendencies, in some enterprise-wide agreements so far signed for these employees (mobile maintenance, sales assistance, booking and commercial information, software development), the main scope of the social partners has been to provide for teleworkers the legal status of employees. To this end they have adapted traditional rules, or defined new control systems and new wage systems.

Act 81 /2017 (Articles 18ff.) has regulated the so-called smart work which is a revised version of telework, implemented in innovative ways through new technological and digital devices. The Act defines this type of work as a form of (execution of) subordinate employment defined by agreement among the parties, also organised by cycles and objectives without precise bounds of time or of place of work, with the possible use of technological devices. The activity may be performed partly within the firm premises and partly outside within the only limits of maximum duration of daily and weekly working time fixed by law and collective agreements.

The regulations are declared applicable to employment in the public administrations in so far as compatible.

The employer is responsible for the safety and proper functioning of the technological instruments assigned to the employee for the activity; he must safeguard the health and safety of the employee performing smart work. To this end he is obliged to inform yearly in writing the employees and the representatives for the safety of all the risks connected with the specific forms of execution of work.

Employers who sign agreements for the execution of smart working must give priority to the applications made by mothers within three years of the end of the maternity leave (stated by Act 152/2001) or by workers with disabled children (as defined by Act 104, 1992).

The agreement concerning the modalities of smart working must be made and proved in writing for administrative regularity; it regulates the execution of work outside, the firm premises, also concerning the forms of the exercise of the employer's powers. The same agreement also defines the rest periods of the employee and the measures technical and organisational necessary to guarantee the 'disconnection' of the employee from the technological instruments of work.

The agreement may be with a fixed term or for an indefinite period, in which case can be terminated with a notice not inferior to thirty days. The employee who performs smart working have the right to economic and normative conditions not inferior to those applied, according to collective agreements to employees who work exclusively within the firm premises. Moreover the agreement between the parties may grant the employee the right to continuous training and to the periodic certification of the skills so acquired. The 'agile work' has the right to be protected according to the general rules of work accidents insurance (Act 1124/1965) also against the work accidents occurred during the ordinary itinerary from home to the place chosen for the performance of work outside the firm premises, when this choice is due to the execution of work or to the necessity of the employee to reconcile work with his personal need, and provided the choice is reasonable.

During the COVID-19 pandemic the use of remote working has greatly.increased. Emergency legislation has favoured the recourse to this type of work by providing that it could be used with a simple communication by the employer to public authorities even in absence of a specific

agreement with the employee.

In order to face the problems arising from the use of smart work during the pandemic the peak organisations of the social parties, under request by the minister of employment, have signed a framework agreement (on 7 December 2021) setting guidelines for the regulation of this type of works by collective bargaining at central and decentralised levels.

VII. Apprenticeship

110. The contract of apprenticeship is a special labour contract whereby an entrepreneur undertakes to teach an apprentice to become a skilled worker (blue-collar) and the apprentice engages to work under the employer's direction. This is the definition of Article 2 of Act No. 25/1955 which contains the first regulation of the contract, repeatedly changed: Act 196/1997, Act 30/2003, Act 247/2007, Act 133/2008, Act 191/2009; Act 167/2011, Act 92/2012 as amended by Act 99/2013, and lately Decree 81/2015. The object of the contract is intended to be not only working for money in a position of subordination but, more important, training to acquire a skill. The apprentice is entitled to a wage, which is less than that of regular workers, fixed by collective bargaining, but the obligation of the employer to pay the apprentice is traditionally considered an accessory to his main obligation to train him.

111. This training function of apprenticeship has been undergoing a deep change with the development of the mass production industry, where the need for skilled jobs has been decreasing and, on the other hand, the specialised professional instruction necessary for it can neither be easily nor generally provided for in the practical training given inside a single firm. The courts have considered the apprentice a regular worker whenever the work is too simple to require training. An attempt has also been made by the Constitutional Court – though only partially and with some ambiguity – to strengthen the job security of apprentices by declaring unconstitutional Article 10 of Act No. 604 of 1966 where it excludes apprentices from protection against unfair dismissals.

The use of apprenticeship has been promoted and enlarged by recent legislation: Act 58/1987; Act 196/1997; Act 30/2003 as specified by Decree 276; Act 92/2012, Decree 81/2015.

This legislation defines and regulates three types of apprenticeship.

Some general rules are common to all the three types: the contract must be in written form and indicate the job content, the individual training programmes, the minimum duration in six months (apart from different conditions and duration fixed by collective agreements for seasonal works). Piecework is prohibited. The apprentice may be assigned to two levels of a classification lower than that of a corresponding employee. Presence of a tutor is required to follow the apprentice standard training. Basic formalities are: registration of the training received by the apprentice, recognition of the professional qualification and skill acquired.

The effective implementation of training according to the rules is a condition for being entitled to the cost reductions of apprenticeship (lower wages and reduction of social security contributions).

Collective agreements are competent to fix training and working conditions, within the principles of the law: specific requirement may be determined by regional administrations, respecting the fundamental principles of national law.

112. A first type of apprenticeship is organised so as to combine training within the enterprise with education in professional schools operating within the regional systems of education and the consequent duties (Article 43 Decree 81). It can be adopted for youngsters of 15 years of age (until 25).

The duration varies according to the professional qualification to be pursued; but cannot exceed three years or four (when necessary to acquire a four years professional diploma).

The content and duration of the training and of education obligations of the employer are fixed by a specific protocol between the employer and the school where the apprentice is enrolled. The protocol has to follow the indication of a ministerial decree, concerning the basic standards and certification of skills (Article 46, Decree 81).

The employer has no duty to pay wages for the hours of training organised within the schools and must pay only 10% of the hours of training within the enterprise (Article 43).

113. A second type of apprenticeship is applicable to young workers beyond school age, from 18 (17 in special cases) up to 29 years. The Act 137/2011 has introduced the possibility to hire as apprentices also employees made redundant by enterprises in crisis – who may be above the age of 29.

The contract is functional for the acquisition of specific skills and professional qualification. The minimum duration is six months, apart from seasonal activities where different duration can be fixed by collective agreements. The maximum is three years, or five, for specific qualifications of artisans.

The training may be provided not only in dedicated courses organised by specialised institutions (public and private) as it was in the past but also inside the enterprise (Act 133/208 Article 23). The importance of this ‘internal’ training has been emphasised by Act 167/2011. Article 44 of Decree 81 has specified that internal training is supplemented with formation organised by public institutions, for a maximum number of 120 hours in three years, but (only) according to available resources. The regions will communicate to the employer within 45 after the hiring of the apprentice the conditions and contents of public education opportunities. These opportunities are quite variable in the different regions.

In any event following this recent legislation, the absence of public courses does not represent an obstacle to the implementation of the contract which consequently can be based only on internal training (on the job).

Collective agreements have a major role in defining the requirements of training, its contents and the modalities necessary to acquire the professional qualifications. The traditional rule was that the number of apprentices cannot exceed 100% of the skilled workers employed by the firm, unless provided differently by collective agreements. Act 92/2012 has increased this proportion to 3 to 2 in enterprises employing more than ten employees. On the other hand the Act has provided that new hirings of apprentices are possible only if the enterprise has stabilised at least 50% of apprentices hired in the previous thirty-six months (for three years the percentage required is reduced to 30%). This limit has been criticised by employers and has been lifted by Decree 81/2015.

114. A third type of apprenticeship can be adopted for young workers between 18 and 29 years of age willing to acquire formal education degrees (secondary school, university degrees, specialisation degrees).

The regulation of this contract is up to the regions. The professional skills acquired during the apprenticeship can be accredited in formal educational curricula. The Budget Law of 2020 (Act 160/2019) has fully exempted the firms employing up to employees from the contributions due for the contracts of apprenticeship of the first type signed after 2 January 2020.

115. In spite of the increased favour and some simplification introduced by a recent legislator, the actual use of apprenticeship has been less widespread than expected, also due to the overlapping of regulations by the state, the regions and by collective agreements. Moreover it has to compete with contracts for an indefinite duration which have often been supported by considerable fiscal incentives (Act 190/2014).

The number of apprentices has been variable over time: according to the last data (Istat, October 2022) it amounts to 406.800.

A. A Special Form of Apprenticeship for Young Workers: Work-Training Contracts – Entry Contracts

116. The high unemployment of young workers induced the government to promote their employment also by introducing a special kind of work-training contract. This type of contract has been regulated in different ways beginning with Act 285/1977 subsequently amended several times: Act 863/1984; Act 196/1997 and Act 30/2003. It was reserved to young workers between the ages of 15 and 26 years and increased to 32 for youngsters living in depressed areas. Statutory regulations were reduced to the minimum. The timing and conditions of work and training are defined in special projects prepared by the interested enterprises and approved by the tripartite regional employment commissions in accordance with national/regional legislation and with agreements stipulated between the most representative local unions and employers' associations. The duration was for a maximum period of twenty-four months, not renewable. The young workers were entitled to a wage, proportional to their working hours, according to the minimum collective tariffs fixed for similar jobs. During the period of the contract, the employers obtained a fairly substantial financial subsidy. The use of this contract became quite common due to its advantages: not only reduced labour costs (reduction of social security contribution) but also normative advantages (liberalisation of hiring contrary to the general rules of public placement, valid until 1996 – *see* below; possibility of using fixed-term hiring freely, again contrary to general rules). It became competitive with apprenticeship also due to the fact that its formalities and training content came to be minimal.

117. In 2002 the European Court of Justice (ECJ) decided that the financial subsidies to this contract were against the European rules concerning state aids (C 310/99 *Repubblica italiana v. Commissione*). Following the decision public incentives were restricted by the government to the most depressed areas of the country (southern regions) where state aid was justified by the aim of fighting the high unemployment (in the north it had been greatly reduced).

The trend to extend some basic rights and protections similar to those of dependent employees to autonomous workers, particularly to solo self-employed and to economically dependent autonomous workers, has continued in recent years. This tendency is present not only in Italy and is supported by international organisations, ILO in the first place, and by some European directives: for example, the proposal of directive on the so-called platform workers, which considers both subordinate and autonomous workers.

118. The contract has been reshaped by Act 30/2003 which also changed the name to *contratto di inserimento*, literally 'entry-contract'. Articles 55ff. of Decree 276/2003 provides that this contract aims at facilitating the entry into the labour market of specific categories of workers: youngsters between 18 and 29 years, long-term unemployed until 32 years of age, workers above 45 years unemployed or at risk of losing their job, women living in areas of high unemployment.

Due to considerable economic advantages the 'entry contract' was widely used. On the other hand its favourable conditions have been considered not justified, given the scarce or non-existent training content. For this reason the contract has been abolished by Act 92/2012 which instead concentrated legal support and incentives in apprenticeship (*see* above paragraph 111).

A further legal instrument directed to favour the transition of youngsters from school to work is the so-called stage, which has been regulated in various forms, originally by Act 276/2003 and lately by Act 148/2011 and 92/2012 complemented by several Acts of Regions which have competence in the matters of vocational training. The law specifies that the stage is not a contract of employment but aims at providing high school and university students with some work experience, useful both in the school curriculum and for future placement (so-called non curricular stage), Act 92/2012 provides that agreements between State and Regions will define common guidelines indicating the basic requirements of stages: including the types of institutions entitled to promote the various types of stage, the conditions of training and of work activity of the student (in order to avoid abuses), and an adequate indemnity to the student.

The budget law for 2022 (Act 234/2021) has assigned to the regions the task to agree on a new set of guidelines concerning the use of non-curricular stage.

In order to favour the transition of young students from school to work, Act 107/2015 provides that all students of the last three years of the secondary schools must attend a period of combined activities, partly at school and partly of stage in selected firms or other organisations. The duration of this period varies from 210 hours in professional schools to ninety hours for the high schools.

These combined activities must be agreed between the schools and the host organisations and be followed by specially appointed tutors. The organization of the activities now under the name PCTO (School guidance paths) has changed over the years is and regulated also by codes of conduct.

§6. Self-Employment/Independent Work

119. Independent workers comprise different groups; apart from employers, 'professionals'; autonomous self-employed so-called collaborators legally autonomous but often economically dependent. In the past these groups were more numerous in Italy than in other European countries and included a certain number of false autonomous workers. Recently while professionals and self-employees of a new generation have continued to grow, other categories of solo self-employees have started to decline, facing difficult to work in the new economy. According to the last data (Istat, October 2022), the total number of independent workers amounts to 4.987.000.

Traditionally Italian labour law has been dealing with subordinate employment. Quite a few acts have regulated some forms of coordinated and continuous collaboration which have been defined 'independent', but in fact for their nature similar to subordinate employment have been subject to many parts of protective legislation typical of the latter.

Act 81/2017 is the first piece of legislation which is directed specifically to independent work. The Act applies to all forms of independent work, as defined by Title III of the Civil Code, excluding small business owners, which are regulated by Act 2083 of the Civil Code.

The Act provides for these workers some basic protections similar to those of dependent employees but with some adaptations linked to the specific need of independent workers: namely the right to paid maternity leave with the possibility of the mothers being substituted by other workers (with the consent of the employer); suspension of the employment contract for a maximum period in case of illness, work accident of the worker; special indemnity in case of unemployment.

Other norms are tailored to the specific needs of the independent workers' rights to be rewarded for inventions made during the period of the contract (apart from cases when the activity aimed at inventions is the object of the contract and is paid accordingly); protection against abusive contractual clauses; e.g., implying right of the principal to alter or terminate unilaterally the contract; protection against excessive delay in payments (according to Decree 231/2002):

- tax exceptions for expenses in continuous education, participation to professional meeting and conventions;
- information and consultancy on labour and professional opportunities through dedicated sections of public employment services;
- the government is delegated to approve simplified rules on health and safety concerning the members of professional firms.

It is also delegated to improve the measures of social protection for members of the regulated professions, authorising private organisations to provide supplementary forms of pensions and health care.

Public administrations are directed to promote the participation of independent workers in public procurements, also diffusing the relevant information.

In order to monitor and coordinate the measures in favour of independent workers the Ministry of Employment is committed to organising a table of discussion with the most representative unions, employer's associations, and associations of independent workers, with the task to elaborate proposals in the areas of professional training, social security and welfare.

I. Work in Associations and in Cooperatives

120. The typical labour contract is a bilateral exchange contract. Italian law accepts that a work activity can be the object of a contract of partnership or association (*associazione in partecipazione*) regulated by Articles 2549–2555 Civil Code. The associated worker participates in the common enterprise and shares its risk; for this reason he cannot be considered subordinate. Cases of work in association concern mainly professional workers who combine their activity with that of other partners. This contract may be used abusively, in lieu of an ordinary labour contract in order to save social security costs (much as in the case of collaboration contracts: *see* above). It is up to the judge to ascertain the real nature of the contract taking into account the effective character of the relationship: a professional, for example, is more likely to be truly associated to a common enterprise than a manual worker.

Act 92/2012 has intervened directly to prevent all kind of abuses by providing that a maximum of three workers be associated in the same 'activity', not counting relatives (the word activity is strictly interpreted as meaning 'enterprise'). Workers in excess of three are to be considered subordinate.

Moreover, a work activity can also be object of a cooperative enterprise (a form of enterprise quite common, particularly in some areas of Italy). This case has been regulated by law: Act 142/2001 and Act 30/2003. The law provides that a person is involved in two different kinds of relationship, one of partnership in so far as he is a member of a cooperative and one of employment (subordinate, autonomous or collaborative, according to the circumstances).

Consequently the Acts extend to this employee only some of the provisions typical of labour law: some collective and union rights, but only insofar as they are compatible with the status of member of the cooperative (Article 9 of Act 30/2003), the right to a remuneration proportionate to the quantity and quality of the work (the basic remuneration is usually fixed by national collective agreements, but extra-bonuses are granted unilaterally by the cooperative enterprise), some basic social security protection (old age pensions, work accidents). For the rest the norms on cooperatives are applicable, including the jurisdiction of ordinary courts.

The Act 117/2017 assembled an organic set of norms in a code of the so-called 'third sector', which groups different types of associations and entities, formed by civil society and operating in the different social and charitable activities, including social enterprises.

§7. The Requirements for Concluding a Valid Labour Contract

I. Legal Capacity to Work and to Contract

121. The minimum wage at which a person may be employed has been traditionally fifteen years (Act 977 of 17 October 1967 modified by Act 345/1999 implementing EU Directive 94/33). The age was lowered to 14 for agricultural work, services with the family, light non-industrial work and in the entertainment industry (safeguarding, in any case, the fulfilment of the child's educational obligations), and was raised to between 16 and 18 for some heavy activities which are considered dangerous to the physical and moral integrity of a child (Articles 5, 6, 16 of the Act). The capacity to conclude a labour contract and to exercise all the rights pertaining to a labour relationship was fixed by the Civil Code at the age of 18 (while under civil law the age of capacity was 21). Act No. 39 of 8 March 1975 has in general lowered the age of majority to 18 and has also provided that where the minimum age of employment is inferior, the minor can also exercise the rights and actions deriving from a labour relationship, which seems to imply a parallel reduction of the capacity to conclude a labour contract. These rules have been changed by the legislation on compulsory education. Act. 296/2006 (Article 1, co. 622) provides that the minimum age must be raised to 16 years to meet school obligations. A provision of 2010 has introduced an exception whereby youngsters of 15 can be employed as apprentices, using this contract to fulfil school obligations.

A. Children and Adolescents

122. Act No. 977 of 1967, revised by Decrees 345/1999 and 262/2000 (implementing EU Directive 94/33) sets special regulations to protect the work of children (below the age of 15) and of adolescents (between the ages of 15 and 18) such as special medical certificates guaranteeing their physical fitness for work, periodical medical checks on their health, limits to night work (forbidden in general between 10 pm and 6 am, apart from cases of force majeure authorised by the labour inspector), limits to working hours (a maximum of seven hours daily and thirty-five hours weekly for children, of eight hours daily and forty hours weekly for adolescents with a compulsory intermediate rest of one hour every four and a half hours worked), a compulsory period for annual holidays – thirty days for children and twenty for adolescents.

B. Women

123. In principle both single and married women have the same capacity to contract as men. In general, working women are guaranteed the same rights as men by Article 37 of the Constitution and by the ILO Convention No. 100, ratified by Italy in Act No. 741 of 22 May 1956. However, women's work was traditionally limited by a wide range of rules of law justified by the need to protect their health and their 'essential functions' (as stated by Article 37 of the Constitution) in the family and in maternity. Some of these limits and conditions are similar to those imposed on the work of minors, for example, prohibition of night work, underground, heavy and unhealthy work (Articles 6, 10 of Act No. 977 of 1967), and special medical check-ups. More restrictive limits are imposed on pregnant women, namely compulsory abstention from work two months before the foreseen date of confinement until three months after it (prolonged in cases of heavy and unhealthy work). These limits, apart from the protection of maternity, have been attacked as being unjustly discriminatory and as restricting women's employment opportunities. Act No. 903 of 9 December 1977 has abolished them. The prohibition of night work, maintained by Act 903, has been abolished by Act 25/1999 (Article 17(1)); now Article 53 of Act 151/2001 and Article 11.2 Decree 66/2003. It is confirmed only for mothers from the time of pregnancy to the first year of age of the child.

The Constitutional Court (Decree 137/1986) has declared unconstitutional Article 11 of Act 604 (on dismissal at retirement age), holding that the reasons which had in the past justified differential treatment of women in this respect (in order to reconcile the family role of women workers with their right to work) have become obsolete, given changing social, cultural and economic conditions. The court decision directly concerns the regime of dismissal at retirement, not the differences of this age as such. The fact that women maintain an option in respect of retirement age was considered justified as a positive discrimination in favour of women, for their peculiar position and double role in family and labour market.

124. But the issue of retirement age – and of early retirement – of women has *been* controversial for many years. Act 335/1995, reforming the public pension system has changed the retirement age for both men and women. In lieu of the fixed retirement age, it provided a flexible period for retirement for both men and women: between 57 and 65 years of age. The pension would vary according to the years of contributions and the years of average expected life after retirement.

Subsequent legislation has raised the minimum age: Act 243/2004 provides that the normal retirement age is 65 for men and 60 for women.

A decision of the ECJ, 13 November 2008 (c 46/2007) has declared that this remaining difference is incompatible with the principle of equal treatment and therefore must be corrected. The Italian government has provided accordingly (Act 102/

2009) and raised progressively to the level of men the retirement age of women in the public service, to which the ECJ has addressed its decision.

Following the Act 214/2011 the normal retirement age is now 67 years for men and women. An anticipation of retirement is allowed for women on condition of some reduction of pension (lately Budget Law, Act 127/2022) (*see* Chapter II, paragraph 4, 17).

C. *Foreign Extra-Community Workers*

125. Special provisions within the EU guarantee the principle of free circulation of manpower and therefore the right of the workers to hold job positions (Community regulations of 1961, 1964 and 1966 and in Italy DPR No. 1656 of 30 December 1965) and Decree 30/2007. Since January 2012 citizens from Bulgaria and Romania who have entered the E. C. can be hired freely. But Italian law is not completely consistent with this principle, because the granting of the residence permit has been discretionary for a long time and often requires lengthy bureaucratic procedures.

More restrictive is the regulation of extra-Community workers, which has been changed repeatedly over time: a major text is Act 286/1998. Since 2013 Italy has to apply European directive 2011/98 which has simplified the procedures for granting admission and unified the request for residence and work permits and the consequent permits. In fact, the presence of foreigners as regular workers in Italy, due to legal limitations and to the difficulties of the Italian labour market, has been traditionally limited.

The pressure has been growing dramatically in recent years, mainly from the Mediterranean and Eastern Europe countries. Many workers are working under illegal conditions. Recent estimates (2018) indicate 5,365,000 are officially residents; 2,455,000 are regularly employed. Recently the rate of employment of immigrants has been growing (more than that of Italians), but the distance has been reduced due to the economic crisis.

Following the increasing pressure of extra-Community immigration, the Italian government has intervened in two directions: in favouring the regularisation of these workers and in redefining the rules of entry). Procedures for regularisation were enacted in 1998/99, 2002, 2009 and 2012. The requests for regularisation have always been particularly numerous for domestic employees.

126. In order to regulate the flux of immigration the government has begun to fix every year a programmed, i.e., limited, number of entry permits both for indefinite and for fixed-term labour contracts, according to criteria harmonised with EU standards.

This instrument, first used in 1996, operated unevenly. It was regulated by Act 40/1998, by Act 189/2002, by Decree 334/2004 by Decree 13 March 2012. The recent pressures of immigrants have interrupted this type of control for some years.

The Decree of 2019 limited the number to 350,000, mostly for seasonal workers, The decree of 2021 has further reduced it to 69.700 again mostly for seasonal workers.

These regulations adopt a rather restrictive approach. The foreign worker may work on the condition that he is granted a residence permit for working purpose; this permit, however, can be obtained only if the worker already has an employment contract (a commitment to hiring new entrants by a 'sponsor' was held sufficient by the previous Act, but this possibility has been abolished).

The procedure for hiring extra-Community workers has proved to be long and cumbersome, which does not favour regularisation. Simplified procedures are provided for hiring seasonal workers and for workers already holding a residence permit.

Each alien applying for a permit must undergo police controls and identification procedures. Recent legislation has also revised the procedures for controlling illegal immigration and for expelling foreigners who enter the country and work under illegal conditions. During the employment contract the foreign worker enjoys full parity of treatment with nationals.

Act 73/2022 has introduced some simplifications in the procedures for hiring foreign workers and for granting them the *nihil obstat* for work.

A common European immigration policy is commonly held necessary, even more so as a consequence of the increasing pressure of immigrants, including refugees, coming from the southern and eastern borders of Europe.

II. Limits to the Conclusion of a Labour Contract Resulting from the Law on the Public Placement Service

127. The historic rule of Italian law was that mediation for concluding a labour contract was necessarily a public function: consequently not only was any private intermediation activity prohibited but employers were prevented in principle from hiring directly the workers they needed and were obliged to resort to workers registered on special lists at the employment offices, the local organ of the Ministry of Labour. Moreover, the employer could not specifically name the workers he requested from the agency but as a rule, only the number of employees needed, specified by their qualification. Request by name was allowed by Act No. 264 of 1949 (the general law on the subject) for all skilled workers and for a fixed percentage of unskilled, but it was severely limited by Article 34 of Act No. 300 of 1970 which allowed for only members of the employer's family and for highly skilled workers (as specified by a ministerial decree) to be requested by name. In line with these provisions, any worker looking for employment had to register at the employment office.

128. These limitations on the freedom of the parties to conclude a labour contract, stricter than in any other European country, have been traditionally justified by the public authority's need to control the match between labour supply and demand in a labour market characterised by high unemployment. They were so strict that in practice they were circumvented. The procedure through the employment office was followed mainly in the case of unemployed workers or of workers looking for a first job, and here too only in a small percentage of cases.

The rigidity of the system made it more and more unsustainable. Reforms have been introduced in the process of time, gradually reducing its scope and finally dismantling it completely. Request by name was admitted for employees on work training contracts (Act 285/1977 and following) and apprentices (Act 56/1987); then it was also allowed for 50% of all hirings (Act 863/1984). The request by name was generalised in the private sector by Act 223/1991 upon the condition of authorisation by employment offices. Also this condition was abolished in 1995.

Direct hiring has therefore become the rule also in Italy. The public monopoly of this function has been challenged before the ECJ, as being against freedom of circulation and services, and was indirectly broken by Act 196/1997 where it enables temporary work agencies to operate (*see* above paragraph 90). Decree 469/1997 has definitely abolished the public placement monopoly by allowing employment services to be also provided by private organisations although under public control.

Due to these changes the public employment offices were requested to change their role from one of mere certification, to one of active service directed at promoting better chances for the unemployed and favour a match between labour demand and offer on the market.

To this extent, the law commits them to provide services and to organise specific promotional actions, particularly for disadvantaged categories and unemployed workers (Decree 181/2000) Act 92/2012 has indicated further essential services due to these persons: periodical interviews, personal counselling, personalised training and job offers. Measures to strengthen these offices are provided specifically for youngsters by Act 99/2013 (*see* below).

129. According to the above-mentioned Decree 469/1997, the Ministry of Labour will retain a national competence (through the network of local labour offices) only on the following matters: (a) migration policy; (b) conciliation of individual as well as collective labour disputes; (c) settlement of collective labour disputes at a multi-regional level; (d) setting up of national informative/statistical service on the labour market; (e) linking with international bodies and coordination of the relations with the European Union.

Decree 469/1997 gave the regions large autonomy in organising the new system of public employment services, which are delegated in practice to the provinces. In each region, a 'trilateral regional permanent committee' should be set up in order to ensure the contribution of the social partners, jointly with the regional and local authorities. This is an example of the institutionalisation of 'social concertation' at regional/local level in Italy. This decentralisation has been confirmed and specified by the constitutional Act 3/2001 which has granted legislative powers to the regions, among others, in labour market matters (placement services, training, incentives to employment), although within the limits of the fundamental principles stated by national legislation.

130. After the abolition of public monopoly over the matter, employment centres are obliged to keep a list of job seekers only for special categories of workers: for the recruitment of unskilled public service workers (a rather odd provision indeed) and for disadvantaged people, mostly handicapped. The hiring of the latter category is regulated by Act 68/1999.

Act 68, modified by Act 92/2012 Article 4, 27° co., has maintained a quota system of compulsory hiring in favour of disabled people, but has reduced the quota from 15% of the workforce of the unit to 7% (two disabled persons must be hired by firms employing from thirty-six to fifty employees and one by firms employing between fifteen and thirty-five employees). In order to reduce the rigidity of the system, employers can stipulate specific agreements with centres for employment (Article 7) whereby they can agree on the best modalities to promote the useful employment of the disabled: the timing, the training needs and opportunities, the choice of individual disabled to be hired (contrary to the rule that still maintains for these workers a request by the number of employees to be hired). Act 14 of Decree 276 provides that employers may fulfil in part their obligation to hire seriously disabled people by sub-contracting work for the amount needed to so-called social cooperatives, which will actually employ the workers.

For other categories of people, there are no limits left to the conclusion of the labour contract deriving from the legislation on placement. The employer is, however, obliged to communicate to the centres for employment the names of people hired within the day prior to hiring (DM 30 October 2007). Prior practices to postpone the notice after the beginning of work were open to abuse (particularly in case of a work accident). The communication must also contain the essential elements of the contract so as to facilitate control on the fulfilment of legal obligations by the employer.

However, unemployed people must report periodically to employment centres (and accept their job and training offers) as a condition of receiving unemployment benefits (Decree 181/2000, Article 4). Act 92/2012 specifies that all employees receiving these benefits must accept the offers of training and of adequate job positions by the centres under penalty of losing the benefits (Act 4, co. 40–47), this rule has been confirmed by Decree 50/2015 (Article 25).

131. Act 152/1997, implementing EU Directive 91/533, specified that the information to be given to the employment offices must be in writing; so indirectly, a written form is required for all labour contracts.

The informatisation of employment services is a decisive instrument to improve their efficiency: so far it has proceeded unevenly in the various regions of the country. Article 15 of Decree 276/2003 intends to promote the informatic organisation of the labour market and to organise the exchange of information on a consistent national basis by setting up a *bourse* of jobs available nationwide.

Since 2011 the '*bourse*' has been set on a portal web, so-called *clic lavoro*, to which all public and private subjects operating on the labour market must be connected. Decree 112/2008 (Act 133/2008) has obliged the employers to keep a unified document where all current employees must be listed and which must contain all the information concerning their employment relationship (seniority, job classification, wages, social contributions). This document is intended to simplify the formal obligations of the employer to the employees and facilitate public controls.

132. The second innovation introduced by Decree 469/1997 was the legalisation of private employment agencies. Article 10 of the decree stipulates that the activity of mediation between labour demand and supply may be performed by undertakings or groups of undertakings, including cooperative companies, which have certain requisites and are authorised by the Ministry of Labour.

The end of the state monopoly in the field of employment service has been decided by Italian law in conformity with a ruling of the Court of the European Communities (11 December 1997) which ruled that the Italian law (Act No. 1369 of 23 October 1960) banning private companies from acting as employment agencies was contrary to European Union competition rules (Articles 86 and 90 of the Treaty).

Act 30/2003 specified by Decree 276/2003, regulated private employment agencies. The Act fixes some basic requisites for the operation of these agencies, beginning with their registration in a special register set up by the Ministry of Labour. The requisites vary according to the activities to be performed by the agencies: personnel selection and recruitment, mediation between demand and offer, support for professional adaptation, provision of temporary employees and staff leasing. Basically, they are similar to those required for temporary work agencies: minimum financial capital, operative extension in at least four regions, adequate skills of managers and staff (but not the exclusive dedication to one function because this limitation has been lifted).

The services of placement must be provided free of charge for the employees (Article 10(10), Act 469/1997) following the general principle of the ILO and of the EU.

Decree 276/2003 confirmed that all private agencies are bound by the principles of non-discrimination (Article 10) and must guarantee the protection of privacy in the acquisition, treatment and diffusion of personal data (Article 8).

Attempts to modernise public placement services have been repeated in recent years, but with scarce and uneven results. The entire system of placement has been revised by Decree 150/2015 as a major part of the labour market reform whose general guidelines are fixed by Act 183/2014; a further revision has been introduced by Act 26/2019, with the aim of reinforcing its organisations and functioning (*see* below 293 ff.).

III. Consent and Formal Requirements

133. The rules governing the conclusion of a labour contract do not differ in principle from the general rules of the Civil Code on contracts. Accordingly, an employment contract needs the consent of both parties, which may also be given tacitly because usually the law does not require any special formality for the conclusion of a contract. Special formalities are required by law for certain categories of workers, namely maritime and airline workers, where a public document or written document is essential to the contract's effectiveness for special clauses (trial clause, the fixing of a term to a contract, covenant of non-competition which must be in writing) and for certain acts of the employer (e.g., dismissal).

134. In practice, the labour contract is traditionally entered into by conclusive conduct; (certification was indirectly required in all cases in which the hiring had to be authorised by the public employment agency). In order to let an employee know his rights under the contract, national collective agreements require as a rule that an employer should provide his employee with a written statement specifying the date when the employment is to begin, the exact place of work, the job position according to the classification scale agreed collectively, the remuneration, the duration of the trial clause (if any), the special discipline applicable to the labour relation (e.g., the collective agreements which are applicable), and all other terms and conditions of work agreed upon by the parties (if any). The law also requires, for example, that the employer specifies in writing the disciplinary rules which apply within the firm (Article 7 of Act No. 300 of 1970) and makes the document stating them reasonably accessible to the employees. These duties of documentation have been generalised by Act 152/1997 following the EEC Directive 91/533, which obliges the employer to provide the employee with a written document stating the essential elements of the employment relationship: the parties' identity, the place of work, the job content, the date of beginning and (prospective) end of the employment, the period of notice and the terms of wages and working time.

135. The validity of the consent and any shortcomings in it must be judged according to civil law rules; violence, deceit, error related to essential elements of the contract are all, consequently, grounds for the annulment of the labour contract (at the initiative of the interested party and within the terms fixed by the Civil Code). In practice the importance of these shortcomings is greatly reduced due to the reduced role of consent itself in the conclusion and shaping of a labour contract which is typically a standard contract, i.e., with a content almost completely predetermined. Even an error in the identity or in essential qualities of the parties (namely of the employee) can be relevant only when it refers to the professional attitude of the employee to do the job requested. The relevance of other personal characteristics is indirectly excluded in principle by Article 8 of Act No. 300 of 1970 which prohibits any inquiry by the employer into elements not influencing the professional capacity of the worker.

IV. Object and Cause

136. According to general civil law rules the object of a contract (the performances due by the parties, here the work performances) must be possible, legally permissible (i.e., not contrary to imperative rules of law, public order or morality) and determined (or determinable) under the sanction of nullity. The cause of the contract (i.e., the relation between the obligations of the parties and, therefore, the function of the contract) must not be contrary to imperative rules of law, public order or morality. In practice, cases of nullity for lack of these requisites are fairly rare; for example, the object would not be possible in the case of the complete and irremediable technical inability of the worker. We will discuss below the special labour law discipline on the supervening impossibility of performance, which largely corrects civil law principles.

V. Labour-Only Subcontracting: Lending of Workers

137. An important type of labour contract traditionally considered as having an illegal cause is the so-called labour-only subcontract, whereby a worker is hired without materials or equipment by a person who is not in fact, the real user, to work for another person having the general control and direction of the performance and actually exploiting it. In such a case, the whole arrangement was illegal and directly forbidden by Act No. 1369 of 23 October 1960.

This Act aims at preventing the exploitation of employees by intermediaries who operate under the fictitious appearance of subcontractors, particularly of services. The rigid prohibition introduced in 1960 proved less and less able in the process of time to cope with the evolution of productive methods and in particular, with the trend to decentralise specific segments of production away from the core enterprise. It often interfered with genuine decentralisation needs without being effective in repressing fraud.

The prohibition of labour-only subcontracting has been derogated by the recognition of temporary work agencies by Act 196/1997 and then by the widening of their functions to include staff leasing (Act 30/2003); subsequently reformed by Act 92/2012 and by Decree 81/2015.

Labour-only subcontracting remains, however, illegal if not organised by authorised agencies and so the need to distinguish it from genuine subcontracting of services remains.

The Dignity decree (Act 96/2018) has reintroduced a specific criminal sanction for the fraudulent labour only subcontracting (which was abrogated by decree 81/2015). The definition of Act 1369/1960 indicated as a key character of illegal subcontracting the fact that the intermediator lacks any real work organisation which belongs to the real employer-user, thereby artificially separating the position of the formal employer from that of the real entrepreneur, normally in order to escape the application of protective labour legislation, social security norms and collective agreements.

The distinction between subcontracting services and of labour has been redefined by and large in the same terms by Decree 276/2003 (Article 29).

138. Since the legal definition is still rather vague, court interpretations are decisive. A basic principle followed by courts is that labour-only subcontracting is presumed whenever the contractor uses machinery, capital and equipment provided by the contracting employer even though a payment is granted for such use. This may be enough to solve the easiest cases, i.e., those in which the subcontractor totally lacks any of these elements or any significant organisation and hence appears at first glance as a pure intermediator of labour. But, on most occasions, the mere reference to the factors indicated above is insufficient and sometimes ambiguous. For example:

(a) when the importance of the equipment is relatively minor with respect to labour, which may be true for very simple activities such as cleaning and maintenance but most often applies to sophisticated activities such as information services;

(b) when some equipment must necessarily be provided by the user of the services because it is an integral part or object of the process (e.g., information services to be applied to an enterprise); therefore, the work must be done on it often under the user's direction for technical reasons. The very meaning of 'equipment' is changing: a software program is it a piece of 'equipment'?
(c) when the contractor or subcontractor has an organisation of his own (i.e., material, equipment) which he uses to some extent while also using the user's equipment in part and/or for some employees.

139. In all cases, which are ambiguous in one way or another, the courts have tried to find other indicators in order to distinguish labour-only subcontracting from job contracting. These indicators by and large concern the modalities and conditions under which the work is performed in order to see the actual link, independence or dependence that exists in relation to the user more than anything else. The most commonly used indicators beyond the provision of equipment are:

– the presence of the contractor's employees on the user's premises and enterprise;
– their subjection to the user's orders and controls on the execution of the work, including the imposition of working time and powers to discipline the user;
– remuneration system for the work done; if linked to collective agreements rules, it indicates labour-only contracting;
– the continuity and exclusiveness of the work done for the user;
– the lack (or presence) of economic risk (undertaken by the contractor).

The evaluation of these factors and of their mix may vary according to the type of work services and/or labour which is subcontracted. For example, the court may be more inclined to recognise labour-only subcontracting when the work and services are of a simple, repetitious nature (cleaning, simple technical computer operations). Lacking significant equipment needed from the contractor and given the minimal autonomy of the operator, it will be rather difficult to prove real and not simulated job contracting, particularly if it is rendered within the user's facilities.

140. Recent court attitudes imply a higher likelihood that real as opposed to simulated job contracting will be recognised, particularly in new areas such as information and business services in general. 'Intellectual' and professional work tends to be more easily qualified as independent and therefore to escape the rigid limitations of Act 1369. This is especially the case when the liberal professions which are recognised and organised by public professional orders (lawyers, business and tax consultants) are involved. This trend is apparently favoured not only by the professional qualities of these services but also by the interest of the people involved in being considered independent workers. A stricter interpretation might expose many small entrepreneurs to serious danger. The motives whereby the enterprise decides to sub-contract work or services even pertaining to its own ordinary economic cycle are not subject to judicial control.

The need for a looser interpretation of job contracting versus labour – only subcontracting has been recognised by Act 30/2003 and Decree 276/2003. Workers employed illegally are considered employees of the real employer-user for all legal effects of the labour relation. These prohibitions have, however, proved very difficult to enforce. The extent and condition of this joint responsibility between employers and the contractors have been subsequently changed. Act 296/2006 (Article 11, co. 911), provides that the employers contracting out services or works are obliged together with the contractor to pay wages and social security contributions to employees (within two years). But Act 92/2012 allows collective agreements to modify or lift this joint responsibility (Article 4, co. 31, (a), (b)).

141. The lending of workers has not been traditionally subject to regulation in Italian law, with the exception of an exchange of workers between small agricultural concerns, a situation expressly provided for by Article 2139 of the Civil Code. However, particularly within enterprise groups, there has always been a widespread custom known as 'command or detach' whereby an employee is ordered to work for a person or firm that is extraneous to the employment relationship while coming within the overall organisation of the latter. Both legal theorists and judges have debated as to whether this kind of 'detachment' may be deemed lawful or whether, on the contrary, it should be forbidden as it constitutes an interference with the carrying out of the job performance, in accordance with Act No. 1369 of 23 October 1960. The generally held opinion is for the lawfulness of such a situation. This depends not so much on the temporary nature of the 'detachment' but rather on the fact that such a detachment is in the interest not only of the person or firm borrowing the worker but also of the original employers; for example, if the employee acquires new skills during his period of detachment, this will ultimately be of advantage to the original firm.

Now the lawfulness of this practice is recognised in general by Article 30 of Decree 276/2003 which defines it in the same terms as those above. The original employer is held responsible for the treatment of the detached employee.

A special rule has been set by Act 99/2013. Employers having signed a 'network contract', may exchange employees among themselves without the need to prove a specific interest to the detachment, as required by courts in other cases of detachment (this norm has modified Article 30 of Decree 276/2003).

§8. Legal Consequences of Nullity and Annulment of a Labour Contract

142. A major exception to civil law principles is introduced by Article 2126 of the Civil Code in the case of nullity and annulment of a labour contract. This norm provides that, in spite of nullity or annulment, the legal and contractual effects of a labour contract remain in force for the time during which the labour relation has in fact lasted, i.e., for the time during which the work has been performed, apart from cases where the object of the cause of the contract is illegal: in this case, the employee can only claim damages – if any – according to the general principles on unjust enrichment. If the work has been done in violation of norms protecting the employees (e.g., norms on night work, on minimum age, or on public employment service) he is entitled to remuneration in any case.

143. Article 2126 has been widely discussed by legal commentators with respect to the general 'dogmatic' problem of the nature of the labour relationship. Prevailing opinion rejects the conclusion that this provision contradicts the contractual origin of the labour relationship chiefly because the effects guaranteed by Article 2126 are limited to the de facto duration of the work with no obligation to the parties to continue it. Therefore the relation can be terminated at will, whereas if the contract was valid a justified motive or a just cause would be, in principle, necessary (*see* below paragraph 219). But there is no doubt that Article 2126 practically reduces to a minimum the relevance of a (valid) labour contract insofar as it neutralises most of the negative effects of its invalidity. Accordingly, the de facto work done is assumed as relevant in itself and deserving to be protected according to the legal and contractual rules applicable to all regular employees.

Chapter 2. The Rights and Duties of the Parties During the Employment Relationship

144. The reciprocal rights and duties of an employer and of an employee derive from different sources. The role of the individual labour contract in shaping them has long ceased to be primary, due to the development of labour legislation and collective bargaining. Both these norms are in principle imperative and incorporated into the individual contract itself and, more properly, directly shape the individual labour relationship, when contractual provisions are either absent or state the contrary. Some revival of the role of the individual contract is favoured by the trend toward liberalisation of some areas of labour law and by labour market changes. Indeed, this revival seems rather limited and confined to skilled employees in areas where there is a tight labour market. Some duties and rights derive from the contractual origin of the labour relationship itself, i.e., from the application of the relevant articles of the Civil Code on contracts in general. We will, however, limit ourselves mainly to the obligations and rights which specifically affect the employer and the employee.

145. The fundamental obligations of the labour relationship, resulting from its very definition (Article 2094 of the Civil Code), are that of the employee to work under the command and control of the employer and that of the employer to remunerate the employee for the work done. The parties, moreover, are bound by a series of other obligations that are accessory or instrumental to their fundamental duties.

§1. Duties of the Employee

I. Duty to Work Diligently and Obediently

146. The employee must perform his work with the care and diligence required by the nature of the work (Article 2104, paragraph 1 of the Civil Code). The law distinguishes between diligence, which is a way of performing the duty, and the duty to obey the commands and directives relating to the execution of the work (Article 2104, paragraph 2). This duty of obedience results from the worker's subordination.

II. Job Classifications

147. The scope of the obligation to work – and therefore the object of the contract – is in principle identified by the jobs agreed upon by the parties. The various jobs which make up the work organisation of a plant are usually grouped together and classified in a scale according to their content through collective bargaining. A group of jobs of common professional content and common evaluation in terms of salary is called *qualifica* by the law, or 'category' according to the traditional terminology of collective agreements. For example, in the metal-workers' national agreement, up to 1973, blue-collar workers were divided into six categories, ranging from completely unskilled workers to highly specialised white-collar workers were divided into five categories and the intermediate group (*see* above paragraph 71) into two categories. Since 1973 the traditional system of classification in most industrial sectors has been changed in order to adapt it to the evolution of work organisation which had made the old category divisions largely obsolete. The classification is now the same for blue- and white-collar workers. All workers are divided into seven or eight levels, which signify mainly a common remuneration; one or two further levels are often provided for 'cadres'.

This classification has meant a reduction in wage differentials between the least and most skilled workers. Within each level, national agreements distinguish between different 'professional profiles', i.e., patterns of jobs having a common professional value to be specified and adopted through plant-wide bargaining. During the 1990s some national collective agreements (e.g., chemicals, telecommunications, banking) have substituted the traditional division into eight or ten levels with a looser classification into four or five broad 'areas' within which more specific profiles may be determined at plant level according to the circumstances. The aim of this broad classification is to increase functional flexibility in the use of manpower. This trend towards more flexibility is accompanied by a (cautious) reopening of occupational wage differentials which can be detected now in many sectors and which has been helped by the abolition of the escalator clause in 1992 (*see* below paragraph 195). The collective agreement for the metalworking industry of 2021 has renovated the traditional classification based on level and groups of tasks, and substituted it with a much looser system of roles and competences, which allows for more flexibility in work organisation and more responsibility of the employees.

148. In general the parties refer to this collective classification in order to identify the performance due from the employee and the corresponding remuneration due from the employer. The basic principle stated by Article 2103 – as amended by Article 13 of the Workers' Statute (Act No. 300 of 1970) – is that a worker must be assigned to and employed on the jobs, and classification, for which he has been hired. The same article, however, acknowledged a very limited power of an employer to change these jobs, under fixed conditions. Under Article 13 an employee could be moved either to jobs equivalent to those for which he has been hired, or to jobs corresponding to a higher classification (*qualifica*) in the scale resulting as a rule from collective agreements. In this latter case he must be paid the corresponding remuneration and, after a period of time fixed by collective agreements, in no case longer than three months, his assignment to the higher qualification becomes definitive (i.e., he may not be reassigned to the original lower job position). This latter rule does not apply when the assignment to a higher position is decided on to substitute for an employee absent for illness, military service, or pregnancy and consequently entitled to keep his post during the suspension of the contract.

149. To be 'equivalent', two (or more) jobs must be paid the same remuneration and have a similar professional content. The decision on what is equivalent may be very delicate and is generally made taking into account the job classifications and career profiles fixed in collective agreements. Court interpretation of the term *equivalent* has been traditionally rather strict; but pressure has been growing to accept a looser approach in order to favour a more flexible use of the workforce. The exact nature of the so-called principle of irreducibility of remuneration has been clarified by case law: 'irreducible remuneration' does not include 'accessory' elements of pay such as indemnities that are linked to aspects which are extrinsic to the job performance itself (e.g., risk benefits to compensate for specific factors such as dangerous environmental conditions, not present in the new job). The principle applies also in cases when there is merely a change in the place where the job is to be carried out without there being a change in the type of job performance (e.g., a benefit deriving from a job being performed abroad would not be retained should the worker come back to work in his native country).

150. Any agreement contrary to Article 13 providing that an employer can unilaterally change the job position of an employee beyond these limitations was considered null and void. In the process of time a reasonable application of the provision has come to be adopted by courts and agreed upon at the plant level through a bargained and fairly broad interpretation of the notion of equivalence, e.g., it has not prevented the parties from experimenting with fairly elastic forms of job rotation. However, a change even to a lower job position is allowed when the change is in the interest of the employee, e.g., because he has become an invalid and consequently unable to keep his previous post (Act 482/1968, Article 20 and now Act 68/1999, Article 4(4)); or because the previous position would be prejudicial to a working mother (Act 1204/1971, Article 3; Decree 151/2001, Article 7); or because the post has been abolished due to industrial restructuring or reorganisation; this latter conclusion has been adopted by courts and indirectly confirmed by Act 223/1991 (Article 4 (11)). Act 8 of Act 148/2011 has empowered local and enterprise collective agreements to derogate to various legal norms, including Article 13.

151. The need to reduce the rigid limits set by Article 2103 to the internal mobility of the employees has been definitely recognised by Decree 81/2015 (implementing Act 183/2015). This innovation is in line with the general purpose of the Jobs Act to respond to the needs of flexibility in employment which are greater than in the past.

The decree acknowledges this need not only at the beginning and in the termination of employment (so-called external flexibility) but also in the normal use of manpower during the course of the contract (so-called functional or internal flexibility).

Other aspects of functional flexibility are recognised by Decree 81/2015 (Article 8) which concern the variations in working time (*see* above).

Article 3 of Decree 81 enlarges the power of the employer to change the range of tasks in which the employee can be employed, in various directions:

(a) The employee can be assigned to all jobs included in the same level of classification, regardless of their 'equivalence', provided that they remain within the original category (blue collars, white collars, cadres). A similar norm was introduced in the public service by Article 52 of Decree 165/2000.

(b) In case of firm's restructuring or reorganisation and in other cases identified by collective agreements, the employer can assign the employee also to jobs included in a different level of classification (one level of difference allowed) without changing his wage, a part from economic treatments linked to the specific job.

(c) Individual employees, assisted by labour unions or in front of the commissions indicated by Article 2113 civ. Code, can also agree to the modification of their level of classification and of the correspondent wages in order to safeguard employment or to acquire new professional skill.

(d) The assignment of the employee to jobs pertaining to a superior level of classification becomes definitive, i.e., cannot be revoked, after six months (previously the time limit was three months).

III. Transfer

152. Article 13 of Act No. 300 provides that an employer can transfer an employee from one place of work (Productive Union) to another only when the transfer is justified by organisational, technical or productive reasons for so doing. Judicial interpretation of this norm is not uniform. In general the courts limit themselves to verifying the existence of these reasons without questioning the merit or requiring the inevitability of the transfer. Some courts have, however, tried to balance the interest of the employers with that of the employee and his family, e.g., by exploring possible alternatives to the transfer.

The issue is particularly controversial when the transfer involves travelling a significant distance. Some courts have decided that such a transfer can only be made with the employee's consent, unless the possibility of such a transfer is expressly provided for in the individual or collective contract or is implied in the nature of the job (e.g., salesman); but this seems to remain a minority opinion.

Decree 104/2022 implementing EU directive 1152/2019 provides that the employer must inform in writing the employee of the place of work where is assigned. Lacking a predominant place, he must indicate the different places of work or the employee is free to determine the place.

IV. Duty of Fidelity (Duty of Non-competition and Duty to Respect Professional Secrets)

153. Under this heading, Article 2105 of the Civil Code provides that an employee must not do business that is competitive with his principal employer or take any job which might damage the latter; that he must not disclose to other persons confidential information pertaining to the organisation or methods of production of the enterprise or use such information to the detriment of his employer.

The law protects the so called whistleblowing of employees according to the principles of EU directive 2019/1937, specified by Italian Act 197/2017, and by the regulations of ANAC, of 1 July 2020.

154. The prevailing opinion has come to exclude that the duty to respect professional secrets should continue even after employment has ended. The duty of non-competition can last beyond this term only by means of a non-competition covenant. This covenant must be concluded in writing, and must indicate the extension of the object and the area of the limits imposed to competition. Compensation to the employee must be provided.

Violation of both duties is ground for disciplinary sanctions, up to dismissal, according to the gravity of the violation, as specified by collective agreements. The disclosure of industrial or scientific secrets is also punished by Article 623 of the Penal Code, with imprisonment for up to two years. The duty to respect professional secrets does not usually mean that a worker cannot use the professional skills acquired on his job or discuss and criticise the economic policy of the enterprise publicly. A delicate problem might arise as to the contents and effects of professional secrets, but has not yet been clearly discussed, from the application of the collective bargaining agreements which grant union representatives the right to be informed by management about investment and other productive decisions of the enterprise.

155. In addition to these two specific duties, the employee (like the employer) is bound to perform the labour contract according to the general civil law principle of good faith. This implies, for example, the duty to keep and return tools and raw materials in good condition (violation with gross fault may be ground for damages but it is in fact dealt with by disciplinary action). The trend, confirmed by the Workers' Statute, is to restrict these 'implied' duties of good faith to the functional needs of production and to exclude their coverage from the whole 'personal behaviour' of the worker.

§2. Duties of the Employer

I. Duty to Employ the Worker

156. Such a duty was traditionally recognised by legal commentators for special categories of workers only: apprentices, employees on trial, or in general those having a specific interest in actually working (e.g., artistic employees). Now the prevailing opinion, which is also that of the courts, believes that a general obligation of the employer to actually use all the employees for the jobs for which they have been hired, and to supply the necessary conditions (tools, etc.), can be derived from Article 13 of Act No. 300 insofar as this norm implicitly protects and promotes the professional attitudes of the workers. The actual enforcement in the courts of this duty may be difficult in practice because a specific performance can hardly be sanctioned and it is difficult for the employee to prove damages (but cases are reported of damages granted, particularly to skilled employees).

II. Duty to Provide Safe Conditions of Work

157. Article 2087 of the Civil Code provides that an employer must adopt in the organisation of his enterprise all measures which, according to the nature of the work, the experience and the technical possibilities, are required to protect the physical integrity and moral personality of his employees. This general, very broad provision is specified by a detailed set of rules, sanctioned by penal and administrative penalties, to guarantee health and safety within the firms, in particular by DPR No. 303 of 19 March 1956 and DPR No. 547 of 27 April 1955 on work hygiene and prevention of work accidents (now rather obsolete and in the process of reform). Articles 437 and 451 of the Penal Code punish as a crime the omission and removal of measures and devices to prevent work accidents (imprisonment of up to five years if the omission is intentional, up to one year if it is due to negligence). The effectiveness of all these provisions is very restricted, in part due to their ambiguity or obsolescence, in part or chiefly due to the lack of efficient public controls on the work environment. In fact Italy has a very bad record of work accidents and professional diseases.

158. Act No. 300 of 1970 (Article 9) has tried to strengthen this control by acknowledging for the workers, through their representatives, the right to check the application by the employer of the provisions aimed at preventing work accidents and professional diseases and the right to promote research into and the implementation of all suitable measures for protecting their health and integrity. The right to control has been fairly widely exercised by employees, through ad hoc representatives and experts trusted by them. Employers refusing such control within an enterprise have been accused of anti-union activity under Article 28 of the Workers' Statute (*see* below paragraphs 386 ff.). The meaning of the second part of Article 9 is less clear. Some commentators believe that it lays down a simple statement of policy hardly enforceable in the courts; others believe that it grants workers' representatives a right to make proposals, to bargain with the employer about them and even to resort to the courts in order to have those proposals, which are unreasonably refused by the employer and which are 'suitable for protecting the workers' health' directly enforced. The second part of Article 9 has never been tested before the courts. But the principle stated by Article 9 has been implemented by Decree 81/2008 (*see* below). Powers to control the work environment to these ends have been granted to the local units of the National Health Service (Act 833/1978); these units often have not reached a satisfactory degree of efficiency.

The matter of safety at work has been deeply influenced by EU directives, beginning with the framework Directive 89/391. This directive (and seven specific directives following) has been implemented in Italy first by Act 142/1992, by the Decree 626/1994, recently modified by Decree 242/1996 and lately by Decree 81/2008 as amended by Decree 106/2009. These decrees define in great detail not only specific safety measures but also the procedural duties of the employer, in particular, to verify the degree and quality of risks present in the enterprise, to evaluate their character in order to implement measures directed to reduce them and prevent work accidents. A detailed document of evaluation must be prepared and kept in the enterprise, periodically adjourned. The employer has the duty to inform of the safety condition of the workplace to the union representatives specifically allowed by law to operate in the firm to their extent.

Specialised employees' representatives are elected in order to supervise working conditions, and have the right to be consulted on all safety issues and make proposals on these matters.

A most serious sanction which consists of the forced suspension of the enterprise activity, has been provided by Act 112/2008, and now by Article 14, Act 81/2008, in case of repeated violation of the rules concerning safety at work.

Some basic principles of Decree 81/2008 are applicable also to para-subordinate workers. Employee's victims of work accidents and professional diseases are protected by a special social insurance system; moreover, they can recover damages including so-called biological damages, those related to the reduction of the integrity of the person as such.

An implication of Article 2087 has been identified by courts which have found sexual harassment to be in violation of the dignity and personal integrity of the individual employee protected by this article: the consequences are civil responsibility and damages, in addition to possible penal sanctions. Also some cases of mobbing have been found to be in violation of Article 2087. This rather broad interpretation of the article was a substitution for specific legislation on sexual harassment and on mobbing. Sexual harassment is now sanctioned by Decree 198/2006 as a form of direct discrimination. On mobbing a bill is pending in Parliament; meanwhile mobbing is severely sanctioned by a considerable number of court decisions.

During the COVID-19 pandemic (2020–2021) public health authorities have enacted a series of measures to prevent contagion: lockdown of activities of different duration and intensity, obligation to wear protective masks, compulsory vaccination for some public employees.

The application of preventive measures in the workplace has been specified by many collective agreements, national and company-wide.

The general measures included in the protocol signed in 23 April 2020 (and adjourned) between the Government and the most representative social parties, aimed at the containment of COVID-19 in the workplaces and have been endorsed by act 40/2020 which provides that employers abiding by the protocol are considered to have respected the duty of safety protection fixed by 2087 civil code and consequently are not responsible for workers contagions.

III. Duties Related to Employment Cards

159. The law (Act No. 112 of 1935) traditionally required most categories of workers to be provided with an employment card (*libretto*), containing basic information on the worker's personal data, professional attitudes, jobs performed and duration of the jobs done. An employer could not hire any worker who did not have this document.

The abolition of the rigid public procedures of hiring has also implied the abolition of the employment card. This is substituted by a personal document of the employee which is relevant to state the acquired skills and professional itinerary of each individual: *see also* Decree 112/2008 which has introduced a 'unified document' on the matter Decree 151/2015 (Article 15) has provided that this document, like others connected with employment procedures, must be organised and kept with the Ministry of Labour in electronic form. The unemployed worker remains obliged to report to the employment offices only in order to maintain the right to unemployment benefits (*see* below).

160. An important obligation of the employer has been recently introduced in order to control the respect of social security regulations (and indirectly also the economic conditions of employment). All employers are obliged to keep a 'unified document' of contributive regularity (DURC) as a condition of being entitled to all benefits and incentives provided by the law and to participative to public tenders. The document must contain all data concerning the employment contract and must certify the fulfilment of all social security obligations.

This duty is intended to control and reduce the black economy which is particularly extended in certain sectors and areas of Italy.

The introduction of this document and of the unified work document (*see* above paragraph 106) has been also backed by a reinforcement of the procedures and sanctions concerning irregular works. The procedures are provided in Act 296/06 Article 1, co. 1192. And Act 78/2014 provides that all interested persons can verify online their contributive position.

Recent European and Italian legislation has given growing importance to the employers duties of information and transparency. Decree 104/2022 implementing European directive 2019/ 1152 has greatly increased the duties stated by decree 152/ 1997. It has specified very analytically, the contents of these duties, concerning all the aspects of the employment relationship, the identity of the parties, the programmes of work, the normal working schedules including their possible variation, the collective agreements applicable to the relationship, the social security rights of the employee and the competent institutions.

This information must be granted not only to subordinate employees but also to para subordinates and even occasional workers.

§3. Directive and Disciplinary Powers of the Employer

161. An employer's directive power is the counterpart of the duty of obedience of an employee. Disciplinary power is the ultimate guarantee of the former and of the implementation of an employee's duty. The power of an employer to take the law (of the enterprise) into his own hands, unique in private contractual relations, is usually explained as a need to promptly punish employee's violations without resorting to less efficient general reacting to a breach of contract or to the maximum solution of dismissal. The general provision of Article 2106 of the Civil Code provides that the violation of an employee's basic duties (diligence, obedience and fidelity) is grounds for disciplinary action by his employer. The exercise of both these powers – originally widely discretionary – has been restricted and controlled through collective bargaining and by the law.

I. Limitations by Law

162. Some restrictions derive from the provisions of Act No. 300 of 1970 which guarantee workers basic freedom of expression and of concerted activity within the plant, and whereby an employer is forbidden to make inquiries into the personal opinions of his employees and into questions which are irrelevant to his professional attitudes. Other restrictions come from Articles 2–7 of Act No. 300.

163. Article 2 prohibits using private police – fairly frequent in the past – inside firms for motives other than the protection of private property, in particular for the purpose of controlling workers' activities. Consequently these guards are forbidden in principle from entering work premises and from denouncing violations of the employees' duties (not related to private property). Article 3 obliges an employer to communicate to interested employees the names and specific assignments of supervisory personnel. Article 4 prohibits in principle the use of audio-visual instruments and other machinery to control the employees at a distance (i.e., without them being aware of it). An employer can only use such instruments when it is necessary for technical, organisational or safety reasons, provided that it is bargained about with the union plant representatives (or subordinately the work committees) or, lacking any agreement, that it is authorised by labour inspectors. All these provisions are obviously aimed at preventing abuses by an employer in the (necessary) surveillance of his employees. Their application has proved rather difficult with respect to information systems of control (badges, data collections, etc.) which can be used simultaneously for safety, organisational reasons and for personal control of individuals.

164. A similar aim is pursued by Article 6 which allows employees to be searched only at the plant exits, when it is necessary to protect the enterprise's property such as the materials or instruments used in production, in a system of arithmetic selection related not to single workers but to groups of them and in such a way as to guarantee their dignity and privacy. The cases in which searching may take place and the relevant conditions must be bargained upon between an employer and the union plant representatives (if there are no works committees); without an agreement they must be decided by the labour inspectorate.

The need to update the regulation of Article 4 in line with the evolution of production and technology has been recognised by Decree 151/2015 (Article 23). The new Article 4 extends the possibility of control at a distance also to protect the enterprise property. Even more important, it entitles the employer to monitor the work tools and the instruments which check the presence of the employees without the need to bargain with the union's representatives and to ask permission from the territorial offices of the Ministry of employment.

The meaning of work tools is controversial, in particular, it is discussed whether it comprises instruments and digital devices which are commonly used by enterprises for production, but at the same time may imply a strict control on the activity of the employers.

According to Article 8 the employer is forbidden, before hiring and during the course of employment, to conduct inquiries, also through third parties, on the political, religious, trade Union opinions of the workers and on any other fact that is irrelevant to the assessment of their professional qualifications.

The effectiveness of this provision is now challenged by the diffusion of digital technologies and of social networks which multiply the circulation of information, including personal data often provided by the workers themselves.

For this reason, the national and European regulations of data protection (decree 101/2018 and European regulation 2016/679) have acquired growing importance for the protection of privacy also of the workers.

165. The violation of Articles 2, 4, 5, 6, is penally sanctioned: a fine from EUR 100,000 to EUR 1 million can be increased up to five times by the judge and imprisonment from fifteen days to one year, which can both be applied in very serious violations. It seems that there have never been cases of actual application of these criminal sanctions.

II. Limits to Disciplinary Powers

166. The only limit which Article 2106 of the Civil Code provided for was that disciplinary sanctions had to be proportionate (or adequate) to the seriousness of an employee's violation, according to collective agreement.

Article 7 of Act No. 300, while confirming the unilateral nature of the disciplinary power, limits its exercise to a rather detailed series of further restrictions, mostly of a procedural nature. An employer must adequately publicise, with appropriate details, the disciplinary rules (violations, each relevant sanction and disciplinary procedures) by affixing them in a place which is accessible to all employees. It is debatable whether it is adequate for an employer simply to provide his employees with a text of the collective agreement fixing these rules (which the employer must anyhow respect). Recent court decisions are on the negative and require actual posting. An employer cannot take any sanction without first communicating the grounds for it to the employee in question and hearing his defence (the grounds must be specifically indicated). For this purpose, an employee can be assisted by a union representative of his choice. Sanctions which are more serious than a verbal reprimand cannot be taken in any case before five days have elapsed from the giving of the grounds in writing.

167. An employer cannot fine an employee more than four hours pay or suspend him from work and his pay for more than ten days. Reprimand (written and verbal), fine and suspension are the usual sanctions. Article 7 prohibits taking sanctions which cause 'definitive modifications of the labour relationship', i.e., transfers or change of job content. When there are no similar provisions in collective agreements, in addition to the ordinary court procedure, an employee affected by a disciplinary sanction can appeal within twenty days to a tripartite conciliation and arbitration board, set up in the provincial office of labour (one representative from each party and an impartial member). An appeal to this board automatically suspends a disciplinary sanction, and for this reason it is widely used by workers.

Article 7 finally provides that disciplinary sanctions cannot be considered two years after their application, i.e., an employer cannot take into account sanctions which were imposed two years or more previously in order to consider the employee's recidivism and therefore apply a more serious sanction for a present violation. Article 7 does not fix any time period for the employer's decision on disciplinary measures; many collective agreements indicate that if the employer does not proceed within a short time (e.g., ten days) from the employee's defence to apply some sort of measure, the defence is considered as accepted.

168. It is a controversial issue whether the detailed procedure provided by Article 7 must also be applied to disciplinary dismissals. In fact these dismissals are considered by collective agreements as the most serious disciplinary sanctions. But Article 7 is somehow ambiguous and seems to refer to Act No. 604 as the only source of regulation of dismissals. The Court of Cassation had originally declared Article 7 in principle inapplicable as regards dismissals, rejecting even the applicability of the first paragraphs (grounds in writing, right to defence, five days' time) on the assumption that these are inseparably linked with the following ones which are incompatible with the discipline on dismissals (they also have a much more general scope of application: *see* below paragraphs 227–228). However, the Court admitted that the procedural guarantees of Article 7 are applicable when they are explicitly embodied in collective agreements. Other decisions held these guarantees applicable for the mere fact that the collective agreement includes dismissals in the list of disciplinary sanctions provided by the agreement. Basic procedural guarantees are in fact, usually reproduced by most national agreements with two exceptions: the rights of an employee to suspend the sanction by resorting to arbitration and the five-day period before the application of the sanction when the violation by an employee is so serious as to represent a just cause for dismissal without notice. In this case, some collective agreements provide that the employee may be suspended from work instead of being dismissed until the facts are ascertained.

Following a decision of the Constitutional Court (No. 204/1982) the procedural guarantees of the first three paragraphs of Article 7 have been extended to disciplinary dismissals. This concept is widely conceived as including all dismissals due to irregular or illegal behaviour of the employee. Another decision of the same Court No. 427/1989 has held these three paragraphs applicable also to disciplinary dismissal in the productive units having fewer than fifteen employees, i.e., below the threshold then valid for the application of the protective norms on dismissals (*see* paragraphs 281 ff.).

169. The principle of non-discrimination represents a general limitation to employers' powers. The general legal sanction derives from Article 15 of the Workers' Statute as supplemented by Article 13 of Act 903 of 1977. The first declares null and void all acts and agreements in any way discriminating against employees because of union affiliation or non-affiliation, religious or political beliefs; the second extends the prohibition to discrimination on the grounds of sex, race, ethnic origin, language. In fact, these norms forbid all major reasons for discrimination and are potentially applicable to all employers' decisions impinging on the employee's position during the life of the employment relationship (*see* paragraph 295). They also apply to pacts, i.e., both individual and collective agreements having discriminatory effects, even though unilateral decision-making by the employer is the one which comes under scrutiny most often. However, the effectiveness of the prohibition is rather problematic (*see* below for anti-union and sex discrimination, which have been the most widely investigated areas).

The normative implications of the principle of non-discrimination are specified by Decree 215 and 216/2003 implementing the European directives 2000/43 and 2000/78 (*see* below paragraphs 198 ff.).

Chapter 3. Working Time and Holidays

§1. Working Time

170. The traditional statutory discipline goes back to Act No. 692 of March 1923, which provides that the hours worked by employees must not exceed eight hours a day or forty-eight hours a week. Act 196/1997 (Article 13) has changed this rule and reduced to forty hours as the normal weekly hours; the norm has been confirmed by Decree 66/2003 implementing EU Directive 93/104, which re-regulates the whole matter (Article 3). No legal limit is fixed to daily normal hours, in order to allow for some flexibility. Indirectly a maximum of thirteen hours derives from the obligation to respect a minimum of eleven hours of continuous rest every twenty-four hours (Article 7, Decree 66). In public service the standard working week is thirty-six hours. Collective agreements of the private sector are empowered to determine the normal weekly working time of forty as an average over a multi-weekly period (not superior to one year): Article 3, Decree 66/2003, confirming Act 196/1997. Consequently, work can exceed forty hours weekly without overtime pay provided the multi-weekly average remains at forty. Act 196 does not significantly alter the cost of labour because since 1973, most national collective agreements have introduced the forty-hour (and five-day) week. A few categories of workers, e.g., in the steel industry, have acquired a right to periodical days of rest which further reduce the working week (to thirty-nine hours). Collective agreements are also empowered to determine the maximum weekly working hours: the average working time cannot exceed forty-eight hours every seven days, including overtime; the average can be calculated over a multi-weekly period, not more than four months, which can be prolonged by collective agreements to six months or even to nine for objective needs specified by the same agreements (Article 4, Decree 66). Since the bargaining round of 1979, labour unions have repeatedly asked to reduce working time below these limits; but their requests have been accepted only in part. The majority of national agreements of 1979 provided for a small reduction in the yearly working hours, while only a few agreements clearly indicated the objective of reducing the working week to less than forty hours.

In the 1987 agreements the metal and textile workers obtained a further reduction of sixteen hours yearly for regular workers (twelve for shiftworkers). In the banking sector the reduction was of twenty-five minutes a week which brings the weekly hours down to fewer than thirty-eight. Many plant and enterprise agreements provided for a more substantial reduction in weekly working time, often coupled to a new shift system in order to allow increased productivity and a more intensive use of machinery (e.g., textile plants, where a thirty-six-hour week in the form of a six-hour/six-day shift system is widespread). Redistribution of working time on a multi-weekly basis (so-called annualisation) is provided in quite a few national agreements. Decentralised agreements often provide for flexible systems of working time, finalised to increase productivity and employment. Flexible work time regimes are inherent to the use of smart work.

171. The attempts of the Italian unions to bargain further working time reductions have met with the resistance of employers who claim that the current annual working time in Italy is shorter than that of most foreign competitors. In fact the actual working time is lower than that fixed in collective agreements. If one takes into account annual vacations and holidays, the number of yearly hours (in total) has oscillated between a maximum of 1867 in the 1990s and a lower average of 1750 in the last years. In order to counteract this trend and favour a more even distribution of working time, the cost for overtime has been increased by Act 549/1995 which imposed an extra for each hour of work between 40 and 44.

Act 196/1997 established significant incentives to the reduction and reorganisation of working time, provided it was bargained collectively. But with scarce results.

The subsequent centre-right government adopted an opposite approach by giving incentives for over time. But this provision was abolished under the impact of the crisis. During the course of the crisis the average number of hours worked has declined; and thousands of employees have been on short-time regimes (*see* below).

The issue of working time reduction has lost momentum until recently when the debate has been resumed, in connection with the possible negative impact of the new digital technologies on the future of work. However, some reduction of working time, mainly of working week, has been introduced by some large innovative firms in response to expectations of particularly young and skilled workers.

The maximum hours fixed by Act 196/1997 do not apply to discontinuous work and to activities of mere custody (caretakers, guardians, etc.) indicated in a list attached to the Act, nor to leading personnel (but similar limits are now fixed by collective agreements). The list has been updated by Article 16 of Decree 66/2003. The limit fixed by the law refers explicitly to actual working hours, with the exclusion of periods of rest.

Decree 66 provides that employees are entitled to a period of continuous rest of eleven hours daily (Article 7) unless provided otherwise by collective agreements and whenever the daily working time exceeds six hours to a period of rest to be determined by collective agreements (in absence of them a minimum rest of ten minutes is fixed by Article 8 of Decree 66). The matter is indeed regulated by collective agreements: for example, the metalworkers' agreement provides that employees working on shifts will benefit from half an hour, regularly paid, for their meal within the plant. Further restrictions on working time, intermediate rest periods and night work were fixed for young workers and for women. These restrictions, as regards to women, have been abolished by Act No. 903 of 1977 (*see* paragraph 123).

Decree 66/2003 has fixed for night work a maximum limit of eight hours as an average within the twenty-four hours (Article 13). The employer is bound to consult the unions prior to the introduction of night work (Article 12) and to provide controls on the health and safety of employees working at night (Article 14). Articles 12 and 13 can be derogated by collective agreements.

172. Special regulations are provided for particular categories of workers, such as maritime workers, miners, employees engaged in transport operations, etc.

173. The daily distribution of working hours is generally decided by management, after consultation with the plant union representatives. On the other hand, the employer does not have the power to reduce unilaterally an employee's working hours with a proportional reduction in wages. In practice, the possibilities of reducing working hours allowed by Italian law always require the consensus of the unions and of the worker concerned; the transformation of a full-time employment relationship into a part-time relationship is subordinate to a direct agreement between the (individual) parties, ratified by the provincial labour office.

The permanent reduction of the working hours normally performed in a given sector, following the stipulation of a solidarity contract (*see* paragraphs 202, 249) must be agreed upon at the plant level by the trade union belonging to the most representative confederations.

§2. Overtime

174. According to the law, overtime is the extraordinary work done after the normal legal hours: traditionally eight a day or forty-eight a week; now forty a week after Act 196/1997. Different limits can be fixed by collective agreements. Decree 66 provides (Article 5) that the use of overtime must be limited and should be regulated by collective bargaining. Lacking agreements, overtime is allowed only following an accord between the employer and the individual employee for a period not exceeding 250 hours (yearly). Unless provided differently by collective agreements overtime is furthermore allowed in the case of exceptional productive need, to avoid risks of damages to persons or properties, during social, cultural events (like fairs, exhibitions).

Originally overtime was subject to specific authorisation by the labour inspectorate; Act 196/1997 provided that this authorisation remains, temporarily, due only for work over forty-eight hours weekly. Decree 66/2003 requires in this case only that information be supplied to the labour inspectorate for firms employing more than ten people, but this duty has been abolished by Act 133/2008. The employer was traditionally obliged to pay a percentage of the total amount of wages paid for overtime to a special public fund for unemployment benefits and to pay a higher rate for it: by law a minimum of 10% of the gross wage, generally increased to 25%–30% by collective agreements plus the extra cost of 15%. However, this percentage was referred to a conventional base of remuneration lower than the actual wage, so that the total cost of overtime was indeed less than that of regular hours.

175. Traditionally overtime has been widely used with collective agreements making it compulsory (while the law declared it optional). In the 1970s, most collective agreements begun to limit explicitly the total amount of overtime (usually to 150 hours per year) and to strictly control the observance of this maximum. This policy has been gradually changed due to its excessive rigidity. A more flexible use of overtime has been granted, within certain maximum limits: e.g., the national metalworkers' agreement provides a maximum of 2 hours a day, 8 hours a week with an annual total of 150 hours per worker. For firms with fewer than 200 employees the annual total is set at 200 hours and for maintenance and installation activities it is increased to 210 hours. The employer is usually obliged to inform the local union delegate of overtime in advance at a special meeting (i.e., after bargaining). More recently, collective agreements have given management a certain number of hours of overtime at its disposal which it need not make known to trade unions: 32 hours annually for shift workers and for all employees in firms with over 200 employees, 40 hours for firms with fewer than 200 employees. Indeed, the actual amount of overtime has been on the increase. Special pay increases are fixed by collective agreements for overtime worked on Sundays, on other rest days (50% or more), and night work (50% or more).

§3. Sunday Rest

176. All workers have the right to a period of rest of twenty-four hours consecutive every seven days, in addition to the eleven hours of daily rest. The rest must be usually on Sunday (Article 36 of the Constitution, Article 2109 of the Civil Code; now Decree 66/2003, Article 9).

Exceptions are provided for special kinds of work, e.g., maintenance, cleaning, repairs and surveillance of machinery, work necessary to guarantee the safety of persons and machinery, and the preparation of raw materials and products (originally Articles 16 and 17, Act No. 370 of 22 February 1934, now Decree 66/2003). The twenty-four hour weekly rest period can be shifted to another day for a series of undertakings and activities provided for in general by Decree 66 (Article 9) and more in detail by ministerial decrees (22 June 1935 and following); namely industrial activities requiring a continuous cycle of operation, e.g., affecting workers in many operations of the steel and chemical industry, seasonal industries where special urgent activities are required to use and preserve products of raw materials, e.g., in fishing, dairy products, oil industry, many fruit canning industries; other industries where working on Sundays is required for technical or public utility reasons, e.g., ship repairs, typographical businesses, newspaper firms, photographic undertakings, museums, hotels, restaurants and the like, broadcasting and television, chemist shops, retail sale of food and drink, transport industry, etc.

Moreover, a general derogation to the rule has been introduced by Act 133/2008 (Article 41(5)°) which provides that the twenty-hour hour weekly rest period can be calculated as an average in a period not longer than fourteen days. In fact the concept of ‘periodical’ rest has been interpreted loosely also by the Constitutional Court. Workers employed on Sundays are entitled to a compensatory rest in the principle of twenty-four consecutive hours, which can be reduced for special categories of workers and activities. Work on Sundays is generally paid with a special increase in the wage rate, e.g., for metalworkers 50%. A common practice in some industries of distributing work on shift of a period of forty-nine days allowing one day of rest after seven days of work (instead of six) has been declared illegal by the Court of Cassation.

177. Work on Saturdays, in a five-day working week, is generally not considered as holiday work as regards the wage rate applicable.

178. Act No. 260 of 1949 and No. 90 of 1954 recognise four national holidays (25 April, 1 May, 2 June, 4 November) and eleven other holidays, plus usually the patron saint's day. Workers paid by the hour, at rest during these days, receive regular pay; work done on these days – for technical or organisational reasons – is remunerated with a wage increase equal to that fixed for work on Sundays. When these holidays fall on a Sunday, the workers receive double pay. Five of these holidays have been abolished by law, Act No. 54 of 1976 – with the consent of the trade unions – in order to increase the number of hours worked yearly and particularly to reduce the phenomenon of 'after holiday' absenteeism.

The decision to reduce holidays has been reversed by most collective agreements as being against the directive to reduce working time. A common provision is that in lieu of five holidays abolished by law the employees benefit from an equal number of compensatory rest days to be taken up individually: e.g., the textile agreement (in rotation, in periods of reduced production activity and consistent with work needs); the banking sector and metal-workers' agreements (with the same conditions). At present the recognised holidays are 12 (7 religious and 5 civil): Act 792/1985 and Act 336/2000.

§4. Annual Vacations

179. The workers' right to an annual vacation is recognised by Article 36 of the Constitution and by Article 2109 of the Civil Code. The length of the holiday is determined usually by collective agreements together with most of the relevant conditions. Act 66/2003 has set a minimum of four weeks (Article 10).

In the past, the length was different for white-collar and blue-collar workers and varied according to seniority. Since 1973 most industrial collective agreements have recognised in general four weeks' paid vacation for all employees. Some agreements, e.g., the metalworkers' agreement, grant a longer period to white-collar workers with high seniority: one day extra for those with more than ten years' seniority and six days extra for those with more than eighteen years' seniority. Quite a few enterprise agreements grant a fifth week of paid vacation. The rules of Act No. 1825 of 1924 are still in force for white-collar workers insofar as they are not ameliorated by collective agreements: e.g., the norm granting thirty days' vacation for workers with more than twenty-five years of seniority. According to collective agreements, a week's vacation is equivalent to six working days, but in the case of a five-day week, the working days used as vacations are counted 1.2 each (to guarantee the same total result of four full weeks or twenty-four days holiday). For employees who have worked less than one year the holiday is reduced in proportion: one-twelfth of vacation for each month's work or a fraction over fifteen days (meaning effective work days and assimilated days such as – usually – days of sickness, work accidents, pregnancy and so on). If the labour contract is terminated before the holiday period, collective agreements usually provide that a worker will be entitled to holiday pay in a similar proportion (not to the actual vacation before the end of the contract). Public holidays are not counted as part of the annual vacation. The same is true for the period of notice (Article 2109 of the Civil Code), and now also the periods of illness. The Constitutional Court has decided that illness suspends the periods of vacation; but subsequent court decisions have recognised the suspension only when illness in fact prevents the normal use of vacation.

180. During their vacation – usually at the beginning – employees receive their regular pay from the employer, as determined by collective agreements; these often exclude exceptional extra pay for special work done (e.g., exceptional night work extra pay). Employees normally working at piece rate receive, as a rule, the average earnings of the three months preceding the vacation.

181. Article 2109 of the Civil Code provides that vacations must be, if possible, continuous, fixed by the employer taking into account both the needs of production and the worker's interest, and must be communicated in advance to employees. In principle vacations must be taken for at least two weeks within the year. In practice times and conditions of annual vacations are often bargained over by the employer with the union plant representatives. Collective agreements usually provide that the period of continuous and collective holiday should not exceed three weeks.

182. The minimum four weeks of vacation cannot be substituted by any indemnity apart from the case in which the labour contract is terminated (Article 10, Decree 66/2003).

Since the rules granting the right to annual vacations – as well as to holidays and Sunday rests – are imperative, all agreements to the contrary are null. But actual work done is protected under Article 2126 of the Civil Code (*see* above), the consequence being that an employee working during the holiday period receives double pay.

§5. Time Off Work

183. Various categories of workers have the right to take time off with and without pay during working hours and/or in certain occasions both by law and by collective agreement.

184. Act No. 300 grants such a right to union officials and union members for union activities, and to publicly elected officials in order to fulfil their duties (*see* below for details).

185. Special regulations give a worker time off with and without pay for other specified public duties, such as being a member of commissions to take care of general or municipal elections or as a witness in judicial proceedings. An employee who has been given notice of dismissal is entitled to reasonable time off to seek new employment.

186. Special provisions in favour of student workers are established by Article 10 of Act No. 300. Workers attending regular courses in state or in publicly certified schools or in schools issuing officially recognised study certificates are entitled to a working schedule which favours attending courses and the preparation of examinations. According to the prevailing opinion, this right can only operate taking into account the work organisation of the enterprise, i.e., to the extent that the latter can be reasonably adapted to the needs of the student. Flexitime could prove ideal; its use is slowly gaining ground. Student workers are not obliged to work overtime and on Sundays and (including those attending university courses) must be given paid days off work to take exams, a minimum of one day for each examination. An employer can demand the necessary documents or certificates to prove the conditions requested by the law. Provisions of Article 10 are often specified and ameliorated through collective bargaining.

Regular workers are entitled to a number of paid hours off work – 150 in general, up to a maximum of 250 for employees who have to obtain a basic degree of compulsory education – to attend courses, related or not to their professional activities, in public or officially certified schools (the so-called 150-hour courses after the number of hours recognised by the first agreement of 1973). The right pertains strictly to the individual student worker while the conditions, terms and criteria for benefiting from the 150–250 hours provided by these agreements are bargained over between management and the union plant representatives, taking into account, as far as possible, individual preferences. The number of workers who can be absent from the firm to attend these courses at the same time must not exceed 2% of the total manpower. Unions have given priority to courses for workers wanting to complete minimum school requirements and have bargained with the central and regional school authorities for the public support needed to organise them (mainly premises, teachers, teaching material). The emphasis has lately shifted also due to persistent underutilisation of the hours available. More diversified and individual use of these hours is being allowed for training and retraining purposes as well.

Act 53/2000 has regulated the matter of time off work both for educational purposes (Article 5) and for family reasons (*see also* Act 151/2001 which consolidates all the legislation on maternity and paternity).

187. More extended benefits to promote the education of workers have been introduced since 1973 by many national collective agreements, following the pattern of the metalworkers' agreement.

The collective agreement of metalworkers of 2021 recognizes the individual right of employees to continuous training.

Parental leave was originally granted only to working mothers (Act 1204/1971, Article 7). This right, to be distinguished from the duty to abstain (*see* below paragraph 188) from work, has been extended to the father in specific cases by Act 903/1977 (Article 7) and generalised by Act 53/2000. The right pertains to each parent for each child in the first eight years of life. The parents can use the leave either separately or simultaneously for a period not exceeding ten months in total (six months maximum for each parent). If the father uses the leave for at least three months the total amount recognised to the family is increased to eleven months and that to the father is increased to seven months (this is clearly aimed at promoting the use of parental leave by fathers). Act 92/2012 has provided the duty of the father to abstain within the first five months of the child's life (*see* below paragraph 217).

The effectiveness of the law is reduced by the scarce economic budget which supports it: the parents are entitled to an indemnity of 30% of the wage for a maximum of six months during work up to the third year of life of the child; after this period the indemnity is due only to parents with very low income. The periods of leave are as a rule counted for seniority. The budget law for 2023 (Act 197/2022) has raised the amount to 80% of the wage for a max of one month until the child age of 6 years.

Decree 80/2015 has further innovated the regulation concerning parental leaves for working mothers and extended these leaves to non-dependent or autonomous workers (*see* below 214).

Decree 105/2022, implementing the European directive 2019/1158, has reregulated the matter, abrogating the previous rules and providing the duty of the father to abstain from work for ten days (twenty in case of multiple births) in the period between two to five months after childbirth, during which period the father has the right to an indemnity equal to 100% of the wage.

Act 32/2022 (so-called Family Act) provides for a comprehensive reform of family policies aimed at extending parental leaves, introducing a universal system of child benefits and incentives to women's work, promoting the autonomy of the young. The universal child benefits provided by Act 46/2021 are calculated according to the economic conditions of the family, age and the members' children. Other principles of Act 32 must be implemented by subsequent regulations. The budget law for 2023 (Act 197/2022) has raised the amount of benefits for small children and for numerous families.

Chapter 4. Remuneration and Benefits

188. Remuneration is the essential obligation of an employer, which characterises the labour contract as a bilateral contract. According to a minority opinion, a promise to perform gratuitous services cannot be enforced as a legitimate contract, as being contrary to Article 36, paragraph 1 of the Constitution granting a worker the right to a just remuneration for his work. Most commentators and law courts recognise such a promise only in exceptional cases, justified by the relations between the parties (work performed by members of parties, philanthropic organisations, etc.), otherwise being suspected of fraud. However, such a gratuitous contract is not considered as a typical labour contract.

189. Services performed within the family were traditionally considered gratuitous as being rendered on the basis of a duty to contribute to the family maintenance and therefore were explicitly excluded from the field of application of some protective labour legislation and social security benefits. Act No. 151 of 1975, reforming family law, seems to consider the services rendered within the family, unless they are the object of a regular labour contract, as a counterpart of, and giving rise to, a right to participate – proportionately – in the earnings of the familiar activity or enterprise.

§1. The Concept of Remuneration

190. The general provision on the subject, Article 2099 of the Civil Code, does not give details of remuneration, but simply states that it can be determined in different forms (payment according to time, at piece rate, profit sharing or product sharing, commissions, payment in cash and in kind), paid in the measure determined by a collective agreement, on the customary terms and conditions of the place of work.

191. In fact there is no uniform legal definition of remuneration, and many controversies have arisen in the courts as to its scope, particularly with respect to:

(a) the various fringe or accessory benefits established either by law or by agreement in addition to basic pay (e.g., overtime pay, productivity bonuses, thirteenth and fourteenth month's pay, indemnities for special heavy or unhealthy jobs, for transport, seniority allowance, cost of living bonus);
(b) payments made by an employer in addition to or in substitution for social security benefits (e.g., payments in case of illness, work accidents, family allowances, annual vacations), usually not related to the actual work performed or paid even if no work is performed.

Traditional opinions tended to consider all these payments in principle as remuneration and to enlarge its notion so as to include all payments made by an employer to an employee which have their cause and origin in the labour relationship. Only the sums for reimbursement of expenses and gratuities are excluded, but both these notions are interpreted very strictly. Expenses must be true and proved as such, lump sums or indemnities not being recognised as reimbursements. Gratuities are hardly conceivable during a labour relationship and never recognised when the employer is obliged to make a payment: this is almost always the case now, also with premiums or bonuses originally having such a gratuitous nature, apart from sums paid only once (*una tantum*). Tips received customarily by an employee are also understood as remuneration.

In recent years this wide judicial notion of remuneration has been criticised as being arbitrarily generalised by the courts without sufficient legal foundation and with negative effects on the increase in labour costs.

Critics claim that such a unitary notion of remuneration for general application does not exist either in the legal or contractual system where different notions are adopted according to the different rules of the law and where a distinction is often made between 'normal' remuneration, 'total' or 'global' and 'basic' remuneration. Each case is to be decided by examining the specific discipline of the law and agreements, e.g., whether 'normal' or 'basic' remuneration (both notions are more restrictive than the other two) must be considered in order to calculate the above-mentioned accessory benefits. This criticism has been accepted by a series of decisions of the Supreme Court of Cassation (1 April 1993) which has almost completely reversed the trend, a demonstration of the great concern with increasing labour costs and with the risk of inflation. Act 402/1996 (Article 3) has indirectly confirmed the same trend, by recognising to collective agreements the power to determine the notion of remuneration, apart from cases explicitly defined law.

192. A wide notion of remuneration is adopted by the legislator in order to assess social security contributions (mainly for old age and disability pensions) with the clear aim of taxing as many benefits as possible. Article 12 of Act No. 153 of 30 April 1969 considers as remuneration 'all gross sums received by an employee from his employer in cash or in kind, as a consequence of his employment relationship', with the exception of: (1) daily subsistence allowances and travelling expenses up to 50%; (2) actual reimbursement of expenses incurred in consequence of employment and proved as such; (3) seniority allowance; (4) cash allowance (for employees handling cash); (5) board-money and indemnities for maritime workers while ashore, up to 60%; (6) gratuities paid *una tantum* for exceptional and non-recurrent reasons, not connected even indirectly to a worker's productivity or to the enterprise's results. This definition is clearly a compromise, in part broader than the one usually adopted by the courts (under Nos. 1 and 5) in part narrower (under Nos. 3 and 4). Act 335/1995 has added a few fringe benefits not included in the notion of remuneration: fees paid by employees for nurseries; expenses paid by employers for clubs, sport centres, vacation houses for sons, price difference of stocks to employees; products of the firm given to employees (above 50% of the gross market price).

193. More restrictive definitions of remuneration are adopted for specific purposes, for example, Article 2121 of the Civil Code provides that in order to calculate severance allowance and pay in lieu of a period of notice, only sums paid as continuous remuneration can be taken into account, which excludes sums payable as remuneration for overtime pay, night shift pay, etc., of an occasional character (a slightly different definition has been adopted in Act No. 297 of 1982, which has modified Article 2121 and the regulation of the seniority allowance: *see* paragraph 254). Act No. 260 of 27 May 1949 provides that during recognised holidays workers paid by the hour receive the 'normal daily total wage', calculated on the basis of a sixth of the weekly contractual working time; it apparently excludes overtime pay even when overtime is not occasional.

194. To sum up, remuneration, while remaining in principle the counterpart of the work performed, has gone far beyond the strict notion of the 'equivalent' of the contractual performance as known to the civil law of contracts in two senses:

(a) because it includes a growing number of payments, made by an employer even if no work is performed (illness, accident, etc.), in cases explicitly provided for by the law or by contract;
(b) because the amount of wages to be paid is not left to the autonomy of the individual nor of the collective parties, but its minimum is determined by law.

The forms of remuneration may be different: payment according to time; piecework, payment in kind, commissions, profit sharing, shares and stock options, seniority bonuses, indemnities, linked to specific conditions of work. The forms and the basic amount of remuneration are fixed usually by collective agreements. Variable wages linked to productivity and performance have become more common in recent years, also due to the decentralisation of collective bargaining (paragraph 479). Individual bonuses are also common, mainly for white-collar workers, professionals and leading personnel.

§2. Minimum Wages: Escalator Clause– Working Poor

195. Italy does not have minimum wage legislation although the problem has been recurrently under discussion. However, Article 36 of the Italian Constitution entitles an employee to receive a wage 'proportionate to the quality and quantity of his work and in any case sufficient to guarantee a free and decent life to him and to his family.' A long established jurisprudential opinion has interpreted this norm as immediately effective so as to grant indirectly any employee the right to a minimum wage determined by the courts, normally equal to prevailing collective tariffs (*see* below paragraph 449). A most important provision aimed at implementing the last part of Article 36 (sufficient wage) has been for a long time the escalator clause. The basic source of regulation was the 1975 interconfederal agreement for the entire industrial sector and extended to commerce, agriculture and public service (*see* below paragraph 412). In spite of divergences in the effectiveness of this system, there is no doubt that it has been able to substantially protect the average wage, particularly for the lowest-paid workers. On the other hand, the fact that the automatic wage increase provided for by this system was equal for all employees contributed greatly to reducing wage differentials, again in favour of lower-paid workers. At the high inflation rate of the period 1977–1985 this effect was increasingly significant and subject to growing criticism within the union movement as well as for being unjustly punitive towards the middle-higher levels of employees and hence discouraging of professional qualifications. Moreover, the high indexation brought about by this system has been held to be a major obstacle to controlling inflation. In fact, growing pressure from the employers – and the government itself – has caused the regulation of 1975 to be changed twice. In 1983 a tripartite agreement aimed at slowing down the escalator clause and was substituted by a governmental decree (273/1984) setting a ceiling to indexation. In February 1986, the 'fixed amount' system of the *scala mobile* was replaced by a percentage system. The abolition of the escalator clause was decided in 1992 by a trilateral agreement, according to a common Italian practice, which confirms that the obsolescence of this mechanism had also been recognised by the trade unions.

196. In subsequent years wage increases have returned to be decided by collective agreements and by their periodical renewal. This collective protection of wages by has been uneven, linked to the effectiveness of the agreements signed for the various productive sectors. Given the private nature of these agreements they have no general binding force; consequently in some sectors of the economy where trade unions are scarcely present the protection of employees wages is limited. Moreover, the crisis of the last years have weakened the bargaining capacity of Trade Unions in general. The convergent impact of these different factors has caused the emergence of an unknown phenomena: the 'working poors'.

The number of these workers, i.e., those earning less than the relative poverty level has been growing particularly during and after the economic crisis began in 2009. Istat data show that their number has grown from 1.9 million in 2005 to 5.6 million in 2021.

To meet the needs of the low-paid workers, quite a few bills have been presented in Parliament to introduce also in Italy legislation on minimum wages, particularly for those workers which are not covered by collective bargaining. Following these attempts Act 92/2012 has provided that minimum wages related to collective agreements provisions must be paid to collaborators working on 'projects' – who are usually not covered by traditional collective bargaining (*see* above).

The introduction of minimum wage was envisaged by Act 183/2014. But the government has abstained so far from implementing this provision and warned the parties that legislation might be passed in case of persistent inactivity and various bills are being discussed in Parliament on this issue and the government is committed to submit its proposal.

The recent approval of the European directive on minimum adequate wages (2021) may favour a new approach to this issue by the Italian government.

Since the social parties, the unions in particular, strongly oppose a legislation directly fixing minimum wages, a possible solution could be to follow the alternative way indicated by the directive, namely relying on collective agreements to protect low-wage workers.The directive provides that this protection is considered sufficient when national collective agreements apply at least to 80% of the employees of a given category; in case this percentage of coverage is not reached, the Member States are requested to provide specific procedures to reinforce the agreements. In Italy, this percentage is reached in many sectors, but not in some marginal and technological categories where the unions are particularly weak.

A proposal of the past minister of labour (2021) was to establish procedures aimed at generally giving binding force to the basic salaries fixed by most representative collective agreements. It remains to be seen what the decisions of the new government will be.

§3. Equality of Treatment

197. According to some opinion, Article 36 introduces indirectly into Italian law the general principle of equality of treatment in wage matters, at least for workers employed by the same employer. But this is a minority opinion not accepted by the prevailing jurisprudence (*see* below paragraphs 445 ff.). A general principle of non-discrimination, however, is fixed by Decrees 215 and 216/2003, in the application of the European directives 2000/43 and 2000/78.

I. Women

198. Article 37 of the Constitution provides that women workers have the same rights as men workers and must be paid equal remuneration for equal work. Minors are also granted the same right to equal pay for equal work. The implementation of the principle of equal pay (and of equal treatment) for women workers has a long and controversial history in Italy which has been marked by Court decisions and legislative innovations. Important laws were passed rather early, the major being Acts 903/1977 and 125/1991. Now the whole subject matter has been reorganised by Decree 198/2006 (Code of Equal Opportunities) which regulates the most important issues.

The first cases of actual enforcement of Article 37 in court go back to 1955. An important impulse to the courts' favourable attitude came from Article 119 of the Treaty of Rome (on the European Economic Community), from ILO Convention No. 100 (1951) ratified by Italy with Act No. 741 of 22 May 1956, and from the Social European Charter of 1961 (Article 4, paragraph 3).

199. For a long time the meaning of 'equal work' was controversial, one opinion interpreting it as equal job classification, another as equal job classification and equal productivity (which in fact amounted to paying women workers even less as they are less productive than men of a similar qualification). The second opinion – backed by the authority of the Court of Cassation and then by collective agreements – became predominant during the 1960s. This led in time to the abolition, as discriminatory, of the traditional practice of collective bargaining to classify women's jobs separately from men's. The full implementation of the principle, which has been confirmed by Act 903/1977 (now Decree 198/2006), caused some reduction in wage differentials between men and women in the 1960s and 1970s. The general gap, however, remains significant and in some cases has been on the increase, according to a general trend to widen occupational differentials (paragraphs 170 and 171) which is reflected particularly in sex differentials.

200. Actual enforcement of the principle by individual women in the courts has been fairly rare for reasons which are self-evident. The formal equalisation of job evaluation between men and women does not prevent women from being in fact undervalued or classified mostly in the lowest-paid jobs, also due to their lower average professional qualification. More specifically, rates of pay in the female-dominated industries, for instance the textile retail trade, tend to be lower than in the male-dominated industries, for instance steel or automobiles.

201. Some aspects appear particularly indicative of sex discrimination. This is the case with wage differentials linked to different productive sectors. The problem here is not to enforce equal pay per se but to overcome historical sex segregation by opening to women traditionally male professions through education, training and positive recruiting programmes.

A second aspect, related to indirect wage discrimination, has to do with possible bias built into existing job classification schemes. Such a bias can be claimed, for instance, when classification criteria are adopted, whether unilaterally or contractually, that evaluate factors such as physical strength, common to men, more than manual dexterity and accurateness (skills which are considered typically female); the result in fact is undervaluing certain kinds of jobs which are female dominated. Similar bias may be found in practices which evaluate certain jobs in traditionally female-dominated sectors less highly than jobs common in male-dominated industries.

For instance, in the textile industries, a skilled woman's job, such as master weaver, is rated less than a skilled man's job, such as a printer in the printing industry. These systems of classification have never been challenged in court and, indeed, are barely discussed among trade unions and handled in collective bargaining. This is also due to the fact that a bias of this kind cuts across the job structure in different productive sectors and overlaps, therefore with discrimination due to job segregation. The discriminatory effect appears more clearly by comparing typically female jobs in the textile or pharmaceutical sectors with typically male jobs in the metal and mechanical sectors.

These latter are better rated because they are considered to be heavier or perhaps simply because the male workers have more bargaining capacity and stronger representation in the unions than the former jobs, in spite of being less skilled. On the other hand, the concentration of women in the lowest traded jobs within a single sector or across sectors may be justified not by bias in the classification system, but by historical gaps and discrimination in education and social organisation of work.

These factors can be redressed only through positive action rather than legal prohibition of formal discrimination. Italian courts have traditionally been very reluctant to recognise wage and other forms of discrimination unless they appear to be direct. The Court of Cassation (Decision 329 of 1979), stated that the concept of equal work or work of equal value is in itself generic and needs further specification. This line of agreement has been contradicted by Act No. 125 of 10 April 1991 (now Decree 198/2006) which has explicitly outlawed indirect discrimination.

The wage differentials between men and women may be due to other reasons: overtime bonuses, shift work allowances (which are more common for men), and personal merit bonuses paid above contractual rates. These latter bonuses fall in principle under the provision of the law, but are hardly controllable either for men or women when they escape union's control. This occurs now more often than a few years ago. The granting of these bonuses on an individual basis (but possibly to a considerable number of employees) is justified as a reward for the employee's qualities such as actual presence on the job, willingness to perform specific work (overtime, rotating shifts, etc.) which are in fact easier for men than women for social and family reasons. Discrimination is even more serious taking into account the fact that homework and other forms of peripheral work, underpaid and under-protected, and part time are mainly done by women.

202. Act No. 903 of 1977 (now Decree 198/2006, Articles 27ff.) has confirmed the principle of equal treatment for male and female workers as regards hiring, wages, job classification, career possibilities, vocational training, some social security benefits (family allowances, pensions in case of death of husbands) and in general all terms of employment. Act 903 did not mention explicitly indirect discrimination – but most legal scholars argued that this was covered by the broad wording of the Act, and among others, by Article 1 where it forbids sex discrimination in the access to any job irrespective of hiring procedures and even though it is pursued with reference to marital status or pregnancy or *indirectly* through any technique requiring sex as a prerequisite for competing for certain jobs. This opinion has been confirmed by Act No. 125 of 10 April 1991 (now Decree 198/2006) which prohibits as indirect (sex) discrimination all prejudicial treatment, even following from apparently neutral criteria which, however, affect proportionately more the employees of one sex (or another) and concern requisites not essential to the actual work (Article 25). The law does not limit itself to sanctioning equality of treatment between the sexes; it also provides for preferential treatment in favour of female workers. Article 3, paragraph 2, stipulates that the periods of abstention from work (recognised by law) for maternity count towards seniority benefits 'where collective agreements do not make special requirements for this purpose' (i.e., actual work done). The legislature recently decided to shift to the state budget some social security contributions paid by employers regarding the hiring of women (in order to compensate the employer for the greater cost of female labour).

203. Act 903 (Article 1) does not consider as discriminatory 'to subordinate to a sex requisite the hiring in artistic and fashion activities and in the pursuance of public performances when such a requisite is essential to the nature of the work'(now Decree 198/2006 Article 27.6). The provision on the essential character of the requisite is of strict interpretation, i.e., it cannot be equated with general business needs nor with a more convenient or efficient performance of the task, but it implies an intrinsic and absolute requirement of the same tasks. Needs of this type cannot be taken a priori as legitimate grounds for the exclusion of women but must be tested in practice in order to judge the appropriateness of certain requisites for hiring.

In the very sectors mentioned by the law of artistic and fashion activities, sex requirements cannot be applied generally but only to those jobs (models, actors) where the identity is linked to sex. The two requisites of 'sector' and 'nature' of work are both necessary, according to Article 1. The interpretation of the word 'essential' is decisive because the same requisite can refer not only to access to work but also to other aspects of the employment relationship, like job classification, career, etc. Judicial tests of this meaning are not numerous given the reluctance, of the Italian courts to analyse cases of indirect discrimination, i.e., the justification of requisites which are apparently neutral but have disparately negative effects on women without being essential to the nature of work. The few court decisions which have touched on this issue under the heading of indirect discrimination are, however, significant: those concerning military forces, police, prison guards have been controversial but have contributed to opening these corps to women. Now this principle is confirmed by Decree 198/2006 Articles 32–33. Controversial opinions have also been expressed on the question of whether reasons of privacy and decency can be justifiable grounds for sex discrimination in certain kinds of employment. The Court of Cassation has tried to deemphasise the question in a case concerning physical education teachers; a law of 1958, which separates boys' classes from girls' classes and provides for a corresponding division of men and women teachers in deference to the custom that teacher, should be of the same gender as the pupil, has been upheld as being an organisational rule which does not imply any discrimination. Opposite opinions have been held with respect to similar cases by other courts. Some court decisions have confirmed that sex can be a justifying factor for restriction in employment only if it is 'absolutely required' for the nature of the work. Accordingly, they have considered unlawful the practice of various public administrations of reserving places in some jobs for the mere fact that they were regarded as traditionally feminine. Collective bargaining is empowered to make further exceptions regarding the principle of equality in the hiring of women when the hiring refers to 'particularly heavy work' (prohibited for women by Act No. 977 of 1967. The norm is confirmed by Decree 198/2006 Article 27, 4). The unions have hesitated to use this power to reintroduce, by agreement, limits to the hiring of women (even for protective reasons). Another limit, although reduced, to the actual employment of women upheld by Act No. 903 was the prohibition of night work. This norm, in spite of a favourable decision by the Italian Constitutional Court, has been considered contrary to the general principle of equal treatment as interpreted by the ECJ and has been abolished by Article 17 of Act 25/1999 confirmed by Decree 66/2003. The prohibition now applies only to working mothers from the time of pregnancy to the first year of age of the child. Moreover, the Acts recognise the right to abstain from night work to the parents of a child below the age of 3 years, to the single parent who is in charge of a child below the age of 12, and to workers who are in charge of a disabled person (as defined by Act 104/1992).

204. Article 15 of Act No. 903, now Decree 198/2006, Articles 36ff., grants the worker discriminated against in hiring and to the unions delegated by the worker, the right to resort to the judge to obtain an order to cease from the discriminatory behaviour and to cancel its effect, following a proceeding shaped after Article 28 of Act No. 300 of 1970 (*see* below paragraphs 386 ff.).

205. An innovative solution is provided by Act No. 125 1991, now Decree 198/ 2006 Article 40, which gives the judge the power to order a plan to remove with positive actions all collective discrimination (*see* above paragraph 175). The reasons for the originally low degree of effectiveness of these norms consisted in the weakness of the enforcement system. A first key point concerns the proof of discrimination. Italian courts have adopted conflicting views on the object of proof.

A solution in line with the EU principles on the reversal of the burden of proof has been adopted by Act 125/1991 (now Decree 198/2006, Article 40), which also allows recourse to statistical data as indicative – and not conclusive – evidence of discrimination. Moreover, the law has reinforced the sanctions against discrimination by giving judges special powers to remove collective discrimination and possibly to award damages (*see* above paragraph 175); by giving the public administration the power to suspend or revoke financial benefits or public contracts to all employers who are proved to discriminate. A further difficulty in proving discrimination concerns the lack of information. In the absence of objective and publicised systems of recruitment or promotion, as is the case in most private firms, the interested woman would in any case not have basic information about applicants and selected employees sufficient to prove her case. Public agencies aimed at promoting and assisting the parties in the enforcement of the law – not only in the field of discrimination – are alien to the Italian tradition.

In 1983, following EEC directives, the Ministry of Labour set up a National Committee for Equality where social and political party experts and women's associations are represented. The Committee has been confirmed by Act No. 125 1991 (now Decree 198/2006, Articles 8ff.) Article 6, No. 7), which grants relatively wide powers to it: research and information on employment problems and prospects for women, investigation and inspection of enforcement of the law (through the labour inspectors), assistance to women subject to discrimination, intervention in grievance settlements.

Act 125, now Decree 198/2006 Articles 11–15, also recognises so-called equality advisers, who are appointed and operate at national, regional, provincial level. They are full members of the local (regional) commissions on employment (*see* paragraph 106) and have powers to assist women in all matters concerning equality, including the power to bring an action in court against collective discrimination (Article 4, No. 6), Act 125 (now Decree 198/2006, Article 37), i.e., discrimination which does not necessarily touch on specific individual employees. The effective use of these powers has been, reduced by the scarce financial and organisational resources put at the disposal of the committee and of the advisers. The resources have been increased by various Acts and lately by Decree 151/2015, which have allowed for a more intense activity. Decree 151/2015 has also revised the National committee on equality and strengthened the role of the equality advisers. The possibility of these 'advisors' acting independently from the government (central and local) remains, however, an open question.

206. A few positive measures to redress discrimination exist in Italian legislation, but no systematic policy has been implemented aimed at promoting equal opportunities for women, in the same way as for other disadvantaged groups. Indeed, doubts were raised as to its lawfulness in the Italian legal system, until Act No. 125 of 10 April 1991 explicitly recognised and promoted positive action (Act 198/2006, Articles 42ff.). The definition of these actions by the law is similar to that developed in other European systems and in particular to that adopted by the EEC recommendation of 13 December 1984: it includes all initiatives finalised to remove the obstacles which de facto hinder equal opportunities between men and women workers. Positive actions are, in principle voluntary and promoted by financial incentives (now Decree 198/2006, Article 48); priority is given to those actions which are agreed upon between employers and representative unions. Public administrations have the *duty* to promote positive action, within one year from the Act (Decree 198/2006, Article 2, No. 6). Positive action can also be *ordered* by the judge: when he ascertains collective discrimination he can order a plan to remove it within a fixed term (Decree 198, Article 37).

Act. 198/2006 has confirmed the existing opinion that sexual harassment falls within the prohibition of direct discrimination (Article 26): it defines sexual harassment as any act or behaviour, also verbal, with a sexual connotation or based on gender that is undesired and is made clear in any way or through actual insistence is perceptible, as offensive to the dignity and freedom of any reasonable person or, through creating a climate of intimidation, is susceptible.

The area of application concerns both sexes and all types of employment contract. Any act or pact that is derived from the discrimination or which is related to sexual harassment is seen as void. Also the promotion or transferrals obtained through unfair behaviour with sexual connotations are made void at the request of the party involved. Any act against the worker who has denounced sexual harassment by the employer or any superiors (such as dismissals, transferrals, and so on) is presumed to be discriminatory.

The protection against discrimination has been progressively extended, under the impulse of European directives, to discriminatory acts motivated by a vast set of factors: race, ethnic origin, religion or personal opinions, handicap, age, and sexual orientation: *see* Decrees 215/2003 and 216/2003, modified by Act 101/2008, implementing EU directives. The prohibition concerns both direct and indirect discrimination, and operates in much the same terms as those stated above, including harassment and mobbing (Article 2, 3, Decrees 215 and 216/2003).

Recently the Italian parliament has approved new norms (Act 162/2021) directed to promote the principles of equal pay and equal treatment for women workers, spurred by the awareness that the gender gap remains high in spite of many past legal interventions.

The average wage gap is around 14% if related to hourly wages but is much higher (over 40%) if one considers the yearly income which takes into account the reduced number of hours worked by women due to part-time often involuntary, intermittent careers and various suspensions of work.

Act 162/2021 has introduced further legal innovations to promote gender parity following the European directive. The Act requires all enterprises employing more than fifty employees to prepare every two years a detailed report on all working conditions of both male and female employees to be submitted to Parliament. Individual employees have the right to be informed by the employers about average wages; and when the average gender gap is above 5% without due justification, the employer is requested to evaluate the wage structure with the unions in order to find appropriate remedies.

Second, the Act has introduced the so-called gender parity certificate stating the working conditions present in the firm and the measures implemented in order to promote gender parity. Holding the certificate is a condition for obtaining various public incentives and preferential treatment in public procurement.

Third, Article 2 of the act specifies the concept of discrimination which comprise all enterprises' decisions concerning the organisation of work and all working conditions which have disparately negative effects on some employees on the basis of sex, age, maternity, care duties.

Specific measures to promote the employment of women have been introduced in the National Recovery Plan (2021–2026).

Finally the budget law for 2023 has approved a reduction of social security contributions to favour the return of women to work after the end of maternal leave, the increase of this leave and has instituted a National Fund to promote wage parity (Articles 33–37).

II. Minors

207. Minors have traditionally been paid less than adult workers in reality and also under collective agreements, and classified in the lowest paid jobs. Different collective tariffs have been traditionally established, sometimes for minors under the age of 21, sometimes for various ages (15–16, 16–18, 18–21, for example); average wage differentials ranged from 20% to 30%.

Wage discrimination due to age has been declared illegal (as being against Article 37 of the Constitution) following the same legal arguments adopted for women by the courts and has almost completely disappeared from collective agreements since 1975–1976. Wage differentials for exist apprentices (*see* above paragraph 103). The impact of these contractual innovations on minors' actual wages and classification is not precisely known.

§4. Pay Systems

I. According to Time and by Results

208. The *summa divisio* is between payment according to time and payment by results, piece-rate being the most common traditionally. The latter forms of payment, although explicitly mentioned by Article 2099, cannot and do not in fact represent the whole wage paid to a worker but only a part. A fixed minimum pay depending on job classification and on the time worked is as a rule guaranteed also to employees paid by results. An agreement to the contrary, i.e., linking the whole wage to results, would probably be considered as being against Article 36 of the Constitution and therefore null insofar as it did not guarantee a just and sufficient remuneration to the worker. In fact, the use and importance of individual piece-rate are decreasing vis-à-vis collective incentives and so is the incentive character of this pay system which tends to be reduced by collective bargaining (by increasing the fixed part of remuneration). Article 2100 provides that a piece-rate is compulsory when an employee works in fixed production by the type of organisation (e.g., the assembly line) or his job evaluation is based on measuring the times of his work performance. The norm is rather ambiguous and apparently obsolete vis-à-vis this trend unless it is understood only as granting these workers higher rates than those of regular workers in return for maintaining a specified and necessary level of performance. The determination of a piece-rate is generally a rather complex process, bargained at the various stages between management and union plant representatives: management has usually the duty to inform the unions and the workers about all the basic elements of the piece-rate, and can only change them when the conditions of the work organisation are changed (Article 2101, Civil Code); in this case the new piece-rate becomes definitive only after a 'period of adjustment'.

It is worth noting that plant-level bargaining often provides for various kinds of flexible wages linked to more or less objective criteria for measuring productivity, which are called with different names: productivity bonuses, premiums, payment of result.

This kind of wages has been progressively generalised, also due to the fact that the law has repeatedly favoured this trend by granting flexible wages collectively bargained a reduction of taxes and social security contributions (Act 247/2007, Act 93/2008, Act 183/2011, Act 92/2012 Article 4 co. 28–29).

These fiscal advantages have been confirmed and extended by the budget law of 2016 (Act 208/2015 Article 1 paragraphs 182–189). By the subsequent budget laws similar reductions are granted to the forms of profit sharing. Moreover this legislation has given to the employees the option to convert these bonuses into welfare benefits of various kinds: support to the education and the care of children, to the costs of transportation, refund of expenses for health care and personal assistance, etc. The budget law for 2023 (Act 197/2022) has further increased the favour of these productivity bonuses by reducing the taxation on them to 5%.

These provisions have been well accepted by the bargaining parties. According to the last data of 2019 a total of 50,847 collective agreements have been deposited between May 2016 and October 2019 to the Ministry of Labour in order to receive the tax advantages; 16,577 of these agreement are still active in October 2019. The employees who benefit from the bonus with tax reductions have been 3,422,000, and 69% of them may opt for a programme of welfare benefits which are mostly tax exempted. The number of agreements deposited for the same purpose in 2020 has decreased to 6784 then again increased to 9015 in 2021.

The criteria used to calculate flexible wages vary: in some cases they are based on qualitative and quantitative levels of production by small groups of workers or units of production; in others they are based on the overall production level of the firm, with an important distinction being made between production resulting purely from work as opposed to all factors of production, starting with investment, or even on the enterprise profitability.

209. However the percentage of the wage linked to such criteria is fairly limited (5%–6%) and is generally accompanied by wage increases of the traditional kind, i.e., which are not linked to parameters of productivity and/or the firm's overall production. Merit pay, unilaterally decided by management, is also used in various forms, particularly for medium-high-level employees and in firms where unions are not present.

210. Payment according to time was traditionally counted by the hour for blue-collar workers and by the month for white-collar workers. Since 1973 most collective agreements introduced a monthly salary system also for blue-collar workers. For white-collar workers the monthly pay system traditionally means that remuneration is paid independently of the number of hours actually worked, and in case of sickness and other unavoidable absences from work. This further guarantee is now extended more and more to blue-collar workers also.

211. As regards profits sharing, Article 2101 of the Civil Code provides that, lacking collective or individual contracts to the contrary, the share is determined on the basis of an enterprise's net profits resulting from the budget duly published (if the budget has to be published).

The Italian system makes wide use of indirect forms of wage such as periodical bonuses (for Christmas, Easter, etc.), bonuses linked to specific circumstances (anniversaries); indemnities, often (but not always) linked to particular conditions of work (underground, specific risks, heavy work, overtime, etc.).

Automatic forms of wages have been widely used in the Italian tradition particularly in two forms usually regulated by collective bargaining: periodical wage increases linked to seniority and wage increase linked to indexation, the so-called escalator clause. Both have been under attack during the 1980s as being an excessively rigid system of payment. The former have been either abolished or progressively reduced and maintain some importance only in some sectors (banking, insurance, schools) and for some employees (managers). The escalator clause, which has been the most important element of the wage structure during most of the post-war period and particularly since the early 1970s, was abolished in 1992 (*see* above).

II. Methods and Terms of Payment

212. Remuneration must be paid to an employee at the place of work contrary to the general civil law rules to make its perception easier. The place of work is also decisive in determining courts' jurisdictions for all labour grievances, Article 413 of the Civil Code procedure. Act No. 4 of 5 January 1953 stipulates that an employer must give an employee together with his remuneration a pay-slip indicating specifically all its elements (basic rate, piece rate, cost of living allowance, etc.), social security contributions and taxes.

213. Remuneration is traditionally paid after the work is done weekly, twice a month or monthly, in cash. Doubts have arisen as to the possibility of paying it by cheque, some lower courts denying it in principle or admitting it only under conditions aimed at favouring the worker who cashes the cheque. Act 205/ 2017

(Article 1, paragraphs 910–914) provides that employers may not pay wages directly in cash to the worker, but must pay through a bank or postal office.

III. Deductions, Seizure, Protection

214. The law protects an employee against excessive deductions of his wage in various ways. Article 7 of Act No. 300, 1970 fixes a maximum level of deductions by an employer for fines (four hours) and disciplinary suspension (ten days). A maximum of one-fifth can be seized for distraint by creditors (apart from alimony credits, where the amount is fixed by the judge). In case of multiple credits the maximum can reach half (Article 545, co. 3–4 cpc). The same maximum level is fixed for setting off credits owed to employers (advances, indemnification for damages, etc.). Finally, workers' credits for wages are protected from insolvencies by a special privilege on all the employer's movable properties, ranked first in the list of Article 2778 of the Civil Code.

215. Traditionally employees not paid at the appropriate time were only entitled to legal interest from the time at which the remuneration was due unless they proved further and concrete damages (in principle, not simply devaluation). Act No. 733 of 1973 empowers a judge to award, if necessary, in addition to legal interest, further damages resulting from cost of living increases by taking into account the official price index of ISTAT used for sliding scale adjustments in the industrial sector. The possibility of cumulating legal interest and further damages were excluded by Act 724/1994 (Article 22(36)) but the Constitutional Court held the norm to be illegitimate, at least for the private sector, because it was an unjustified limitation on the worker's right to a sufficient wage recognised by Article 36 of the Constitution (Decree 459/2000).

Chapter 5. The Suspension (of the Execution) of the Labour Contract

216. The need to protect employees, mainly to guarantee their income and job security, in cases when work cannot be temporarily performed for reasons independent of the will of the parties, has given rise to a legal and contractual discipline which is basically different from the principles regulating the execution of bilateral contracts in general. These principles stipulate that the temporary impossibility to execute the contract independent of the parties' will justifies the non-fulfilment of the obligation by the debtor and correspondingly the counterpart due by the creditor (suspension of both obligations). If the impossibility lasts for a longer period until the debtor cannot be held bound to perform his obligations or (more important) the creditor no longer has any interest in receiving it, the contract is automatically terminated (Article 1256 of the Civil Code).

217. Both these rules are to various extents modified by labour law in favour of employees. The trend is to safeguard the existence of the labour relation, reducing causes of termination as far as possible to causes of suspension of the contract and maintaining, as far as possible, the right of an employee either to remuneration or to an indemnity in lieu of remuneration. A basic distinction, usually made in Italian law, is between reasons for suspension due to an employee's impossibility to work and reasons of impossibility (or of difficulty) to receive the work by his employer.

218. The suspension of the execution of the contract can also be decided by consent between the parties, under conditions to be agreed upon. The consent of an employee to accept suspension without pay, for example, in the case of economic difficulty of the firm, is not to be implied.

§1. Suspension Due to the Employee

219. Articles 2110 and 2111, as amended, of the Civil Code are the general provisions for cases of sickness, work accidents, pregnancy and maternity, compulsory military service (both first call to armies and recall). In such cases an employee cannot be discharged for a period of time determined by law, by collective agreements, according to custom or to equity. Even at the end of the period, the general civil law principle that temporary impossibility to perform the contract led to its automatic termination is modified to the extent that the labour contract continues until the employer (or of course the employee also) decides to terminate it. These periods of absence from work are counted for seniority (a provision originally excluding the first call to arms from this latter protection has been declared unconstitutional). Article 2110 also provides that in cases of sickness, work accident, pregnancy and maternity an employer must pay his employees lacking an equivalent form of social security, remuneration or part of it in the amount and for the time determined by the law, by collective agreements, by custom or according to equity.

I. Sickness, Work Accidents

220. Employees' protection in these cases has been remarkably increased in process of time mainly by collective bargaining. During sickness the suspension of the contract, with job protection, lasts for periods usually determined by collective agreements according to the employee's seniority, generally with the exclusion of employees on trial. For example, the private metalworkers' agreement of 1987 provided for periods of six months for workers with more than six years of seniority. These periods can be prolonged to nine, thirteen, fifteen, eighteen months in cases of a relapse into the same sickness within a maximum period of two months.

221. Beyond these periods an employee is usually entitled, under collective agreements, to a further period of leave of absence, unpaid (four months according to the metalworkers' agreement). During these periods employees can be dismissed only in the (extreme) case where a just cause is proved (*see* below). At the end of the period it is debatable whether an employee still sick can be discharged at will with notice (under the rule of Article 2118 of the Civil Code, *see* below) or only if an employer proves that there is a justified reason for dismissal under Act No. 604 of 1966: the justified reason being a specific organisational or productive need of the enterprise which prevents the employer from continuing the labour contract. The majority of the courts hold that the employee can be legitimately discharged in this case by considering the persisting sickness either a justified reason or a case of impossibility to perform (such as to justify the termination of the labour contract). A similarly controversial question concerns the employer's possibility to discharge an employee who is frequently absent for short periods of illness which individually do not exceed the length of time guaranteed by Article 2110 and by collective agreements. According to Court of Cassation decisions, the criteria established by collective agreements are to be followed in principle; these agreements often consider the case and determine the maximum length of absence protected by totalling the short periods of illness (in a given time span). Lacking such a provision it is up to the judge to determine, according to equity (Article 2110, Civil Code), the maximum length of absence to be protected after which the continuing illness legitimises termination of the contract by the employer. In cases of work accidents the suspension lasts until recovery is officially certified; in cases of professional disease, until the employee receives the inability indemnities provided for by the law.

222. The right of an employee who is sick or a victim of a work accident to the security of income is different for blue-collar and white-collar workers. The latter is entitled to receive regular wages directly from the employer (which is consistent with the idea that white-collar workers are hired and paid independently of the work actually done) up to a period of time fixed by a collective agreement, and part of the salary for a further period.

The wage obligation of an employer can be prolonged in the case of a relapse into the same illness.

223. Blue-collar workers receive – beginning a few days (usually three) after the start of the work suspension, and lasting for a fixed period – an indemnity from social security institution equal to 60% of the regular wage (traditionally from INAM in cases of sickness; after the institution of the national health service and the suspension of INAM, this is to be substituted by INPS; INAIL in cases of work accidents). Since 1973, most national collective agreements have provided that an employer must pay his employee the difference up to the regular wage for a period of time-related to the employee's seniority, and part of the wage for a further period. In the metalworkers' agreements and other national agreements the periods of time and the total income guarantees are the same for blue-collar as for white-collar workers. These protections are granted also if the sickness or the accident is due to the employer's carelessness or negligence (it is doubtful whether remuneration is due also in cases of gross negligence).

Accidents outside the workplace are usually considered by collective agreement as sickness. A general regulation of these cases for white-collar workers is set forth by the old Act No. 1825 of 1924 but has been largely superseded by more favourable collective agreements. Recently some collective agreements have introduced sanctions in case of abnormal absenteeism, including loss of wage for the first days or loss of bonuses.During the COVID-19 pandemic, Act 27/2020 has intervened to protect workers held in quarantine by providing that this period of absence is considered as sickness for the purpose of the right to indemnity.

Act 81/2017 has also recognised autonomous workers right to a limited suspension of the contract, and a limited indemnity in case of sickness, work accidents, and maternity.

224. Collective agreements impose specific and detailed duties on an employee to inform his employer about sickness and accidents, usually within two days in case of sickness (a medical certificate must be submitted within three days) and immediately in cases of work accidents. Without such information an employee is considered absent without justification. A duty to be at disposal for medical checks, during certain hours, is also imposed by law (*see* paragraph 140). Sickness and work accidents suspend the period of notice.

II. Pregnancy and Maternity

225. Women workers have special protection in cases of pregnancy and maternity under Act No. 1204 of 30 December 1971; now, all the regulations on maternity are assembled in Act 151/2001. First of all women cannot be dismissed from the beginning of pregnancy until one year after the child's birth, and in this period a woman who resigns has the right to indemnity in lieu of notice as if she was dismissed. The labour contract can be terminated only when just cause for dismissal is proved, in the case of the enterprise terminating its activity, the end of the specific work for which the woman has been hired, or the elapse of the term of the contract. In order to avoid possible abuses Act 151/2001 has provided a special regulation also in case of resignation of the mother whereby the resignation is valid only if validated with the public inspectorate of labour. This protection applies also in case of adoption and is extended to the father who has used the right to abstain (*see* below). Act 92/2012 has reinforced the procedure of validation and extended the protection from the first year of age of the child to the first three years.

A woman must abstain from work from two months before the probable date of the child's birth (or more if the work is dangerous for the mother's health) until three months after. During this period she is entitled to 80% of her regular pay from social security and the period is counted as actual work as regards seniority, annual vacation and the thirteenth month. Collective agreements usually oblige an employer to pay the difference up to the regular wage. The woman must also abstain from heavy or dangerous jobs (if necessary having the right to be transferred) during the whole period of pregnancy; she can abstain from work for a further six months beyond the compulsory period of rest, and has the right to time off work in the case of the child's sickness.

226. Some rights reserved to the mother by Act 1204 have been gradually extended to the father, also following the pressure of court decisions and of European directives. The right of the father to abstain from work has been first recognised only in specific serious cases; it has been generalised by Act 53/2000 (*see* above paragraph 157). Act 92/2012 has provided a duty of the father to abstain from work for one day, paid with full wage, within the first five months of a child's life, and the option to abstain for two more days also fully paid; but the latter days are subtracted from the days of compulsory abstention of the mother.

Decree 80/2015 implementing Act 183/2014 has improved in many respect the regulation of this matter. The use of a period of compulsory abstention from work has been made more flexible in case of premature birth and child hospitalisation. The right to parental leaves have been extended from the past period of eight years of the child to twelve years. Paid leaves (30%) can be used up to six years of the child and for poor families, up to eight years.

Similar provisions are extended to cases of child adoption and custody. The parental leaves in case of the mother's impediment have been extended to the father regardless of the employment status (i.e., not only to dependent workers). In addition, the father is obliged to take four-days off (fully paid) to be used within five months after the child's birth and may use another day in substitution of the mother, with her consent (Act 232/2016, Article 1, co. 345). Special leaves are provided to women who are victims of violence and are involved in specific programmes of protection. Decree 105/2022 has reregulated the matter and in particular increased the duty of the father to abstain from work (*see* above paragraph 187).

III. Military Service: First Call and Recall to Arms

227. While in both cases job security and seniority are granted to all workers, including those performing social services in lieu of military service (Act No. 653 of 1940, Act No. 303 of 1946, Act No. 370 of 1955, Act 64/2001), a form of guaranteed income during the suspension of the contract is provided for (Act No. 653 of 1940) only in cases of a recall to arms and in favour of white-collar workers. The scope of these norms has been reduced because compulsory military service has been abolished by Act 226/2004, beginning on 1 January 2005. Workers recalled to arms are entitled to receive the equivalent of their regular wage from a special social security fund (INPS) for the first two months of absence and subsequently the difference between the military pay and the regular wage. An equitable guarantee of income should be derived for blue-collar workers from the general principle of Articles 2110 (first paragraph) and 2111 (second paragraph) which stipulate that, lacking any form of social security indemnification, an employer should pay part of the wage at least according to equity. Act No. 370 of 1955 further provides that a worker who is recalled to arms cannot be discharged up to three months after he has returned to work. He is considered as resigning if he does not return to work within a short period after the end of military service.

228. The principles set forth by Articles 2110–2111 are exceptional and therefore cannot be extended beyond the cases explicitly mentioned.

Other cases in which the labour contract is suspended for reasons (different from impossibility) pertaining to the sphere of the employee have already been mentioned: annual vacations, time off work (paid and non-paid) and leaves of absence to perform public duties, political and union activity, to attend courses of study, parental leaves etc.

Special leaves of absence with or without pay are granted to workers by collective agreements on the occasion of important family events, e.g., sickness and death of close relatives, marriage. In the latter case, all workers, not on trial, are usually entitled to 15 consecutive days of absence with regular pay; the same right is to a woman worker who resigns to get married.

Special leaves are granted to parents with seriously disabled children (Act 151/2001 and Act 104/1992), and to disabled workers for specific needs (Article 10(4) Act 68/1999) and to drug addicts to favour medical treatment (Act 162/1990). Suspension of the execution of the contract due to strikes will be discussed below (Part II).

§2. Suspension Due to the Employer and to the Enterprise

I. Generalities

229. The general principles of civil law have undergone profound changes and integrations also in cases where the work is interrupted or reduced for reasons pertaining 'to the sphere' of the employer. The traditional rule is that an employer must continue to pay his employee if the suspension 'depends on him', whereas he is free from any obligation if it depends on supervening impossibility to receive the employee's performance. At a civil law level, temporary impossibility can lead to the termination of the contract under the conditions already stated (Article 1256 of the Civil Code).

230. The concept of 'impossibility' – and the distinction between it and mere 'difficulty' – has always been very controversial: according to prevailing civil law tradition, impossibility is to be interpreted rather strictly, i.e., limited to extreme cases of force majeure (such as the burning down of the factory or its closure by public authorities), and not usually including circumstances connected with the enterprise, although not due to any negligence of the employer (such as economic difficulties).

231. Most collective agreements guarantee blue-collar workers the right to remuneration in all cases of short suspensions of work (usually up to sixty minutes a day) whatever their reason, i.e., even due to force majeure. For suspensions due to force majeure lasting more than sixty minutes a day the worker must be paid only if he is ordered to stay at the employer's disposal, otherwise general civil law rules apply. Time lost because of force majeure or because of a suspension agreed between the individual or collective parties can be recovered by working no more than one hour per day and within thirty days from the suspension.

232. According to the general principle already mentioned, white-collar workers are entitled to their regular salary from the employer whatever the reason for the suspension or due to the reduction of the enterprise's functioning (the principle was originally characterised by two inter confederal agreements of 1946). This privileged position has been modified by the law on salary integrations (*see* below).

II. Salary Integrations: Lay-Offs and Short-Time; Unemployment Benefits

233. A major problem faced by labour law concerns the suspension or reduction of work for economic reasons (lay-off and short-time). According to a strict application of the civil law rules on impossibility, the employer would have been bound in any case to pay the workers their regular wages, because most of these cases could hardly be considered force majeure. But this conclusion was obviously unrealistic, and in fact rarely sustained: it would have caused an employer to dismiss the workers (which he could at that time do at will). The problem has been solved by a series of legislative provisions which created for the industrial sector a special public fund (*Cassa Integrazione Guadagni*) financed with contributions of both employers and employees, to guarantee part of the income to blue-collar workers during such a period (white-collar workers having the right to be paid in any case and are much less affected by lay-offs). Various acts during the whole post-war period greatly broadened the original scope of the Fund's intervention (Act No. 464 of 1972, Act 164 of 1975, Act 223/1991), Act 296/2006; Act 247/2007, Act 191/2009 (Article 2, co. 130), Act 92/2012. Act 148/2015 has reorganised the system (*see* below).

234. Following these changes the Fund has become the major instrument of public protection for workers' income vis-à-vis the periodical crisis and characterising processes which characterise the modern industrial economy. Indirectly the Fund also protects job security, since resort to it by an employer is intended to enable him to overcome his economic difficulties with public help and to avoid collective dismissals. The number of hours of work paid by the Fund has reached high peaks in periods of economic crisis: and contributed to keeping the number of mass dismissals relatively low (*see* Table 3): 578 million hours in 1981; over 750 million in 1984; in 2010 11.97 million, in 2012 10.90 million, and an absolute maximum during the COVID-19 pandemic 2.960.616 hours.

Table 3 Interventions by the Fund (Number of Hours)

	Ordinary Interventions	*Extraordinary Interventions*	*Total*
2000	84.656.408	62.877.102	147.533.510
2012	340.333.095	400.324.809	740.657.904
2015	183.776.222	400.598.524	584.374.746
2017	104.888.482	209.950.902	314.839.384
2018	95.656.895	116.609.623	212.266.518
2020	1.979.786.234	182.305.760	2.960.686.616
2021	932.175.631	186.914.824	1.790.681.563
2022 (jan-nov)	217.789.425	178.845.583	424.783.676

235. Act 223/1991 regulated a special type of social protection (which lasted for many years and terminated at the end of 2016). With the aim of containing the use of lay-offs and a short time to cases of actual temporary enterprise crisis, the Act has provided that when the crisis appears to be definitive and if the employer is not in a position to re-employ his employees, he can initiate a procedure of 'external mobility'. The procedure was essentially similar to that of collective dismissals (*see* below) and, indeed, at the end the employees are dismissed. But they are entitled to receive a special indemnity from the Fund similar to the salary integration (higher than the ordinary unemployment benefits for a period variable according to seniority, age and geographical area (ranging from twelve to thirty-six months). Employees in 'mobility' are put in a special list and enjoy priority in being hired: i.e., employers must select from this list, where other disadvantaged people are included, a percentage of the new employees is variable according to the area (between 12% and 20%). However, employers hiring these employees on contracts for an indefinite period could receive substantial benefits, mainly in the form of social security contribution reduction. This system of mobility has been terminated in 2016:

(1) A common criticism of this discipline is that the good monetary protection guaranteed by the Fund is not matched by public administration's capacity to use the Fund effectively as a means of industrial policy and not as a mere 'assisting institution'.
(2) The need to change the system has brought to a comprehensive reforms, first by Act 92/2012 and then by Decree 148/2015. The new regulation confirms the traditional distinction between two kinds of Funds: one for ordinary and one for extraordinary interventions.

(3) The former occurs in cases of (a) temporary market difficulties of a firm; (b) difficulties due to transitory events not attributable to employees or to the employer, including seasonal bad weather. The latter operates in cases of cessation of the activity of the enterprise or branch; (c) solidarity contracts. The Fund's ordinary intervention applies to industrial sectors, building construction (with a special fund), workers cooperatives, agricultural cooperatives (regardless of the size of the firm).

(4) The scope of application of the extraordinary intervention varies. It applies to firms with more than fifteen employees operating in the industrial sectors, constructions, co-operatives and artisan firms affected by the crisis of the dominant enterprise (which provides more than 50% of the business) cleaning and canteen services affected by the crisis of the contractor, agricultural cooperatives, security services, etc. In the commercial, logistic, tourist, sectors, the fund is applicable only to firms with more than fifty employees.

(5) The fund intervenes, regardless of the number of employees, in case of firms operating in air transportation, airport activities, and for employees of political parties and trade unions.

236. In spite of subsequent extensions of the Fund some sectors and areas, in particular of small enterprises remained excluded. In order to 'protect' these cases a new form of intervention so-called derogatory interventions, was introduced (Act 350/2003, Act 185/2008): whereby the Fund could provide income support on a case-by-case basis, following agreement with the unions and authorisation of the Ministry of Labour – usually with the contribution of the Regions. This type of intervention has come to be more and more used during the years of serious economic crisis.

After the reform of 2015 the coverage of the Fund for enterprises of all sectors is almost complete. But the need to extend and prolong the duration of the Fund is still present, particularly in order to meet serious crises of specific firms, areas and sectors. Derogations therefore have been provided by various provisions: Acts 136/2018; 130/2018; 145/2018 (Article 1 paragraphs 248–259, 282). The duration of fund intervention has been variable over the years.

237. The amount of salary guaranteed by the fund has been traditionally 80% of the ordinary wage within a maximum ceiling, partially indexed (every year); in 2018 the ceiling was EUR 995.21 monthly for workers earning up to EUR 20,148.34.

For those earning more, the ceiling was EUR 1,193.71. The reform of Act 234/2021 has abolished this difference; consequently beginning January 2022 the ceiling applicable to all workers is EUR 122,251.

According to Decree 148/2015 the ordinary intervention may last up to a maximum of thirteen weeks consecutive which can be extended up to a maximum of fifty-two weeks (in a biennium mobile) within a ceiling fixed in proportion to the total working time. The same production unit cannot be authorised to use the fund, ordinary and extraordinary, for more than twenty-four months in a five years period.

The duration of the extraordinary intervention varies according to the reasons of the lay-off or the reduction of worktime: twenty-four months in case of firm's reorganisation; twelve months in case of firm's economic crisis.

238. A total limit of twenty-four months in a five years period is fixed when the firm uses both types of fund intervention, ordinary and extraordinary.

The salary integrations authorised cannot exceed 80% of the total working time of each unit in the given period; this limit aims at favouring the adoption of decision of the firms to adopt forms of short time instead of total suspension of work activity.

The fund ordinary intervention is granted, at the employer's request, by the social security Institute (INPS) which runs the Fund, where the trade unions are represented (in a minority). The extraordinary intervention is granted, at the employer's request by ministerial decree following a procedure of information and consultation with union representatives. The employer is requested to submit detailed programme of reorganisation, indicating the reasons for the fund intervention, the number of employees involved, the measures to handle possible redundancies. Moreover the parties must ascertain that other solutions, in particular solidarity contracts, are not feasible.

239. In order to protect categories of workers not included in the Fund, Act 662/1996 (Article 28) provided that the social parties can set up by collective agreements sectorial funds run by the same parties under ministerial control, and financed by a contribution on wages of not less than 0.5% plus additional contributions by the employer. This voluntary self-regulated form of social protection has been well accepted by the parties; important funds have been operating in the banking and insurance sectors and in the categories of artisans.

Decree 148/2015 has extended the possible use of these bilateral funds in favour of enterprises with more than five employees. The contributions vary. For the funds established by collective agreements they are fixed by the same agreements, but with an additional contribution for employers who actually use the fund. For the so-called alternative funds (e.g., in the artisan sector) the contributions are not less than 0.45% of the wages.

The enterprises not covered by bilateral funds are included in a special fund operating within INPS (where the contribution varies between 0.45% and 0.65% of wages, according to the sure of the firm).

Decree 148/2015 has reregulated the system of financing the Fund. The ordinary intervention is financed with a contribution by the employers variable according to the sector and type of enterprise (from 1.7% of wages to 4.7%). The contributions for the extraordinary interventions amount to 0.90% (0.60% paid by employer 0.30% by the employee).

These contributions are lower than those fixed in the past, but are supplemented by an additional contribution by the employers who actually use the fund in the two forms (ranging from 9% to 15 of the wages due for the hours not worked).

This contributory system is intended to be self-financing. The objective of the legislator is to avoid any recourse to state subsidies which was frequent in the years of economic crisis. The cost of the so-called derogatory intervention of the fund in fact has greatly increased since 2008.

240. The employer is obliged by law to communicate in advance (apart from cases of force majeure) to the unions the dimension and duration of the lay-off or of the short-time and to examine with them all resulting problems by which workers' interests might be affected. In the selection of the employees to be laid off or put on short time, the courts require that the employer follows objective criteria. Usually they are collectively fixed and the most common are seniority, family conditions, organisational needs of the firm, used in combination. Act 223/1991 requires that the selection, while remaining an employer's prerogative, be examined jointly with the unions; moreover it requires that in the case of extraordinary interventions, the employer applies a criterion of rotation among the employees to be laid off. The rotation may be avoided if it is impracticable for technical-organisational reasons; the Minister of Labour may arbitrate in case of disagreement between the parties and impose the rotation.

241. A special kind of arrangement directed to reduce the burden of economic crises on the employees is the so-called solidarity contract. This was introduced by Act 863/1984: Article 1 promotes collective agreement (enterprise-wide) which provide for a reduction of working time for all employees of a given firm in lieu of a lay-off of some of them or of collective dismissals. Following these agreements the Fund will pay 50% of wages cost for the reduction of working time for twenty-four months (the other part of the loss will rest with the employees). Subsequent legislation has raised the Fund contribution to 60% and then 80% (Act 33/2009), and has granted incentives to the employer.

These modifications have made the solidarity contract rather convenient to both parties; in fact it has been increasingly used during the economic crisis.

242. The regulation of this solidarity contract has been confirmed by Decree 148/2015 (Article 31) to put in line with the new rules on the Fund Intervention. The duration has been extended to thirty-six months.

A second form of solidarity contract aims at fostering employment by giving incentives to employers who reduce work time and, at the same time, hire new workers. The incentives were introduced first by Act 863/1984, and lately by Act 296/2006 (*see* below paragraphs 241 ff.) but have been rarely used because they were considered by the employees not sufficient to compensate for the loss of income. These incentives have been confirmed by Article 41 of Decree 148/2015, which reshaped the use of solidarity contracts to favour the gradual retirement of employees. Two years before retirement age employees who are part of the solidarity contract can accept to work part-time, and will receive part of their pension in addition to the reduced wage.

This conditions of gradual retirement have been reformed by the stability Act for 2016 (Act 208, Dec. 2015, Article 1, co. 28) and made more convenient for the employees. Those who accept part-time on an individual basis (with no need to be included in a solidarity collective agreement); continue to accumulate full social security contributions paid by the state useful for their future pension. Employers are required to pay to the employees a sum equivalent to amount of their social security contributions in addition to the wage due for the part time.

These pattern provisions remained in force until the end of 2018. A new discipline has been approved by Act 34/2019, with a different approach (*see* Contract of Expansion).

The established system of Fund protection has been subject to great pressure during the COVID-19 crisis of 2020–2021 which has caused the suspension and interruption of many economic activities.

As a remedy the government has introduced a further case of Fund intervention, 'Covid suspension', which has been operating for periods of different duration often prolonged, exempted from extra costs for the employers and extended to small and smallest enterprises in derogation to general rules.

In addition, monetary bonuses of various entity have been granted to many categories of precarious employees (e.g., seasonal) and to autonomous workers who were traditionally deprived of any social protection.

For them a special welfare provision has been introduced by the budget law of 2021 (so-called ISCRO) on an experimental basis for three years, which consists of a sum equivalent to 25% of the semestral income perceived in the last years on the condition that the worker income has been reduced by 40% due to COVID-19.

This provision is the first welfare measure of this kind recognised to autonomous workers, which is advocated to be improved and extended to all self-employed workers.

Given the limits of these emergency provisions, Act 23 of 28 March 2022 has approved a reform of the regulations concerning the suspensions of work for economic reasons that, while maintaining the basic structures of the Fund fixed by act 148/2015, has extended its intervention, following the principle of 'differentiated universalism', to all sectors and firm dimensions, unless these are already covered by bilateral funds, and to all types of employers previously excluded: apprentices, home workers. The same Act has provided that employees who receive the benefits of the Fund must follow specific training courses finalised to maintain or adjourn their skills.

Act 134/2021 has promoted a so-called 'accord of employment transition', whereby enterprises employing more than fifteen workers which have terminated the ordinary Fund intervention are allowed twelve further months in order to implement measures of reemployment; moreover it has prolonged and strengthened the contract of expansion, and increased the incentives to solidarity contract.

A special procedure has been added to that regulated by act 223/1991 (*see* above), by Act 234/2021 Article 1, com224–238, concerning the cases in which enterprises employing over 250 employees, usually multinational, decide to relocate their activities abroad and to terminate those in Italy.

These enterprises are obliged to give advance notice of ninety days of their decision to relocate to the unions and to national and regional authorities, including the reasons and the timing of the decision, and also to submit a plan directed to limit the economic and occupational impact of the relocation, including programmes of reskilling of the employees and the possibility of asset transfer.

A collective accord with the unions is favoured by special conditions approved by the Fund concerning salary integration to the workers. Lacking the agreement the enterprise is free to proceed to collective dismissals of redundant workers, but the costs of the dismissals are increased.

A series of reforms have been approved during the economic crisis of recent years with the aim of favouring the rescue instead of the liquidation and bankruptcy of companies (in particular Decree 14 of January 2019, known as 'code of enterprise crisis and insolvency').

§3. So-Called Contract of Expansion

243. Article 26 quarter of Decree 34/2019 (converted into Act 58/2019) has regulated the so-called contract of expansion. This contract substitutes the contract of solidarity for fostering employment regulated by Act 148/2015 (*see* above paragraph 241). According to this Act during 2019–2020 the firms which employ more than 1,000 employees and intend to introduce processes of technological innovation, reindustrialisation or reorganisation may sign an agreement with the unions and the Ministry of Development whereby they are authorised to anticipate by five years the retirement of employees with their consensus. These employees are entitled to a monthly indemnity which includes the public indemnity for unemployment. This provision reduces considerably the costs on the employers in comparison to those of other forms of early retirement.

The contract must indicate the number and types of employees whose activity will be reduced or suspended during the process of reorganisation. In addition it must specify the number and the professional qualifications of the employees to be hired following the agreement.

The employer is obliged to implement a plan of training and reskilling of the employees included in the contract. The application of this contract has been prolonged for 2022–2023 by Act 214/2021.

Unemployment Insurance

244. Legislation which regulates unemployment insurance, beginning with the Act 181/2000, has provided controls on the status of the unemployed and directed employment offices to offer to the unemployed, particularly the long-term unemployed, concrete training and job opportunities (source Act 181/2000). These proposals correspond to a policy directive aimed at promoting an active approach to labour market problems and needs.

Employees are obliged to accept these offers under penalty of losing unemployment benefits. The enforcement of these activation policies has been uneven, particularly weak in some southern regions of Italy, due to the scarce effectiveness of the employment agencies and of public controls, to the weakness of labour markets (and also to the scarce 'civicness' of the beneficiaries).

245. Unemployment benefits have been traditionally low. They have been progressively raised: up to 40% of the normal wage by Act 388/2000; then to 50% by

Act 80/2005 and to 60% by Act 247/2007 (for the first six months then decreasing to 40%), by Act 92/2012 to 75% for the first six months, within a ceiling of 1,180 monthly, then decreasing by 15% and again by 15% after twelve months. The conditions necessary to receive the benefits were rather strict (two years of seniority and one year of actual employment in the two years precedent to unemployment). These conditions can be fulfilled only by regular stable employees.

246. Act 22/2015 has revised the system introducing a new form of benefits the so-called NASPI. NASPI is granted to all unemployed people having at least thirteen weeks of contributions in the four years preceding the termination of employment and thirty days of contributions in the last year.

This new regulation has included in the system most unemployed people. However, if the scope of the benefits is extended, their duration has been limited: NASPI is granted for a number of weeks equal to half the weeks of contributions in the last four years. Moreover, the NASPI maximum amount is EUR 1,300 and is reduced by 3% every months after the fourth month of actual utilisation.

A special indemnity (called DIS-COLL) of reduced amount and duration is granted to the continuous and coordinated collaborators unemployed who have at least three months of contributions in the year precedent to the end of their employment and at least one month of contributions or a month of employment in the year of termination of employment. The amount is 75% of the monthly income of the collaborator with a ceiling of EUR 1,300, but is reduced by 3% per month after the fourth month.

247. The decree has introduced a new type of indemnity called ASDI, for people who have used the ordinary benefits for the maximum duration, are still unemployed and are in a condition of need as ascertained by means of testing with a system called ISEE (Decree 159/2015).

ASDI lasts for a maximum of six months and amounts to 75% of the last NASPI, in any event not exceeding the social assistance bonus (around 500E monthly).

In the first year of application (2015) priority is given to workers who are members of a family with minors and to workers near retirement age.

ASDI is the first case of welfare benefit not related to actual contributions; a sort of anticipation of minimum income.

The right to NASPI and ASDI are conditioned to the participation of the beneficiaries in activation programmes; which is a common requirement for all beneficiaries of welfare provisions: (Decree 150/2015 Article 25) (*see* below).

§4. Minimum Income

248. The increased poverty among the population and also among the workers has convinced the legislator to introduce also in Italy, like in most European countries, a form of guaranteed minimum income.

A first version rather limited in coverage and amount was approved in 2017 (Act 33/2017) with the name of income of inclusion (RES).

The subsequent provision approved in 2019, with the name 'income of citizenship', greatly extended its coverage and contents (Decree 4/2019 converted into Act 26/2019). The provisions of the Act are directed to fight poverty and to promote the access to work and the social inclusion of persons at risk of emargination. The income is given to families composed of Italian citizens and regular immigrants resident in Italy for ten years; having an income below 9,360 yearly or more according to the number of family members; and a patrimony lower than a certain amount. The beneficiary, if able to work and unemployed, must sign with the public labour offices an agreement which implies the obligation to accept an offer of work and if necessary, to follow training courses.

The offer of work must be accepted on penalty of decadence from the benefit if it is located within a certain distance from the residence of the beneficiary: for the first offer is 100 km or 100 minutes of travel and then decreases for the second and third offer.

When the needs of the beneficiary are more complex, he/she is assigned to the competent offices of the municipality and must sign with them a 'pact for social inclusion' which provides for the measures necessary to promote social inclusion.

The amount of the economic benefit may reach a maximum of EUR 9,360 yearly, according to the conditions of the family. In fact the average so far is lower (around EUR 500).

In the first year after the approval of the law a great number of requests have been presented (850,000 families over 1,400,000 persons) but less than expected have been accepted. The main shortcoming in the implementation of these provisions is that while the economic indemnities to the beneficiaries have been granted, the measures for their activation in work and social activities are lagging behind; and so are the controls on the requisites.

Decree 150/2015 has introduced (Article 17) a special bonus to employment agencies to promote reemployment of workers who lose their job. The bonus is, coupled with personalised services (including training), to support the search for new employment opportunities. The amount of the bonus is related to the employment profile of the beneficiary and is paid according to the actual performance and result (as defined by Ministerial decree).

The beneficiaries of this special assistance must participate in all the activation measures under penalty of losing the bonus.

Decree 4/2019 has reserved this bonus only for beneficiaries of the income of citizenship;, but this limit has been abolished.

The budget law of 29 December 2022 (Act 197/2022), in anticipation of a reform of the citizens no income has reduced the duration of the benefits to a max of seven months for people able to work, and has restricted the conditions for receiving these benefits by providing that they will be terminated if the person refusing one (adequate) job offer.

Chapter 6. The End of the Individual Labour Contract

§1. General Ways of Terminating the Individual Labour Contract

249. The different ways in which a labour contract can come to an end are enumerated and regulated in part by the general law of contract and in part by specific provisions of labour law. The application of the general principles of civil law to the labour contract has been progressively reduced as a consequence of the emergence of a more detailed special provision. The basic trend of this provision is to promote the stability of employment in favour of the employer, restricting in various ways the possible reasons which can prejudice it according to civil law.

§2. Mutual Consent, Judicial Dissolution, Impossibility of Performance

250. The general principle that a contract can be terminated by mutual consent in the same way as it can come into existence is held applicable to labour law by most legal commentators. It is often pointed out, however, that this means of terminating the labour contract must be tightly controlled, because it could easily be used to circumvent the imperative norms of the law regulating dismissals (e.g., requiring a term of notice, a justified reason for the dismissal) in which case the mutual consent would be nullified. In practice, there has apparently been no judicial test of this way of terminating the labour contract.

251. The judicial dissolution for breach of contract (Articles 1453ff., Civil Code) is commonly excluded by legal commentators and by the Supreme Court as a method of terminating the labour contract, because it is considered to be substituted by the special means of termination for just cause without a term of notice (*see* paragraphs 272 ff.).

252. More uncertain is the applicability to the labour contract of the general principle according to which the supervening impossibility of performance terminates de jure the contract if it is definitive or if it lasts so long that the employer can no longer be held bound to comply with his obligations since the employer no longer has any interest in it (Article 1256, Civil Code).

253. The most important reasons for impossibility on the side of the employee (compulsory military service, illness, work accidents, pregnancy and maternity, etc.) are considered by law to be a cause of suspension of the labour contract and exclude the power of the employer to dismiss the employee unless for just cause. On the side of the employer (or of the enterprise) cases of absolute impossibility as commonly understood under civil law are fairly rare, and the special provisions for lay-off and short time cover most of them. Most probably, even the few circumstances which make the performance of the contract *definitely* unlawful or impossible (and which are not protected by special provision) cannot be considered as just reasons for termination de jure nor just cause for termination without notice but justifiable reasons for the dismissal of the worker. The worker, therefore, maintains his right to a period of notice or to an equivalent indemnity. This has been held true, for example, by the courts, in cases of absence of the employee due to illness prolonged beyond the maximum term of suspension (*see* below). The right to the indemnity in place of term of notice is in fact recognised by law on behalf of the worker's heirs in case of the employee's death (Article 2118, 2nd paragraph Civil Code) and Article 2119, second paragraph, explicitly declares that bankruptcy and forced administration of the enterprise are not just causes for dismissal without term of notice.

§3. Death of One of the Parties, Transfer of the Enterprise

254. The death of the employee automatically terminates the contract. The same is not true for the death of the employer except in the (exceptional) case where the activity of the employer is essential to the continuation of the employment, e.g., professional activity, certain cases of domestic work, etc.

255. The general rule is that the labour relationship continues in spite of the change of the employer if the enterprise continues. According to the law in fact the transfer of the enterprise does not automatically terminate the labour relationship (Article 2112, Civil Code). This applies also to transformation by merger or takeover (argument from Article 2498, last paragraph and 2504, last paragraph, Civil Code).

Article 2112 provides that the employees of a transferred enterprise continue to enjoy the seniority acquired before the transfer, and that the new owner is liable for all benefits of the employee if the new owner was aware of them at the time of the transfer, or if they resulted from the books of the enterprise or from the labour documents of the employee. Under the provision introduced by Act No. 604 of 1966 and by Article 18 of Act No. 300 of 1970, the mere fact of a future transfer cannot in itself justify dismissal. It would be necessary for the employer to prove that the transfer implied, for example, a reorganisation of the enterprise such as to justify a reduction of personnel and that was likely to happen only to the beneficiary and not to the transferring employer. The first regulation of Article 2112 Civil Code has been repeatedly modified, by Act 215/1978, by Act 428/1990 (Article 47), which implemented EU Directive 77/187, and lately by Act 18/2001 implementing EU Directive 98/50.

256. Act 18/2001 adopts a wide concept of transfer of enterprise, wider than that of the previous Acts, including all transfers of 'organised economic activity aimed at the production or exchange of goods or services'. Also a section or branch of an enterprise can be included provided it is 'functionally autonomous': Act 30/2003 and Decree 276 (Article 32) specify that the capacity of the unit to operate autonomously need not pre-exist but may exist at the moment of the transfer.

The identification of the elements characterising the legal notion of transfer is important because if they are not present the employees transferred do not benefit from the protection granted by law. These norms are held to be applicable also to employers not entrepreneurs like non-profit organisations and professional offices.

The concept of enterprise has been further extended in line with decisions of the Italian Court and of the ECJ, which hold sufficient for the application of Article 2112 the existence of an organised group of employees capable of entrepreneurial initiative, even though deprived of specific material instruments.

In other respects the regulation of 2003 confirms the basic principles of the old law. It maintains the liability of both the old and the new owner for all credits of the employees, because it retains the previous condition of awareness. The employee can free one of the owners from his obligations only before the special tripartite commission provided by Article 410 Civil Procedure Code or in a trade union conciliation (Article 411 CPC, *see* below paragraphs 280 ff.). Act 30/2003 confirms that the transfer does not constitute per se just cause or justified reason for dismissal and it also confirms the derogation from the principle of continuity of the employment relationship (and of seniority) for enterprises affected by economic crisis properly acknowledged and for enterprises undergoing bankruptcy procedures or controlled administration (or equivalent), on the condition that an agreement is reached with the most representative unions which provides partial guarantee of further employment for the employees of the firm transferred. The Act has admitted a trade-off between continuity of seniority and employment safeguard.

Act 18/2001 also guarantees that the collective agreements regulating the transferred employees will continue to apply after the transfer until their termination or unless other collective agreements, national or enterprise-wide, are applicable to the new employer. The pre-existing agreements can be substituted by the new ones only if they operate at the same level, e.g., national agreements are substituted by new national agreements but not by enterprise agreements.

Finally the Act subordinates the transfer to a procedure of previous information and consultation of the trade unions; both parties interested in the transfer must inform the trade unions (at territorial and plant level) twenty days before the decision of its reasons, consequences for the employees and remedies provided for the same employees, and must, on request, jointly examine the matter with the unions. The violation of this procedure is an unfair labour practice (*see* below paragraphs 386 ff.) and may lead to damages, invalidation of the effects prejudicial to the employees or, less likely, of the transfer itself.

§4. Other Reasons

257. Other general causes of termination of the labour relations are the nullity and invalidation of the labour contract, insofar as they do not have retroactive effects (*see* above Article 2126, Civil Code).

258. The contract of employment concluded for a definite period of time can terminate, again according to the general principles of civil law, because of the expiry of the term. If the labour contract is concluded for a precisely indicated job, under the conditions provided for by the law, to be considered limited to the duration of this job, the completion of the job can also terminate the relationship.

§5. TERMINATION WITH NOTICE AND FOR A JUST CAUSE

I. The Provision of the Civil Code

259. By far the most relevant – and most precisely regulated – ways of ending the individual labour contract are termination (*recesso*) for just cause without a term of notice and termination (*recesso*) by serving a term of notice. The original provision of these two ways of termination is contained in Articles 2118 and 2119 of the Civil Code and is common to the dismissals by the employer and to the resignation by the employee. Article 2118 provides that each party can terminate an employment relationship for an indefinite period on the giving of a period of notice as established by collective agreements, by practice or equity, or by paying an indemnity equal to the regular pay for the period of notice. Article 2119 provides that each party can terminate a contract for a fixed term before the expiration of the term or a contract for an indefinite period without notice for just cause, i.e., due to a fact that prevents the continuation, even temporarily (for the period of notice or until the expiration of the term) of the labour relationship.

260. Termination at will with notice is common, under civil law, to all contracts for an indefinite period; in the case of the labour contract, it was originally conceived as a protection of the worker's freedom not to be bound for life (argument from Article 1628 of the old Civil Code of 1865). The ideology of formal equality between the parties to a contract justified the granting of the same freedom to the employer.

All arguments advanced by legal commentators to justify a limited judicial control, at least over discriminatory dismissals (based on the violation of the constitutional principle of trade union freedom) have been rejected for many years and have not been passed on the test of the judiciary until 1966.

II. The Term of Notice

261. The main protection of the worker against dismissal – but also of the employer against resignations – was the right to receive advance notice thereof, or the corresponding indemnity. Another monetary protection was (and still is) the so-called seniority allowance (*see* below paragraph 295).

262. The term of notice, for white-collar workers, takes effect only from the end or middle of each month (Act No. 1825 of 1924). Its length varies according to the qualification and seniority of the employee: e.g., the private metalworkers' agreement of 1987 grants to blue-collar workers a term of notice ranging from six days, forty hours (up to five years of seniority) to twelve days (above ten years of seniority), and to white-collar workers a minimum of one month (for the lowest category of white-collar workers with up to five years of seniority) and a maximum of four months (for the two highest categories of white-collar workers with beyond ten years of seniority).

263. A general regulation of the length of notice for white-collar workers, often improved by collective agreements, is set by the old Act No. 1825 of 1924 (from a minimum of fifteen days to four months). The collective agreements concluded for top and middle managers (*dirigenti*) usually grant them much longer terms of notice (up to six months and more). The term of notice which must be given by the employee who resigns is usually equal to the terms of dismissal (*see* Act No. 1825 of 1924 for white-collar workers).

264. Whereas there is no doubt that the labour contract subsists fully throughout the term of notice with all obligations and duties of the parties, it is controversial whether the same is true when instead of giving the term, the party (in particular the employer) pays the equivalent indemnity. The prevailing opinion has been that the indemnity is not an alternative to the term of notice, and that therefore the labour relationship with all rights of seniority continues in any case until its conclusion, even though the employee does not in fact work during this period. The solution – often confirmed by collective agreements – may be practically very relevant, because the continuation of the labour relationship during the term implies that all changes that have occurred in the meantime, e.g., in the amount of wages (due to a cost of living adjustment or a renewal of a collective agreement) must be taken into account in particular to calculate the seniority allowance, which is proportionate to the last wage.

Recently the courts have adopted the opposite solution, but they tend to reach a similar conclusion, e.g., to take into account changes intervened during the period of notice.

III. Termination by the Employee

265. The provision of Articles 2118 and 2119 are still in force for resignation, i.e., the employee may terminate the contract by giving notice or by paying an indemnity under Article 2118 and is entitled to terminate the contract without notice or before the term if the employer breaks a fundamental term of the contract (just cause). Act 92/2012 in order to prevent abuses has required specific validation of resignations signed by employees (mothers and fathers) during the period of maternity (*see* above).

Decree 151/2015 (Article 26) with the same objective has provided that resignations and the resolution by mutual consent must be rendered under penalty of nullity, using specific forms prepared by the Ministry of labour and transmitted in electronic form to the employer and to the local offices of the Ministry. Moreover the employee may withdraw the resignation and the consensus within seven days from the transmission.

§6. INDIVIDUAL DISMISSALS

I. Limitations by Collective Agreement

266. The principle of dismissals at will in the contract for an indefinite period has been, on the other hand, undergoing progressive limitations, first by collective agreements and then, more radically, by law. Individual dismissals have been regulated in the post-war period by a series of interconfederal agreements, concluded for the industrial sector in 1947, 1950 and, finally, in 1965.

267. The 29 August 1965 agreement provided that in plants employing more than 35 workers, an individual employee dismissed either for ordinary reasons (with notice) or for disciplinary reasons (for just cause without notice) could resort to a conciliation procedure (between the provincial unions and employers' associations), then, with fixed terms, to arbitration (informal).

268. The actual operation of the agreement, and of its predecessors, has been only in part satisfactory; it has been strongly influenced, much more so because of the relative weakness of the provision, by the character of labour-management relations, i.e., it is better in the medium-large firms of northern Italy, where relations are more stable.

II. Legislative Protection: In General

269. The first general legislative protection against unfair dismissals was introduced by Act 604 of 15 July 1966, still partially in force.

III. Dismissal Because of Marriage

270. An especially strong provision was granted in 1963 to women workers by Act No. 7, which declared null and void dismissals for reasons of marriage and all agreements considering marriage a reason for termination of the labour contract (then a rather widespread practice). Any dismissal decided between the publishing of the banns of marriage (if the marriage ensues), and the year after the marriage, is presumed to be in violation of this law; so is the resignation by the woman during the same period, unless personally confirmed before the labour office (*see* above). The nullity of these Acts implies that the woman must be paid the regular wage, by the employer, until reinstatement. The woman can be legitimately discharged in the period mentioned only in three cases established for pregnant women and mothers: just cause, end of the term, and cessation of the firm's activity.

IV. The Form of Dismissals

271. The first limit established by Act No. 604 refers to the form of individual dismissals. The employer is bound to communicate the dismissal, in writing, to the interested employee and to make the grounds explicit at the worker's request. According to Act 92/2012 the worker's request is no longer necessary, i.e., the ground for dismissals must always be made explicitly by the employer.

Act 108/1990 has made compulsory this form for all employers and provided that the request must be made within fifteen days of dismissal and that the employer must respond within seven further days (Article 2). This requirement of form implies that having once adopted certain grounds, the employer cannot rely on different ones to justify the dismissal, e.g., before the courts. The sanction for violation of Article 2 is the inefficacy or, more precisely, the nullity of the dismissal.

V. Justifiable Reason and Just Cause

272. A substantial limit to the employer's power to terminate the labour relationship results from Article 1 of Act No. 604. The norm makes explicit what already resulted from the 1965 agreement, namely that the dismissal in a contract for an indefinite period can be legitimated only if supported by just cause (as defined in Article 2119, Civil Code) or by 'justifiable reasons'. The notion of 'justifiable reasons' is defined by Article 3 of Act No. 604 as being of two types: 'a serious violation of the worker's contractual obligations' (the so-called subjective reason) or 'reasons concerning the productive activity, the organisation of work and its regular functioning' (the so-called objective reason). Dismissals, discriminatory on account of union, religious or political grounds are for the first time explicitly declared null (Article 4, confirmed subsequently by Article 15 of Act No. 300 of 1970).

273. The 'justified reason' of the first type corresponds basically to the general ground for dissolving any bilateral civil law contracts. The seriousness of the violation – which must refer to specific contractual obligations and not to general duties such as 'loyalty' or 'trust' or 'mutual confidence' – is to be appreciated by the judge. He can freely take into account the disposition of collective agreements, which generally establish an indicative list of justifiable reasons and of just cause for discharge. Examples of justifiable reasons are repeated and unjustified absence from work for more than four days, insubordination, serious damage to the employer's property or to his materials due to negligence, working without permission within the plant for third persons or for oneself, without using the employer's materials, repeated violation of minor discipline after two suspensions. In principle, facts of the private life of the employee tend to be considered irrelevant, unless they directly influence his professional capacity or reliability: e.g., stealing by a bank employee. This trend has been indirectly confirmed by Article 8 of Act No. 300 of 1970, which prohibits investigations by the employer into a worker's opinions and into facts irrelevant to his professional capacity.

274. The seriousness of the violation can be established, and often is, by taking into account previous minor violations of the employee (sanctioned by way of disciplinary measures). This is generally the case with, e.g., low productivity, which according to collective agreements must be argued in writing to the employee before the decision to dismiss him.

275. The distinction between 'justifiable reasons' of this type and 'just cause' as defined by Article 2119, Civil Code, which legitimates termination without notice before the full term of the labour relationship, is very subtle. Generally, the latter is held, by judges, and by collective agreements, to be a more serious violation of the worker's contractual obligations, e.g., stealing, rioting in the plant, willingly damaging plant materials and machinery; here again excluding personal factors, unless they influence the employee's professional capacity or reliability. The courts consider just cause also other facts than specific violations of contractual obligations, which compromise the trust relationship among the parties (e.g., use of drugs), with the specification that the decision must take into account all the relevant elements and the context of the employment relationship. Act 183/2010 (Article 30, 3 para) has provided that the decision must take into account in particular the indications of collective agreements on the concepts of just cause and justifiable reason.

Bankruptcy and controlled administration of the firm are not considered just causes (Article 2119, Civil Code). It is a generally accepted principle that the grounds amounting to 'just cause' must be immediately announced by the employer as soon as he knows them, otherwise he cannot rely upon them to justify the dismissal.

276. The objective reasons for dismissal include not only grounds pertaining to the organisation of the enterprise, such as 'job suppression' – the abolition of a job position for economic or organisational reasons (indeed, the same reason as for collective dismissals, although related to a single discharge) but also to the relationship between the organisation and the individual worker, e.g., a recurrent illness making the worker's profitable employment in the work organisation impossible.

277. A major controversy concerns the scope of judicial control when the employer justifies the dismissal – individual, but also, as we will see, collective – on grounds pertaining to the organisation of the enterprise or the functioning thereof. The traditionally prevailing opinion is that the courts can only judge whether the reasons advanced by the employer actually warrant the single (or collective) dismissal, without any control over the merit of the employer's decisions, covered by the constitutional guarantee of free enterprise. This position has been confirmed by the legislator: Act 183/2010 (Article 30, 1 co.) and Act 92/2012. An opinion of growing importance has come to question also the social adequacy of the employer's decision so as to allow the dismissal only as an *extrema ratio*, i.e., when the employer has no possibility of recovering the employee(s) for production purposes, even by resorting to professional retraining, transfers, lay-offs or short-time (*see* below).

VI. Remedies Against Unjustified Dismissal

278. This matter has been very controversial and has been regulated differently in the course of time: Act 604/1966, Act 18/1970, Act 108/1990, 92/2012 Decree 23/2015, implementing Act 183/2014 and lately, Act 96/2018 ('Dignity Decree').

According to Act No. 604, if the dismissal was held to lack just cause or e-established reason, the burden of proof resting on the employer, the latter was bound to reinstate the worker within three days, or, alternatively, to pay a special indemnity assessed on the same basis as the 1965 agreement. This solution, which does not in fact guarantee reinstatement to the discharged employee, was radically changed by Article 18 of Act No. 300 of 1970 and by Act 108/1990. Article 18 empowers the judge (*pretore*) to order reinstatement in any case of unjustified, discriminatory or formally vitiated dismissal. Discriminatory dismissals, because of union activity or affiliation, can also be contested through the special procedure of Article 28 of the same Act No. 300 (*see* below paragraphs 444 ff.).

279. The worker illegally dismissed was entitled to damages measured according to the global wage due from the day of the dismissal to the time of the effective reinstatement and to the payment of social security contributions for the same period (Act 108/1990). This is justified because the labour relationship is legally e-established by the decision invalidating the dismissal. This means, for example, that all seniority rights acquired by the employee before the dismissal are maintained.

280. The innovations introduced by Article 18 as to the remedy against unfair dis-missal have completely replaced the provision of Act N. 604 and of the collective agreement of 1965 on this point. Accordingly, the possibility of the employee resorting to informal arbitration, provided for by the agreement and by Article 7 of Act No. 604, is considered no longer available, and the *pretore* (now Tribunal) has exclusive jurisdiction over dismissals.

VII. The Scope of Act No. 604 and of Article 18

281. The protection granted by Act No. 604 against unfair dismissal had a limited coverage (like the collective agreement of 1965). It did not apply to employers employing up to thirty-five employees (Article 11, 1st paragraph) to collective dismissals (Article 11, 2nd paragraph), to upper and middle management (*dirigenti*), to workers who had reached retirement age and those who were on a probationary period (for a maximum of six months). The limits of coverage related to the dimension of the employer were stated in a different way by Act No. 300. While Article 11, first paragraph, of Act No. 604 declared the provisions available to the employer employing more than thirty-five persons, Article 35 of Act No. 300 made the new provision of Article 18 applicable to all productive units employing more than fifteen employees in industry, five in agriculture (*see* below). Productive units located in the same municipality could be added together for the purposes of Article 35.

282. The different terms of reference used by the two Acts raised a difficult problem of interpretation, e.g., as to the provision applicable in cases of a firm employing more than fifteen or thirty-five employees altogether, but divided into productive units each of fewer than fifteen employees. The Supreme Court held that Article 18 applied, and therefore a worker unjustly discharged could demand reinstatement to any productive unit of commercial firms and industrial firms which employed more than fifteen workers (even though the firm did not reach thirty-five employees). The mere monetary protection of Act No. 604 applied to productive units smaller than that, provided that the firm had more than thirty-five employees in total, and to employers not entrepreneurs, whereas Article 2118 will apply when neither of these two sizes is reached.

283. A popular referendum was organised in 1989 directed to abrogating the limits of coverage stated in Article 35 of Act 300 and consequently extending the full protection (reinstatement) to all employees also of the smallest units. In order to avoid the vote, Act 108/1990 was passed, which reshaped the whole matter from this point of view.

First, Act 108 confirms that the strongest protection toward unfair discharge (reinstatement) applies in all cases of discriminatory discharge whatever the size of the unit, and to employees working in units above fifteen in size; but it adds the employees of firms employing more than sixty – whatever the size of the individual units. Second, Act 108 extends to all employees working in units/firms below the size indicated (and to employees of political, religious, cultural organisations) a monetary protection; an indemnity varying between two and a half-year and six months of full salary (according to criteria such as the size of the unit). The Act provides that to calculate the size of units one must also include employees on work-training contracts and part-timers (in the proportion of their time of work) who so far had been excluded. The Act furthermore gives to employees unjustly discharged the right to ask for a monetary compensation up to fifteen months of salary in lieu of reinstatement. Finally, it provides that employees cannot bring a suit before having pursued the conciliation procedures stated by collective agreements or in front of the tripartite commissions established by Articles 410–411 Cod. Civ. Procedure (*see* below paragraph 280). In the case of failure of the conciliation, each party can ask for arbitration according to the provisions of collective agreements or by an ad hoc tripartite body. The arbitration judgment is effective within thirty days with the same effects as stated in Article 411 Cod. Civ. Procedure.

VIII. Variation of Contract and 'Constructive Dismissal'

284. The identification of dismissal may not always be easy, and may have to be inferred from a series of circumstances, not including an explicit declaration by the employer in this direction. This may be the case when the employer introduces substantial changes in working conditions – mainly in job positions – which affect the employee adversely. According to the traditional opinion, sustained by the superior courts, if the employee consents expressly or implicitly to these changes, i.e., by continuing to work under the new conditions although protesting against them, this leads to a 'consensual variation' of the contract and the employee may not then complain that he has been 'dismissed'. This opinion is being questioned by some commentators and by the decisions of certain courts, which refuse to consider as an acceptance of the proposed variation adverse to his interest the mere fact of the employee working under the new conditions and are willing to give relevance to any sign of protest by the employee to deny acceptance. In this case, the worker can claim back at any time his previous job and the relative wage, while it is up to the employer to make explicit his intention to dismiss him in order to avoid this consequence. If the employee, faced with a substantial variation adverse to his interests, decides on the contrary to resign, this can be regarded in fact as a constructive dismissal (although very few cases have tested it).

IX. Effectiveness of Protection

285. Article 18 has proved to be one of the most commonly used norms of Act No. 300, and much more effective means of protection against dismissals than Act No. 604. However, the limits to coverage are such as to exclude from the protection of Article 18 the majority of Italian workers, given the extensive fragmentation of the economy. To employees of small units a monetary protection is granted by Act 108/1990 (*see* above paragraph 265). Freedom to discharge under Article 2118 of the Civil Code Remains valid for domestic employees, for workers having reached retirement age (now 67). But the protection under Article 18 is extended to seventy years if the employed decides to stay up to seventy.

It is more difficult to evaluate the effectiveness of reinstatement. A survey (1975) based on a sample of cases throughout the country showed that although more than 72% of dismissed employees manage to obtain a favourable decision from the *pretore*, only a small percentage are actually reinstated: in the majority of cases dismissed employees accept a monetary transaction to end the case. Another broader survey (1982) gave partially different results; it indicated that a court order of reinstatement is respected in a higher percentage of cases, particularly in depressed areas of the country where it is difficult to find another job. More recent surveys, however confirm that reinstatement is actually rare. The effectiveness of the reinstatement order is higher for discriminatory dismissals under Article 28 of Act No. 300, where the order of the *judge* is penally sanctioned (*see* below paragraphs 444 ff.).

X. Modification of Article 18

286. The protection of unfair dismissals granted by Article 18 has been extremely controversial; its change has been seen on the one hand by the government as a testing ground to make the labour market more flexible by loosening a protection deemed to be too rigid; on the other, it has been defended by the unions as a fundamental protection, and even symbol, of workers' rights.

In 2002 the centre-right government proposed a modification of Article 18 directed to raise the threshold of its applicability (above the limit of units employing more than fifteen employees). This proposal was refused by all the unions; after long negotiations a more limited modification of Article 18 has been accepted by the unions, with the exception of CGIL, and by employers, and became part of the social pact of July 2002 (*see* below). According to the agreement, Article 18 would not apply for an experimental period of three years, to employees newly hired by firms in addition to the fifteenth employee (i.e., to the sixteenth, seventeenth etc.). But this compromise solution was abandoned by government. The scholarly discussions and political controversies about the law of dismissals have continued in the following years. The pressures to change Article 18 in order to make this law more flexible have gained ground, also following the indications of the European Union authorities. These pressures contributed to the decision of the Monti government to propose a bill reforming the law, which was approved as Act 92/2012.

287. The regulation of Act 92/2012 substituted the previous regime where the only sanction of the unjust dismissal was reinstatement, a diversified system of four types of consequences: two of them include reinstatement and two only monetary sanctions.

The first and most severe sanction, similar to that provided by the former regulation, is maintained when the dismissal is found to be discriminatory, or null because it decided in case of marriage, for an illicit and decisive reason, and when it is ineffective because communicated orally.

This sanction applies to all productive units regardless of the number of employees, and also to managers. In these cases the judge will order reinstatement of the employee in his job plus an indemnity equal to the last global wage due from the day of dismissal to the actual reinstatement (including social security contributions) deducted what the employee has earned in others activities. The indemnity cannot be less than five months of global wage, even if the employee is reinstated in a shorter period.

If the employee does not accept within thirty days the offer of the employer to return to his job, the contract of employment is terminated. But the employee can renounce to the reinstatement and obtain in lieu of it an indemnity of fifteen months of global wage.

A second type of sanction is provided:

(a) When the dismissal for a disciplinary reason is held unjustified by the judge because the fact attributed to the employee does not exist or is considered to be ground only for sanctions less serious dismissals (fine or so) by collective agreements or by applicable disciplinary codes.
(b) When a dismissal for objective reasons is held unjustified because the fact motivating the dismissal is manifestly not existing.
(c) When the dismissal is due to physical or psychical of the employee or is decided during in the protected periods of illness of the employee.

In these cases the judge will order reinstatement plus an indemnity up to a maximum of twelve months of the last global wage, deducted what the employee has earned in other activities and also what he could have earned using the normal diligence.

The meaning of the formula 'fact attributed' has proved very controversial. According to some opinions the law considers the material fact attributed to the employee; but a different position widely followed by the courts, interprets the norm as referring to the fact 'legally significant' i.e., to be evaluated by the judge according to the character of illegality, the seriousness of violation, and also to subjective elements (fault, fraud). The second interpretation has allowed the judge wide discretion in deciding the case and to extend the sanction of reinstatement even beyond the ratio of Act 92 which intended to consider this sanction marginal.

The formula used by the norm concerning economic dismissals for 'fact manifestly non-existing', has been usually interpreted as referring to 'pretextuous dismissals'. Economic and budgetary reasons (if not merely transitory) are considered a sufficient objective reasons for dismissals.

In cases of unjustified dismissals different from two mentioned above the judge will declare the employment contract terminated but will condemn the employer to pay an indemnity of an amount variable between twelve and twenty-four months of the last global wage, taking into account the number of employees of the unit, the employer seniority, the firms economics, the overall conditions and behaviour of the parties.

In case of dismissals lacking adequate motivation or decided in violation of the procedures stated by Article 7 Act 300/700 (guarantees in case of disciplinary sanctions) and by Article 2 Act 604/1966 (previous notice to labour offices of the intention to discharge employees for objective reasons), the law indicates a reduced form of monetary sanction, from six to twelve months of last global wage.

The monetary sanction was intended by the law to be the common remedy for unjustified dismissal. But the results have proved to be more uncertain depending on judicial interpretations.

Finally it worth noticing that Act 92/2012 has introduced a special form of judicial procedure for cases concerning dismissals. The intention of the law was to simplify the procedure and to facilitate faster judicial decisions. But the new procedure has proved rather ineffective and consequently has been abrogated by Decree 81/2015.

288. The controversial application of the norm of Act 92 concerning dismissal, in particularly the diverging interpretation adopted by court's decision has contributed to foster the request, coming mainly from the employers, for a new legislative intervention capable of guaranteeing more flexibility and certainty in the law of dismissals.

This demand received answer by Decree 23/2015, implementing Act 183/2014, which again modified the law of dismissals, both individual and collective.

In order to reduce the oppositions to the bill by the unions and by left-wing parties, the government i.e., to apply the new regulation to the dismissals of the employees hired after the coming into force of the decree (7 March 2015), while maintaining the previous regulation of Act 92/2012 to the employees already is force. The number of employment contracts subject to the new regulation is bound to grow in the future, with the increase of employees newly hired, including employees who change employer. In fact labour mobility from one post to another is considerable even in time of crisis decided to introduce a sort of two-tier solution.

Decree 23/2015, innovates only the type of sanctions for unjust dismissals while the legal concepts of just cause and justified reason remain unchanged. According to the decree, the sanction of reinstatement is limited to dismissals which are found to be discriminatory, null for violation of imperative norms, or communicated orally. In all other cases of unjust dismissal the employer is condemned to pay an indemnity of various amount.

The cases of discrimination and nullity, and hence the area of a possible reinstatement of the employee, are identified according to the traditional criteria.

When the judge finds that the dismissal lacks just cause or justified reason – objective or subjective – he will condemn the employer to pay an indemnity equal to two months of global wage per year of service, ranging from a minimum of four to a maximum of twenty-four months. For firms below fifteen employees the indemnity is reduced to one month of pay per year of service, ranging from a minimum of four and a maximum of twenty-four months, of pay.

The only exception to the sanction of indemnity is provided in case of dismissals for disciplinary reason when the judge finds that the 'material fact'; attributed to the employee does not exist. In this case the judge will order to the employer to reinstate the employee in the job and to pay an indemnity up to a maximum of twelve months of pay plus damages measured according to the global wage due from the day of dismissal to the reinstatement, deducted what the employee has earned in other activities or could have earned using the normal diligence.

The decree specifies that the judge cannot take into account the seriousness of the fact attributed to the employee – i.e., its proportionality to the sanction – but only decide about its existence. The specification reveals the intention of the legislator to limit the discretion of the judge in deciding the sanction of unjust dismissal, a discretion which was based in the past on the test of proportionality.

A further innovation is that the decree has cancelled the distinction, as far as sanctions are concerned between individual and collective dismissals, distinction which had been observed in the past. The only difference concerns the special procedure applicable to collective dismissals (*see* below). Consequently, the same rules will apply for the future to the latter as to the former: i.e., in both cases, the judge will decide reinstatement only in case of discrimination or lack of written form. The employer will have to pay an indemnity of the same amount as in all other cases of unjust collective dismissals, including in case of violation of the procedure or of the criteria for the selection of employees to be discharged (according to the previous legislation, these cases implied reinstatement).

Another important innovation of Decree 23/2015 inspired by practice of other countries (Germany in particular) is directed to prevent judicial litigation by promoting a consensual solution of disputes about dismissals. According to the decree the employer – within sixty days of dismissal, may offer to the employee in the forms indicated by Act 2113 Civil Code (certification Commission, local labour Offices, conciliation assisted by social parties) a sum of one month of global pay per year of service, from minimum of two to a maximum of eighteen months of global wage. The employee who accepts the sum gives up the right to sue the employer in court.

This conciliation mechanism is rather favourable because the sum offered by the employer is slightly lower than the maximum indemnity that the employee can receive from the judge in case of unjust dismissal, but the sum exempted from taxation and social security contributions. Moreover the employee who accepts the conciliation avoids the risk of an unfavourable judge decision.

The constitutional court has been called to decide over various questions of constitutionality concerning provisions of Act 13/2015 on individual dismissals.

The Court has accepted only one of the objections of constitutionality concerning the indemnity to be paid to the employee dismissed without cause. It has declared unconstitutional and consequently annulled the norm of the Act which links the amount of the indemnity only to the years of service of the employee (Decision 194/2018).

To respond to this decision, Act 3 of the 'Dignity Decree' (modifying Decree 23/2015) has increased the amount of the indemnity to a minimum of 6 and a maximum of thirty-four month's salary.

It remains to the courts to decide the criteria according to which fix the actual amount of the indemnity to be paid in individual cases.

Moreover Article 3 of the Decree provides that the employer, in order to avoid a legal disputes must offer to the dismissed employee a sum not less than three and no more than twenty-seven times the monthly salary. Previously the range was between twelve and eighteen month's salary.

Recent court decisions have extended the possible sanction of reinstatement, mainly using a wide interpretation of the concept of 'material fact' mentioned above, whose non-existence justifies the reinstatement. In particular have decided for reinstatement not only in cases of non-existence of the material fact but also when the fact attributed to the worker is held by the judge not to be illegal and also when the fact is considered by collective agreements to be ground not for dismissal but only for minor disciplinary sanctions.

The Constitutional court (decision 155/2022) has declared illegitimate the specific legal requirement of dismissal for objective reasons that the non-existence of the fact be 'manifest'.

Following interpretations of the ordinary courts and of the Constitutional court the sanction of reinstatement has become again central and the sanction of indemnity has been less important.

Finally, it is worth mentioning that during the COVID-19 lockdown the government, in order to prevent possible mass dismissals, has temporarily prohibited dismissals, collective and individual, for economic reasons. This prohibition has been gradually lifted during 2021.

§7. Collective Dismissals

289. The law of collective dismissals has developed separately from that of individual dismissals. The major source of provision for the industrial sector was for a long time – until Act 223/1991 which now regulates the matter – the interconfederal agreement of 5 May 1965, which reproduced with certain improvements the agreement of 20 December 1950.

290. A complete regulation mainly procedural, of the matter was introduced by Act 223/1991 which implements EU Directive 129/75 (modified by Act 236/1993 and by Decree 151/1997). Act 223 applies to entrepreneurs employing more than fifteen employees and defines as collective dismissals those concerning at least five employees, over a period of 120 days, in the same province, as a consequence of reduction or transformation of activity or work. This notion, which has two requisites (common reason for the dismissal and a minimum quantity), is interpreted widely: it includes e.g., technological dismissals and the total closure of the enterprise. Decree 110/2004 has extended this protection to all non-entrepreneur employers (following a decision of the ECJ).

291. The Act provides for procedural guarantees, i.e., prior to the discharge the employer is obliged to inform in writing the plant union representatives and the most representative territorial unions about the reasons for the decision, the number, positions, professional profiles of the redundant employees; the timing of the implementation of the decision; and the measures adopted to remedy its social consequences. The unions may ask within seven days for a concertation procedure, which must be completed within forty-five days. Lacking agreement, a further conciliation procedure is provided before the provincial labour office. The whole procedure must be concluded within seventy-five days. At the end of the procedure the employer remains free in his final decision; but the law encourages a consensual solution by reducing the costs of discharge in case of agreement and by providing alternatives such as solidarity contracts, early retirement plans, etc. (*see* above).

292. In the selection of the individuals to be discharged, the employer must follow objective criteria fixed by collective agreements or, in their absence, stated by the Act: in combination, productive and technical needs, family conditions, seniority. The employer must also communicate in writing the dismissals to the interested parties, and inform the unions and the labour office of the data concerning all the dismissals and of the criteria followed in the procedure.

Finally, Act 223 has strengthened the sanctions for violation of the rules. In fact, all violations empower the judge to order the reinstatement of the employees according to Article 18 of Act 300/1970. The violation of the trade union information procedure also amounts to an unfair labour practice, which can be repressed according to Article 28 of Act 300 (*see* below paragraphs 444 ff.).

But Act 92/2012 has provided that violations of the communication procedure can be corrected by a collective agreement concluded in the course of procedure.

Decree 23/2015 has excluded the sanction of reinstatement if the employer does not respect the priority criteria for selecting the employees to be dismissed, apart from evidence of discrimination. Here too the sanction provided by Decree 21/2015 is an indemnity of variable amount (*see* above).

293. Italian law does not impose in general a social plan on the employer in the case of collective dismissals. However, a specific obligation in this respect is provided by Act 234/2021, with respect to employers employing more than 250 employees. When the employer intends to close the enterprise or an autonomous productive unit, he must notify the reasons, timing and dimension of the closure to the representative Unions and to the Ministries of Labour and Development ninety days in advance, followed by a plan aimed at limiting the consequences of the closure comprising the relevant measures, no longer than twelve months. The dismissals are suspended until the exam with the Unions and the Ministries is concluded. The employees discharged collectively are entitled to the so-called mobility indemnity (*see* above paragraph 197) if they have at least twelve months of enterprise seniority and may benefit from the priority in new hiring, as indicated above (*see* paragraph 230). This indemnity lasted until the end of 2015.

Even more important, the wide use of subsidised lay-off has greatly reduced the resort to collective dismissals: sometimes this has represented a negative element of rigidity in the Italian labour market (*see* above). But this is the case especially for large firms, because small units, which are the most common in Italy, have been recently exempted from lay-off protection. This is another example of the dualism of the Italian labour market, which has been corrected by Decree 148/2015.

294. The unions have also been very active in preventing collective dismissals, but again mainly in medium-large firms. Many collective agreements (plant- and company-wide) deal with measures for avoiding redundancies, such as transfer between jobs, retraining, curtailing of subcontracting, use of short-time work; in a few cases these agreements commit the company to not reducing personnel for a fixed period of time or to making the necessary investments according to restructuring plans verified with the unions.

Early retirement has been widely used and favoured by law; it has been progressively restrained by Act 92/2012 and by Act 214/2011. It remains possible for a limited period, paid by the enterprise or by special fund present in some sectors (Banking, insurance). Partial early retirement has been introduced by the stability Act 2016. A different version can be adopted through the so-called contracts of expansion (Act 58/2019, *see* above).

Some major groups have bargained wide-ranging plans that comprise the whole restructuring process and their consequences on manpower. This has given way to new institutional forms of participation (e.g., joint bilateral committees for monitoring the process in IRI, ENI, Montedison) and intense involvement in the process on the part of trade unions.

§8. Severance Indemnity: Now End of Contract Indemnity

295. At the termination of the employment, whatever the method used to effect it, the worker is entitled to receive from the employer, in addition to any other sum of money (e.g., the indemnity replacing notice of dismissal), a special allowance originally called seniority indemnity (*indennità di anzianità*) now severance indemnity (*trattamento di fine rapporto*). This indemnity, rather peculiar to Italian labour law, has undergone a long evolution. It was established at the beginning of the century, at first for white-collar workers only, then also for blue-collar workers, and was due only to employees discharged not for just cause (Article 2120, Civil Code). It was assessed on the basis of the last total wage and in proportion to the years of service rendered with the same employer. The exclusion of the allowance in cases of dismissal for just cause corresponded to its main function and nature, which was to compensate the employee for his faithful service to the firm and to assist him financially in relation to his loss of employment, in addition to the insufficient social security benefits existing at that time. Act No. 604 of 1966 recognised the right of the employee to the allowance in *any* case of termination of employment. This has been widely interpreted by the Constitutional Court itself as a strong argument indicating that the indemnity has acquired the nature of an indirect element of wage, whose payment, and the determination of whose size, is deferred to the end of the employment.

296. For white-collar workers, the minimum amount of the indemnity was determined by law (Act No. 1561 of 1960) and it amounted to one month of the last salary for each year of service in the firm. This minimum was augmented by collective agreements in some sectors (e.g., in banking from one and a half to two months) especially for employees with longer seniority and for managerial employees.

297. For blue-collar workers, the amount was determined by collective agreement, and it was much lower than for white-collar workers, e.g., in the metalworkers' agreement it ranged from two weeks per year for workers with low seniority – up to ten or eighteen years – to two and a half weeks per year for workers with more than eighteen years of seniority.

298. In the last years the maintaining of the seniority allowance has been criticised for various reasons: because the development of unemployment compensation and of public pensions has deprived it of the original providential function; because its costs have greatly increased due to inflation; because the method whereby it is evaluated hinders labour mobility and favours the irrationality of the wage structure, privileging the automatic value of seniority vis-à-vis the professional standards of employees.

These arguments suggested some changes but not the abolition of the allowance. Act No. 297 of 1982, instead of assessing the allowance on the basis of the last wage multiplied by the years of service, provides that every year a certain amount of wages (roughly one month) is set aside to be paid upon termination of employment. This system of calculation applied only for service after 1982. Since the end of 1989 the amount of the indemnity has been equal for blue-and white-collar workers, and is only partially protected against inflation.

The use of indemnity has been made flexible to some extent. While the previous regulation did not entitle the employee to any part of the sum before termination of the agreement, Act 297 provides that a maximum of 70% of the indemnity acquired can be asked for in advance given certain conditions (minimum eight years of seniority, no precedent request, for sanitary expenditure and purchase of a first house). Act 335/1995 has also provided that a percentage of the severance indemnity may be devoted to contributions to private pension funds; and that for newly hired employees all the indemnity must be dedicated to this end, but only if the employee subscribes to a pension fund. Act 493/2004 and Decree 521/2005 have confirmed this trend.

Act 252/2005 and Article 1, co. 749–766, Act 296/2006 have set a deadline (the first semester of 2006) for employees who adhere to these funds: after this deadline the allowance to which they are entitled for the future, is automatically transferred to the fund, unless they explicitly refuse this.

Newly hired employees have the same options within six months since the beginning of the contract. Such an 'opting out' mechanism has considerably contributed to sustain the financing of the pension funds. However, a large number of employees, in some sectors the majority, have decided to keep the indemnity for personal use and also in favour of their employers (who can use it for self-financing).

Act 190/2014 (Articles 26ff) and Decree 29, 28 February 2015 have provided that employees can ask to transfer the annual instalment of the indemnity directly to the monthly wage. But this opportunity which was intended to support consumptions has been scarcely used by employees, probably due to unfavourable fiscal treatment.

§9. Protection in Case of Insolvency

299. Article 2 of Act No. 297 of 1982 has set up a special guarantee Fund with the aim of replacing the employer, in the case of the latter's insolvency, as specified by Article 2, in the payment of seniority indemnity. The setting up of this fund may be considered only as a partial application of EEC Directive 80/92 and in fact Italy has been condemned twice by the ECJ. Finally, the directive has been implemented by Act 428/1990 which extends the protection of the Fund to all wages due by the insolvent employer for the last three months of duration of the employment relationship. According to Article 1, second paragraph of the EEC Directive on the protection of subordinate workers in the case of insolvency by the employer, Italy has declared that the directive does not apply in the following cases: (a) to the crews on maritime ships, and (b) to those workers who receive benefits through the legislation in force concerning guaranteed incomes in case of a firm's economic crisis (i.e., all those who already receive benefits from the Cassa Integrazione Fund).

Chapter 7. Public Policies to Promote Employment

300. Since the late 1970s a number of government measures in the field of economic policy have been enacted in order to grapple with the problem of unemployment and to protect the job security of workers. These measures are numerous, often overlapping and of uneven effectiveness.

A set of measures is specifically directed to protect job security and therefore to defend existing employment: such protection has been rather effective, according to some even too much so, because it has been to the detriment of new employment (*see* above paragraph 241). The most important protection is granted by the legislation discussed above on the salary integration fund in cases of lay-off and short time (paragraphs 227 ff.). 'Solidarity contracts' are special measures inspired by the idea of work sharing adopted in two versions. The former is linked to lay-off (*see* above paragraph 197). The second had a more proactive attempt: it implies specific incentives for enterprises willing to hire new personnel and at the same time reduce working time and correspondingly wages. This version of the solidarity contract has hardly been used, because the incentives have proved insufficient to compensate the employees for the loss of wages and has been abrogated be Act 34/2019 (*see* above paragraph 237).

A set of measures, introduced originally by Act 223/1991, aims at reinserting redundant employees in work, by means of priority rights (*see* above paragraphs 241 ff.) and provides specific incentives both to the employee and to the employer. The former receives a lump sum equal to the mobility indemnities due to him if he wants to set up a business of his own plus a sum to pay the expenses for change of residence; and he may continue to work part-time and for a definite period without losing priority rights to full employment. The employer receives a reduction in payment of social security benefits if he hires a redundant employee even part-time and for a fixed term (now only in case of a contract for an indefinite duration).

Early retirement has been widely used, particularly in industries undergoing structural crisis such as steel (Act 193/1984), shipbuilding and sea transportation (Act 856/1986). This policy has proved very costly and in some respects counterproductive, also in view of the trend to postpone the retirement age. Now a special type of early retirement has been introduced by Act 34/2019 (*see* paragraph 243).

301. As well as redundant employees, other categories receive preferential treatment in hiring, in particular invalid and handicapped people (for whom a quota of compulsory hiring is reserved by Act 68/1999), and young people. For the latter category incentives are provided in case of hiring through the contract of apprenticeship and through work-training contracts (Act 863/1984 Act 30/2003). These incentives are often increased by regional legislation. Act 416/1995 (Article 8) and Act 196/1997 have firstly promoted the use of the *stage* as a means of favouring the transition of youngsters from school to work; they also aim at favouring *stages* of youngsters from the south in northern enterprises, by providing for the reimbursement of expenses (travel, lodging, etc.).

Special efforts have been recurrently made to give additional support to jobs and enterprise creation in depressed areas of the country, mainly southern regions, where unemployment is now mainly concentrated. A major instrument has been Act No.

64 of 1986, which was concerned in general with the so-called extraordinary interventions in southern Italy provided a wide-ranging series of financial help to firms submitting job and enterprise creation programmes on conditions stated by law and controlled by the administration. The cumbersome procedures of these laws and the lack of public institutions capable of promoting these programmes have greatly reduced the effectiveness of these interventions.

302. A more recent policy has been to promote not so much individual initiatives but local development investments by giving preference and special fiscal advantages to new investments decided within the framework of development plans agreed upon between state and local institutions, preferably with the parties' consent (the so-called territorial pacts and area contracts of development). In these areas unions and employers are called upon to sign flexibility contracts (on flexible wages and worktime in order to contribute to attract investments). These special incentives to enterprises investing and hiring in depressed areas are also intended as a partial compensation for the progressive equalisation of social security benefits between southern and northern Italy which has been required by the European Union. The 'fiscalisation' of social security benefits traditionally provided for southern regions has been held contrary to European rules on competition (Article 92, paragraph 1 of the Treaty) and reduced progressively until total abolition.

Specific incentives have been granted to cooperatives established among young workers in depressed areas and for youngsters willing to set up a business according to plans approved by a special agency (Act 44/1986 and Act 416/1995). A major effort has been made following EEC guidelines and drawing on European structural funds to reorganise public and private investments in basic infrastructure: such infrastructure is particularly scarce in southern Italy and this represents a major obstacle to economic development and to the creation of employment.

303. The long-term unemployed in depressed areas have been employed in so-called socially useful works (which were introduced by Act 451/1994 and subsequently modified several times lately by Act 81/2000). These are works mainly of assistance to persons, care of the environment, urban and cultural goods restoration which were offered originally to employees who benefited from mobility indemnity or salary integration in case of lay-off (*see* above paragraphs 248 ff.). These employees are bound to accept the offer, following the idea of workfare, i.e., that it is their duty to give social services as a compensation for the social welfare they receive. Socially useful works were subsequently extended to long-term unemployed, in which case they receive from the social security institute INPS an indemnity for a maximum of twelve months (for 100 hours of work). Act 81/2000 has provided incentives for hiring of these workers by private enterprises and also by local authorities (municipalities). In spite of this the transformation of these works into ordinary employment has proceeded, although with difficulties and slowly in some regions of the country; in other, particularly southern, regions these works have been repeatedly prolonged as a substitute for public assistance. The competence to regulate and administer them has been mostly transferred to the regions themselves.

304. A specific incentive for the long-term unemployed in southern regions which had a good success for a few years was the so-called loan of honour, i.e., a loan of up to EUR 50 million (about USD 30,000) for starting forms of self-employment. The loan was granted upon selection by a specialised agency and specific training courses aimed at promoting the managerial capacities of the beneficiaries.

Perhaps the most effective measures in fighting unemployment in the depressed areas of southern Italy have been fiscal advantages to enterprises for new investments and specifically for hiring additional employees (for an indefinite period). This measure has been renewed several times: Acts 388/2000, Articles 7 and 8, 289/2002, Article 63, Act 106/2011 (Article 2) which grants a tax credit of 50% of labour costs for twelve months, to employers hiring persons disadvantages in a sense indicated by EU regulation 800/2008. These incentives have contributed to promote employment in those areas; even though unemployment remains higher and the rate of employment is still lower in the south.

Act 191/2009, has extended the benefits granted to employers for hiring long-term unemployed, to the hiring of all unemployed of 50 years of age. Moreover it has recognised to private employment agencies a bonus of EUR 1,200 for each worker unemployed or a laid off which they manage of reemploy for an indefinite period and a bonus of EUR 800 if the employment is for fixed term.

A different kind of incentives is provided by Act 139/2012 for the hiring of highly skilled people. These measures have been reshaped by Act 92/2012 which provides specific incentives (reduction of social contributions) for persons over fifty unemployed for over twelve months; for women of all ages unemployed for six months in depressed areas of the country and unemployed for twenty-four months regardless of residence. Some of these measures can be cumulated with those of Act 106/2011 and possibly with regional incentives, which confirms the scarce consistence and uncertain effectiveness of the system in spite of the considerable amount of resources devoted to it. A special incentive similar to that in favour of youngsters is provided by the Budget Law for 2020 (Act 160/2019) to promote the hiring of people with university degrees.

Lately a major programme has been launched, following European guidelines and supported by European Funds, which is directed to promote the employment of young people (so called *Youth Guarantee*). The programme which actually started in May 2014, commits all the institutions active in the labour market: public services of employment and private agencies, regional and local labour offices, and social parties to implement various measures useful to favour the access of youngsters (between 18 and 29 years, 34 years in southern regions) to regular employment. The measures are: work experiences in schools, counselling about job opportunities, evaluation of personal skill, periods of stage, training courses, support to self-employment. The youngsters who register with the labour offices and the employment agencies throughout the country, will be offered the opportunity to benefit from the various measures according to their needs.

The programme which is administered by the regions, has attracted the interest of many youngsters. According to official data of the Ministry in August 2022, 1.685.243 youngsters, have registered. The public offices have taken charge of

85.2% of them, 65% of whose have been offered specific help and offers: mainly stages, incentives to hiring and education. 531.000 have been employed, mainly with contracts for an indefinite period.

Recent legislation has increased the incentives to promote youth employment, namely a 100% reduction of social security contributions to the employers hiring with a contract for an indefinite period young people below 36 years of age, within a ceiling of 6000 Euro for a maximum period of three years (four in southern regions). Similar incentives are provided for the hiring of workers suspended from work due to economic crisis and for people unemployed (budget law of 2021, confirmed by budget law of 2023).

Attempts at reorganising employment policies and in particular at rationalising the multitude of incentives and other promotional measures have been repeatedly made but so far with little success.

INPS and INAPP (national institute for public policies analysis) keep adjourned a detailed schedule of the main categories of incentives which can be consulted, in Italian, in the INAPP website.

The list adjourned on 23 June 2022 by INPS indicates the following types of incentives, together with legal sources and main contents:

- Apprenticeship: last regulation Act 160(2019.
- Young people: last regulation Act 205/2017 (Article 1, co 100–108, 113–114).
- Act 178/2020 Article 1, co 10–15.
- Women: act 92/2012 Article 4, co 8–11.
- Act 178/2020 Article 1 co 16–19.
- Employers: DD Anpal 52/2020.
- DL 104/2020 Article 6 co 1, Article 7 co 1.
- DL4/2022 Article 4 co 2.
- Southern regions: Act 178/2020 Article 1 co 161–168.

§1. Active Labour Policies and Training

305. In recent years greater attention has been devoted to rationalising labour policies and emphasising their active role in promoting and not only protecting employment. This objective has been pursued in different ways: by finalising the different incentives to job creation (a task which, however, is far from completed; by reorganising the public services at the decentralised level and putting them in competition with private employment agencies (*see* above). Now both private and the public centres have specific obligations to organise positive action in favour of unemployed and disadvantaged persons such as interviews, counselling services, personalised training and job offers, etc.), by giving greater responsibility to local governments (regions, provinces) and also to the social parties in the administration of these policies.

Act 30/2000, confirming and specifying previous trends, has recognised bilateral organisations (funds or organisations of various forms) set up by the social parties important roles in many aspects of labour policies in which they already had some experience (mediation between demand and offer, placement services, certification of labour contracts, vocational training both initial and continuous during the course of employment, salary integration in case of lay-off (integrative or even substitutive of the public system), supplementary pension funds.

Various attempts to reform and strengthen the public placement services have been made in the last years, from 1997 to 2003, to 2012 until the Decree 150/2015 (*see* above paragraph 132).

The Decree has established a National Agency for active labour policies, with major competences in the matter. The Agency coordinates the activities of all the centres and actors authorised to operate in the labour market, which are regulated as a 'network' the agency and incorporates 'Italia Lavoro' which has been so far a special entity dedicated to promote labour policies in various areas of the country.

The functions of the Agency must be exercised within the guidelines set by the Ministry of employment and by regions, which maintain regulatory competence regarding public placement services and active labour policies. The functions of the Agency comprise all the most important activities in the matter, some of which so far had been separate (Article 9): the coordination not only of public placement services but also of activation policies for the unemployed; the definition of the standards of essential services to be provided by local placement offices; the methodology for defining the profile of the unemployed relevant for their reemployment; the operation of the unitary information system of the labour market; the promotion and coordination of programmes financed by the European social funds; the surveillance on the bilateral funds competent for professional training and for labour policies (Acts 388/2000 and Decree 276/2003); the assistance in cases of crisis concerning enterprises located in different areas of the countries, intervention (also direct) in areas where essential employment services are not respected; the definition of the modalities and of the amount of the bonus for the reemployment of displaced workers. Other functions may be attributed to the Agency including the direct handling of employment services, on the basis of specific bilateral agreements with the regions.

Indeed these agreements will be important in determining the actual implementation of the system, because the regions maintain major powers in the field of labour policies and these policies will have to be shaped according to the economic and social conditions of the various areas of Italy, which are quite differentiated.

Decree 150/2015 has also redefined the status of unemployment; the requisites of unemployed workers to be eligible for the relevant benefits, and their duties to maintain them, which are defined in personalised 'pact of service' (Articles 19 ff.).

Moreover, the Decree regulates the conditions and duties necessary to receive the special bonus for reemployment granted to workers who have been unemployed for more than four months.

The design of this reform is ambitions, but its effectiveness has been less than expected due to the serious understaffing of the public placement offices, the weakness of the national Agency and the uneven initiatives and organisations of the regions (*see* below).

§2. VOCATIONAL TRAINING

306. Vocational training has been considered a major prerequisite and instrument useful to promote employment (Act 196/1997). The competence to regulate and organise vocational training rests now mainly with regional governments while the state gives general guidelines and keep relationships with the European Social Fund. Often the regions have proved less effective in using the existing resources, both national and European, precisely in the southern areas where training is most needed.

The major innovation has been to promote vocational training – not only as a complement of basic school education but also as a continuous lifelong activity. The vocational training centres are of uneven quality. Certification and quality control procedures are provided so that the 'credits' acquired in vocational training can be used also in the school system. A contribution of 0.30% of wages paid by the parties into a fund jointly administered has been finalised to support continuous training (Act 388/2000 Article 118, 1° c.). Act 92/2012 has committed all interested institutions, state, regions and local authorities, to set uniform criteria and priorities to promote continuous training – as defined by the Act, and integrate all data concerning this implementation; and has set up a 'national system for the certification of competences' (Act 4, co. 65–68). Apprenticeship, work training contracts and *stages* have been re-regulated with the aim of making them more functional to the transition between school and work, lately by Decree 81/2015 (*see* above paragraph 110–116).

The National Recovery Plan, following the directives of the NGEU, has approved an unprecedented and comprehensive set of investments and reforms finalised to relaunch the growth of the Italian economy which has been stagnating for years and to make it more sustainable both from a social and environmental point of view.

A major objective of the Plan is to promote the quantity and quality of employment. In fact at the end of the Plan period (2006) the average employment rate is supposed to increase by 3.6% with specific concern for the employment of women, of young people and in southern regions.

One mission of the Plan has promoted the employability of workers with a specific programme (2022–2025) of active measures (called GOL) financed with EUR 4.4 Billion, which aims at taking care of 3 million of people within 2025: 800.000 of whose in lifelong learning, particularly in digital skills. The programme is implemented by the regions, under coordination of the National Agency. In November 2022 the programme took charge of 620.000 youngsters.

Women, youngsters and southern regions are considered to be the priorities of the Plan, because most of its measures and programmes must be directed to improve the working and living conditions of these groups of people and territories.

With respect to young people a first set of measures aims at improving their education, from kindergarten to tertiary schools and to fight early school leaving.

With the aim at facilitating their transition from school to work the Plan has strengthened and financed the system of educational guidance, the various forms of stage, the contract of apprenticeship and the programme called Youth guarantee (*see* above).

A special programme has been financed for promoting the so-called civilian service which organises the involvement of young people in social and cultural activities (for eight to twelve months) where they can acquire skills and qualifications useful in the labour market (leg. decree 40/2017 and Min. Decree novembre 4/2019).

Moreover the economic autonomy of youngsters is being promoted by various measures: tax exemptions for school attendance, fellowship and college residencies, in particular for tertiary education, reduction in the rents of housing, preferential loans to buy houses.

In addition to prolonging the incentives to employers for the hiring of youngsters, the Plan has provided (Article 47/Decree 77/2021) that in all public works financed with European funds of the Plan, 30% of the hiring must be reserved to young people under 35 years of age. A similar percentage must be reserved for the hiring of women, with possible motivated derogations of the 30% in sectors (like building trades) where objective impediments exist to the employment of women.

Article 47 is a rather exceptional measure whose implementation will need to be closely monitored

In order to pursue one of its major priorities the Plan has committed all the public institutions, central and local to devote 40% of all investments and resources to the southern regions.

The effectiveness of these policies will depend on the capacity of all actors, public administrations, enterprises and social organisations to implement the multitude of programmes defined by the Plan.

In order to strengthen this capacity, which is traditionally weak particularly in the southern regions, new hirings in the public service have been planned and special programmes are provided to give technical support and assistance to the local administrations.

§3. Irregular Work

307. The Italian labour market is characterised by an abnormal quantity of irregular work: sometime totally irregular, i.e., not complying with all fiscal, social security and labour law regulations, sometime performed with partial evasion of the same regulations. This is the case e.g., of part-timers who are paid reduced wage, but in practice work full-time amount of irregular work ranging between 12% and 15% of the workforce. Irregular work is concentrated mostly in southern Italy, which confirms the dualism of the Italian economy, and reaches its peak in agriculture. Recent estimates indicate a number of irregular workers around 3.2 million, corresponding to 12.4% of GDP.

Attempts to fight this black labour market have intensified in the last years, beginning with Act 196/1997 and continuing with Acts 383/2001, 210/2002, specifically for the construction sector, Act 248/2006 (Article 36 bis).

The Acts have established special procedures, and promoted special agreements (called contracts of 'realignment') for the gradual regularisation of this work: in particular by allowing employers to pay wages, and consequently taxes and social security contributions, lower than regular ones, but increasing them up to the normal in a given period of time (e.g., from 50% of the standard to 100% in three to five years). During this period employers are relieved from the fines due for the evasion of taxes and social security obligations and can settle preceding obligations by paying a given lump sum.

The social parties have been involved in the monitoring of the procedure, as have the local governments, in order to allow a gradual regularisation also of other aspects of enterprise activity, e.g., urban requirements, health and safety regulations, commercial conditions, etc.

Act 210/2002 sets up tripartite local commissions to supervise and control the whole procedure, including providing special forms of inspection.

Act 248/2006 provides that the labour inspectors can order the suspension of construction works if more than 20% of employees are working irregularly or in case of reiterated violation of the norms on working time.

The results of the various norms have been far from satisfactory, even though a certain number of jobs 'created' in the last years seem to come from the regularisation of black labour. Incentives and controls can be useful but are hardly sufficient. They must be backed by general policies promoting a more flexible labour market, reducing the indirect labour costs which affect particularly the weak areas of the country and the weak sectors of the economy (very small marginal firms and low-skilled employees).

Moreover, in southern Italy no labour policy can be effective per se unless supported by economic policies directed to promoting local development.

The National Recovery Plan commits the labour authorities to implement a Plan specifically aimed at fighting irregular work, which has to go hand in hand with the investments and reforms financed by the Plan.

Chapter 8. Covenant of Non-competition; Inventions by Employees; Statute of Limitations

§1. Covenant of Non-competition

308. The general legal duty of non-competition by employees provided for by Article 2105 of the Civil Code ends with the termination of the labour contract, and the workers regain their entire freedom of labour. The employer, however, may be interested in limiting this freedom after the termination of the labour contract, particularly for employees who are highly qualified or specialised. Article 2125 of the Civil Code – still in force, despite various doubts as to its constitutional legitimacy – recognises this interest by admitting the possibility of a specific agreement between the employer and the employee directed to restrain the labour activity of the latter on the following conditions, imposed under penalty of nullity, and aimed at balancing the employer's interests with the employee's freedom of labour: the agreement must be in writing; it must have a maximum duration of five years for leading personnel, and of three years for other workers (a longer duration agreed upon is automatically reduced to the legal maximum); it must be kept within precise limits of space and activity; a specific compensation must be granted to the worker. The amount of compensation is to be determined by the judge according to equitable considerations, taking into account the extensions of the limits imposed on the worker's freedom. The compensation must be specifically determined, and cannot consist of a mere additional quota of the remuneration paid during the labour relationship (because a short duration of the latter could arbitrarily reduce the amount). The limits of space and of activity must be applied together in order to guarantee the worker a reasonable freedom to continue to use his professional knowledge without changing the place of work: e.g., in the case of an enterprise operating over the whole national territory, the employee must still be free to use his capacity with enterprises producing different goods.

§2. Inventions by Employees

309. Article 2590 of the Civil Code stipulates that the worker is entitled to be recognised as author of the inventions formulated during the labour relationship. The basic regulation was set by Act No. 1127 of 29 June 1939 (Articles 23–24). This Act has been substituted by Decree 30/2005 (Article 64) as modified by Act 131/2010 Article 37 which, however, substantially confirms the old rules.

Rights and duties deriving from the invention are regulated on the basis of three types of service invention, i.e., those invented by employees engaged for this very purpose; dependent inventions, those invented by employees in the course of the labour relationship, and relating to the activity of the enterprise or done during working hours, exploiting the time and facilities of the work position in the enterprise; inventions made by the employee in his own time, with his own materials, but using the professional knowledge acquired in his job. The ownership of the first type of invention belongs to the employer (Decree 30/2005, Article 64 co. 1). The ownership of the second type of invention is also due to the employer; the employee is entitled to an equitable compensation relating to the importance of the invention, if a patent is recognised (Decree 30, Article 04, co. 2). In the third case, the ownership of the invention belongs to the employee, but if the invention relates to the same field of activity as the enterprise, the employer has a right of pre-emption – to be exercised within three months – to use the invention, and to buy it at a price fixed to take into account all the aids possibly received by the employee from the firm in making the invention (Decree 30, Article 64, co. 3). Act No. 190 of 1985 (Article 5) has provided that the compensation due for the inventions (apart from service inventions) can be determined by collective agreements.

Act 81/2017 has extended to autonomous workers the rights resulting from their inventions, a part from the case when the activity leading to the inventions is part of the contract.

§3. Statute of Limitations

310. The general rules are stated by the Civil Code Articles 2946 and 2948 Nos. 4 and 5. According to these rules, claims arising out of the individual labour contract (including those arising from its termination) become superannuated generally five years after the facts (the ordinary term of ten years is generally inapplicable). So-called presumptive superannuation, i.e., which can be overcome through decisive oath or judicial confession by the debtor about the payment of the sums, is of one year in the case of payments due at periods no longer apart than one month (Article 2955, No. 2, Civil Code) and of three years in the case of payment due at periods longer than one month (Article 2956, No. 1, Civil Code). These rules on superannuation are of a public order and cannot be modified or waived (Articles 2936, 2937, Civil Code).

311. These regulations have been declared partially unconstitutional by the Constitutional Court in a series of decisions. Decision No. 66 of 1966 declared that the terms of superannuation could run not from the fact, as provided for by the Civil Code, but only from the termination of the labour relationship. The argument of the Court was that failure to exercise his right (mainly the right to be paid for the work done) by the worker himself during the life of the contract could be considered as amounting to a waiver. It was therefore subject to the limits of Article 2113, which declares invalid the employee's waiver of rights deriving from imperative norms of law (most labour law provisions) and empowers the employee to ask for an annulment until three months after the waiver or after the end of the labour relationship, whichever comes later.

312. The Court's decision was based on the fact that the provision of superannuation was contrary to Article 36 of the Constitution, which guarantees the inalienable right to a just and equitable wage, to annual vacations and weekly rest. Consequently, the new term of beginning the superannuation should refer only to the three basic rights of the workers sanctioned by this article. This issue is controversial, but in practice these rights cover most kinds of labour grievance.

313. The scope of the court's decision No. 66 has been restricted by subsequent decisions of the same court, and of the Supreme Court. On the assumption that the non-exercise of the worker's rights during the labour relationship is justified only because of the worker's lack of protection against dismissals, the courts excluded the applicability of the 1966 decision, therefore admitting the validity of the civil law rules on superannuation if job security is guaranteed to the employee: first of all in public employment, in labour relations with public economic institutions and, after the approval of the Workers' Statute, protection against unfair dismissals to all labour relations with private enterprises to which Act No. 300 is applicable (*see* above paragraphs 233 ff.).

314. In 1979 the Constitutional Court once more intervened in this troublesome matter. On the one hand, it reaffirmed the basic principle of its previous decision that the validity of the civil law rules on superannuation depends on the legal protection afforded to employees against unfair dismissal. On the other hand, this validity is not to be automatically admitted whenever Act No. 300 is applicable (as it was according to the previous decision); it is up to the judge to decide whether the protection against unfair dismissal is adequate enough to justify this conclusion if Article 18 of Act 300 is applicable.

The different levels of protection against unfair dismissals introduced by Act 92/2012, by Decree 23/2015 which modify Article 18 of Act 300, and lately by the Court interpretation of these rules which have given again greater importance to the possibility of reinstatement of the worker unjustly discharged, have changed and made uncertain the rule on superannuation.

A recent decision of the Court of Cassation (n. 26246/2022) has decided that, in spite of the increased legal protections afforted to employees in the last years, this protection does not guarantee full stability to them. Consequently, contrary to the civil law rules on superannuation, the term of this will run only from the termination of the employment contract.

315. Collective agreements often provide the so-called terms of decadence, i.e., limits of time beyond which certain claims and grievances pertaining to the labour contract cannot be raised by the employee. These collective clauses are held valid by courts provided they do not make the exercise of the workers' rights too difficult (Article 2965, Civil Code). This usually means that the time limit must not be shorter than six months after the termination of the agreement (the term provided for by Article 2113 of the Civil Code for workers' waivers and transactions).

§4. Waivers

316. Article 2113 of the Civil Code whose original disposal has already been mentioned was changed by Act No. 533 of 11 August 1973. The invalidity is extended to waivers and transactions concerning all rights of the worker deriving not only from imperative norms of the law but also from collective agreements; the waivers can be contested by the interested workers within six months from their date or from the end of the labour contract, whichever comes later, by any written document – even extra-judicial – expressing this intention. This invalidity limits the individual worker's capacity to dispose of certain basic right to protect the minimum standard and conditions of work, on the assumption that the individual position of weakness during the labour relationship prevents him from handling and settling properly the controversies arising out of this relationship. This *ratio* is not present – and the sanction of invalidity does not apply – when the settlement of disputes occurs through public conciliation or through the intervention of the unions (*see* below).

317. The receipts often given by the worker at the end of the labour contract stating that he has received all that was due to him, and that he has nothing more to claim, are not considered by the courts as waivers, and do not prevent in principle any claim from being raised by the worker, unless the receipt contains an explicit waiver.

Act 206/2021 implemented by decree of 28 July 2022 has extended to labour disputed the institute of the so-called assisted negotiation, regulated by Act 409 Code of Civil procedure. The accord reached by this negotiation is protected like the waivers and transactions under Article 2113 Civil Code,

Chapter 9. The Settlement of Labour Disputes

§1. Judicial Settlement

318. In Italy, labour disputes fall under the jurisdiction of civil courts and, until 1973, followed in principle the rules of procedure established for civil matters by the Code of Civil Procedure of 1942 (with certain adaptations provided for in Articles 429–457 of the same Code). Special courts, and implicitly labour courts, are prohibited by Article 102 of the Constitution. This provision, enacted in response to the fascist regime, which had abused special courts, can scarcely be said to meet the needs of modern society, but no one has to date thought an amendment to the Constitution possible. Article 102 does not ban specialisation completely, since it authorises 'specialised sections of the ordinary courts for specific subjects' in which 'qualified citizens not drawn from the judiciary may participate'. Proposals to establish such specialised sections for labour disputes (with participation by laymen) have not met with much support, and have been strongly opposed by some unions (CISL). Since 1970, and even more so since the procedural reform of 1973, the interest in such a solution has almost completely vanished, because the ordinary civil courts, and in particular the *pretori* (usually young and more open-minded judges) have been seen to handle efficiently and competently the growing number of often very delicate labour disputes which have been brought before the judiciary under the new regulation enacted during this period.

319. The provisions of the code relating to collective labour disputes lost their validity with the suppression of the corporative order in 1943, with which they were closely connected. As a consequence, collective disputes concerning rights, whether to do with the interpretation of a collective agreement or to do with a statute, are unknown as such to civil procedure: i.e., although a dispute may in fact involve a collectivity of employees or employers, it can be brought to court only when divided up into many individual claims (sometimes preceded or substituted by a 'pilot action'), and each court decision is binding only for the individual case. Act No. 533 of 11 August 1973, has entirely substituted Articles 429–457, introducing important innovations as regards both the proceedings of individual labour disputes and the distribution of jurisdiction among the various branches of the judiciary.

320. The *pretore*, comprising a single professional judge, has general first instance jurisdiction in all labour disputes in the private sector and among other instances, in matters of social security. Article 29/1993 and lately 165/2001 have extended this jurisdiction to the labour disputes in the public sectors, which have been 'privatised' by the same Acts. The *pretore* is not a specialised court in the sense of Article 102, but where the local office of *pretore* is made up of several divisions, labour disputes only are customarily assigned to one or more *pretore* (e.g., in Milan about 80 *pretori*, out of about 20, hear labour disputes only). Act 51/1998 has transferred the competence of the *pretore* to the Tribunal, but still acting with a single professional judge.

321. The proceedings before the judge have significant differences from ordinary civil practice, conducted mainly in order to increase the speed, informality and accessibility of the procedure. Act No. 533 provides, first of all, for the concentration of hearings and the drastic shortening of the time limits for the completion of the various stages of the procedure. The case should be concluded within sixty to seventy days of the submission of the claim (before 1973 the average length of a case in the first instance was over three years); in practice, these terms are met only in some offices, mainly in northern Italy, provided with enough judges and technical staff to implement the law.

322. The judge has been given significant powers of initiative (investigative) to acquire evidence independently of the parties concerned (calling new witnesses, ordering the so-called free interrogation of the parties, ordering direct inspection of the workplace, asking for written or oral opinion of union representatives, etc.). Oral evidence is allowed to prevail over written evidence, as in criminal trials, and at the conclusion of the final hearing the judge's decision must be pronounced immediately. Judgments ordering the reinstatement of an employee unjustly dismissed or condemning the payment of credits deriving from individual labour relations in favour of the workers are *ope legis* (automatically) temporarily enforceable. Act 353/1990 has extended the provisional enforceability also to the decisions in favour of the employer.

The special procedure regulated by Article 28 of the Statute of Workers' Rights will be considered below.

323. The decisions of the *tribunale* can be appealed before the Court of Appeal, whose decisions can in turn be appealed before the *Corte di Cassazione* (Supreme Court).

324. The Supreme Court, according to the general principles, is not a third source of judgments, since it reviews only questions of law. The most important ground for attack is the 'violation or falsification of a legal norm'. At present, the provisions of collective agreements, consistently with their private character, are not considered 'legal norms' unless they have been incorporated into statutes according to Act No. 741 (*see* below). The obstacle is often overcome, however, by appealing against a *tribunale* or Court of Appeal decision on the ground that a norm concerning the interpretation of a contract was erroneously applied (Articles 1362ff. of the Civil Code).

325. Act No. 533 has created a special section of the Supreme Court exclusively for the handling of labour disputes, which makes judgments with a constant number of five voters (instead of the usual seven). Although in Italy, as in civil law of all other countries, precedent is not binding, a decision of the *Corte di Cassazione* is likely to be followed by the labour courts, at least in order to avoid a possible subsequent overruling by the Supreme Court itself. In recent years, this has not prevented the appearance of bitter, and not merely temporary, differences of opinion between the lower courts and the *Corte di Cassazione*.

326. Differences of opinion exist within the lower courts themselves and often concern crucial aspects of labour relations, both collective and individual, which have been made subject to judicial decision, by the labour legislation beginning in the 1970s, above all by the Workers' Statute. This legislation, and the increased speed of the labour procedure made possible by the Act of 1973 have, on the whole, raised the importance of the judiciary in determining the shape of labour relations law and the nature of political mediation, rather than strictly legal adjudication, in their decisions. It is also noteworthy that attempts at conciliation by judges, made compulsory by law, are more and more successful (probably in the majority of cases, although precise data are not available).

327. Labour disputes were exempted by Act No. 533 from all the usual taxes imposed on civil cases, so that the parties have to bear only the attorneys' fees, generally awarded by the court against the losing party. But the exemption has been abolished. Now all cases pay a contribution in proportion to the value of the dispute (*see* recent Act 183, 2010), but the amount is half of that fixed for civil cases: the exemption is maintained for those having the right to legal aid.

The worker is most often assisted by the legal office of a union and by attorneys connected with it, in which case he may have to pay a very low fee or no fee at all, even when he loses the suit. The possibility of resorting to legal aid is also granted by law, but on very strict conditions, so that it is in fact very little used.

§2. Extra-Judicial Settlements

328. Act No. 533 of 1973 has set new rules in order to discipline and to encourage the settlement of labour disputes by state agencies, and contractual settlement under collective agreements. Conciliation before the labour office, very frequent until 1973, but handled informally by labour officers, has been institutionalised by creating stable commissions of conciliation in each province throughout the country (Article 410 Italian Civil Procedure Code as amended by Article 533). The commissions are tripartite, i.e., composed of the director of the provincial office (a public officer), or his delegate, who presides over it, eight full and eight supplementary members, representing in equal number (four and four) the workers and the employers, designated by the most representative unions at the national level. The commission can be divided into subcommissions where there is a considerable number of disputes to be handled (in practice, they operate with one representative of the office, one of the unions and one of the employers) and local commissions can be set up in the local branches of the labour office. These commissions may be called upon for conciliation of disputes by any individual employee, or employer, also through a labour organisation of his own choosing. The commissions are competent with reference to individual disputes of right. Disputes arising out of new bargaining requests are dealt with informally by the labour officers themselves. The distinction here, however, is more formal than ever, since, before the commission disputes are settled by negotiation rather than by adjudication, and the single conciliation may de facto influence all individual cases concerning the same matter.

If the conciliation is successful, the record, authenticated by the president of the commission, can be granted executive effects by a 'decree' of the first instance judge, i.e., it can be immediately enforced. The same executive effects may be attributed to the record of a conciliation agreement reached directly between the social parties (unions and employers), without the intervention of the Commission, after it has been filed at the labour office in order to be authenticated and ratified by a decree of the judge (Article 411, Cod. Civ. Proc.). Decree 124/2004 (Article 11) has provided for a new form of conciliation, promoted by a single member of the labour offices, in the course of inspection procedures.

329. A major innovation of Act No. 533 has been to provide explicitly that conciliation (waiver or compromise) reached before the labour office (as well as those reached in court) cannot be attacked under the general principle providing that the worker may not waive his own right (Article 2113, Civil Code). The assumption underlying Article 2113, that a compromise was most often brought about by the waiving of rights by the worker due to his state of inferiority, has been held not to be justified in cases of conciliation guaranteed by public office. This conclusion should be adopted, according to the majority opinion, similarly for conciliations reached directly between the social parties (after its authenticity has been ascertained by the director of the labour office and its formal regularity by the *pretore*). The innovations effected by Act No. 533, including the immunity of conciliation from subsequent attacks by individual workers who have repented of the settlement, have given great force to both conciliation before the labour office and inter-union conciliation, which are by far the most frequent means of settling labour disputes (*see* paragraphs 328 ff., 614 ff.). The previous attempt at conciliation both in private and public labour disputes is made compulsory by Decree 80/1998, implementing Act 59/1997 concerning organisation and labour relationship in the public administration, which also regulates informal arbitration.

But Act 183/2010 (Article 31) has changed the rule and rendered the attempt of conciliation again optional – a part from cases when the validity of a certification procedure is contested (*see* below paragraph 337) and in cases if economic dismissals (Act 92/2012).

330. Act No. 533 has introduced major modifications also into the discipline of the arbitration of labour disputes (of rights). Articles 806 and 808 of the Code of Civil Procedure prohibited the individual parties from resorting to 'formal' arbitration in labour disputes and, similarly, the parties in a collective agreement from including a clause obliging individuals to resort to arbitration rather than the courts. This prohibition was justified under the fascist ideology of avoiding all evasions of state jurisdiction in labour disputes, but also by the more general notion that arbitration, like a compromise, leads to a disposition of the unwaiverable rights of workers (Article 2113 Civil Code).

331. Act No. 533 and Act 25/1994 took a (slightly) more favourable view of arbitration, by allowing individual labour disputes to be decided through arbitration only if provided for by collective agreements. The law, however, maintains rather strict limits to arbitration. The arbitrators cannot be authorised to decide according to equity, or exclude the right of individuals to attack their decisions, on penalty of annulment. This discipline concerns the so-called ritual or formal arbitration, i.e., enforceable as a court's judgment after the award has been filed with a first instance judge (now *tribunale*), who examines its compliance with formal regulations. The award may be attacked for the reasons indicated by the Code of Civil Procedure (Article 829) due to nullity of the decision (irregularity in the nomination of the arbitrator, violation of rules of law, etc.) and to a violation or false application of rules of law and of collective agreements.

332. There is, however, another type of arbitration, the so-called informal arbitration, not regulated by the provisions of the code, which originates in a blank agreement between the parties to compromise. The award, in these cases, has, consequently, the same force not as a judgment, but as an agreement (i.e., in case of non-compliance the aggrieved party has to bring a suit to court in order to obtain enforcement).

333. Act No. 533/1973 explicitly allows this type of arbitration only provided for by the law or by collective agreements, on the condition that the right of the parties to resort to the judiciary is preserved. The award may be attacked by the individual employer or employee for the reasons which vitiate any contract (error, violence, fraud, incapacity of the parties and of the arbitration, etc.) and for violation of imperative provisions of law and of collective agreements. This latter expression is so wide that the award stability is very weak: binding provisions of law and collective agreements are counted by the thousands.

334. This regulation has been changed by Act 80/1998 which specifies the modalities in which collective agreements can set up arbitration procedures and also modifies the conditions of validity of the arbitrator award. According to these provisions when the award has contested the tribunal, as labour judge, is called to 'decide about its validity'. The expression 'validity' is ambiguous. It might allow a stability of the award greater than in the past; but this interpretation is challenged by other opinions and in fact the weakness of arbitration remains.

335. Act 183/2010 (Article 31) has innovated this regulation with the aim of favouring this alternative forms of dispute resolution (AdR). It provides three types of informal arbitration: one regulated by collective agreements; one established during the conciliation procedure in front of the tripartite provincial commissions; a third in front of an arbitration board set up by the individual parties – but following strict procedural rules. In the second and third types the Act allows the arbitrators to decide on equity, respecting only the general principle of the law and the limits deriving from European law. The arbitrator's decision is reinforced particularly in the case of a decision on equity where it can be attacked only for violation of procedural rules. In other cases it should be possible to attack the decision also for violation of all legal and contractual norms (as it was traditionally). The innovations of Act 183 concerning the arbitration on equity and the possibility to agree on arbitration by clauses inserted in the individual contract of employment even though only if provided by collective agreements have raised strong objections by the unions and by some political parties: which have caused strong resistance to the application of these norms. This confirms a traditional attitude of the Italian system about the use of arbitration.

The fear that arbitration might lead to uncontrolled waivers of workers' rights has been the traditional reason for opposing it among the unions (with the exception of CISL, consistently with its belief in industrial autonomy), and among judges and members of the Bar (who probably resist it also through a sort of institutional self-defence). The sole case of (informal) arbitration in frequent use is provided for by Article 7 of Act No. 300 of 1970 concerning disciplinary sanctions (paragraphs 155 ff.).

336. This mistrust of arbitration, and its limitations reflect a general philosophy concerning grievance procedures as such. It is recognised that the unions' support is essential to the individual employee in facing the employer even in the procedural phase of labour relations: that the unions strongly influence the individual worker as to whether to file or not to file certain claims, and can legitimately use apparently individual grievances and their settlements in order to obtain collective objectives. But the basic principle, common to all voluntary systems for the settlement of labour disputes, is that the individual worker's grievance remains his own, and that certain basic interests and rights of the individual should not be subject to the absolute discretion of the collectivity. This fundamental tenet derives not only from an individual approach prevailing in the law but also, at least in part, from the assumption that an absolute ownership of labour grievances by the unions, although more efficient in controlling them, would prejudice essential goods, including the capacity of collective bargaining administration to be as fair and responsive as possible to the rank and file. Once it is allowed that certain rights, including those recognised by collective agreements, are to be granted anyway to the individual, it follows that arbitration must be bound to respect them, the ultimate guarantee thereof being the judiciary.

§3. Certification of Labour Contracts

337. Act 30 of 2003 and Decree 276/2003 have introduced a procedure for the certification of the new atypical labour contracts provided by the same Act: work on projects, intermittent work, job sharing, part-time, work in cooperatives (and in association, regulated by Articles 2549–2554 Civil Code). The aim is to prevent and reduce disputes over the legal nature of the various forms of work, which is indeed a good purpose because the proliferation of atypical work has increased the risk, already high, of judicial litigation. Decree 257/2004 and Act 1838/2010 (Article 30) have extended the procedure to all labour contracts.

The procedure is activated voluntarily, at the joint request of the parties to the contract, before specialised commissions of certification which can be set up with the following entities: provincial labour offices, bilateral bodies set up jointly by the social parties, public and private universities (Article 76): Act 266/2005 has added two more entities the directorate of the Ministry of employment, and the councils of employment counsellors (Act 12/1979).

In order to facilitate the certification procedure, the Ministry of Labour will issue codes of practice and standard schemes, taking into account court decisions concerning the various elements relevant to the legal qualification of the contract (Article 78).

The parties to the contract can challenge in court the certification issued by the competent bodies adducing consent defaults (error, violence, deceit) or arguing that the certification is legally improper or that the actual implementation of the contract differs from the conditions which have been ascertained in the procedure and certified. The judge's decision on the invalidity of the certification is effective from the beginning of the contract (*ex tunc*), the decision on the deformity of interpretation is effective from the time when the deformity began. In deciding, the judge must take into account the parties' behaviour during the procedure of certification. This procedure is not a substitute for the judge's decision (which would be impossible in the Italian system). Its effectiveness will depend on the capacity of the certification commissions to convince the parties of the correctness and consistency of their decisions.

But an important consequence is to prevent any investigation by the labour inspectors and of the social security offices on the nature of the certified contract.

Decree 81/2015 (Article 2, co. 3) has provided that the parties can ask to ascertain by certification the presence or absence of the requisites which determine the legal nature of the collaboration contract and consequently the application of the norms concerning either subordinate or autonomous employment.

Part II. Collective Labour Relations

Chapter 1. Trade Union Freedom

§1. Historical Background

338. In Italy, as in most European countries, the first attitude of the law was to deny the workers (and the employers) the freedom to organise. The Penal Code of Sardinia (1859), extended to the rest of the country, with the exception of Tuscany, after unification (1861), punished as a crime any form of a coalition of employers intended to 'induce abusively and unjustly the workers to a diminution of salary' (Article 385) and of workers intended to 'suspend, hinder or make more costly the work without reasonable cause' (Article 386). The criminal repression of labour coalitions, following the pattern of the famous Act Le Chapelier of 1871, reflected the principle of free competition and the direct relationship between individuals and the state.

339. This lasted in Italy until 1889, when the Act was repealed by the new Penal Code Zanardelli, which opened a period of relative tolerance towards organised labour. Under this code strikes and lock-outs in the private sector of the economy were no longer punishable as such, unless put into effect with 'violence or threat' (in public service they still remained criminal offences). The fall of criminal sanctions did not exclude a strike and lock-out being unlawful in civil law, as a violation of the obligations deriving from the individual labour relationship. Moreover, the notions of 'violence and threat' were often broadly interpreted by Italian courts, which have always played an important role in shaping the law of industrial conflict, so as to make many strikes unlawful, particularly those considered most dangerous for social peace because of their aims, form or their participants (e.g., in the agricultural sector).

340. The coming of the fascist regime brought back full repression of the labour movement. In 1925, with the agreement of Palazzo Vidoni, the confederation of industrial employers (Confindustria) recognised for the fascist labour unions the monopoly of workers' representation, sanctioning de facto the end of free trade unionism; as a counterpart it obtained the dissolution of 'works committees' (*commissioni interne*), bodies elected at the plant level by all employees, which had been very active and highly conflict orientated, particularly in the immediate post World War I period, during the 'occupation' of the main industrial plant (summer 1920).

This de facto situation was sanctioned legally by the Act of 3 April 1926, the fundamental fascist law regulating collective labour relations. This Act formally accepted trade union freedom and consequently the possibility of more unions (this being done mainly to prevent objections and refusal of admittance of fascist unions by the ILO). Nonetheless, only one union for each category of employers and employees could be legally recognised by the government (Article 6, paragraph 3), provided that it organised a minimum of 10% of the category (as defined by the same government). Through recognition, the union acquired legal personality, at public law, and was therefore subject to tight control by the state. Among other requisites it had to be guided by men 'of safe national faith', lacking which its governing bodies could be dissolved and the union put under public forced administration. All these provisions were clearly predetermined to make legal only the fascist unions; the very freedom not to join these unions was sharply limited because the members of fascist unions and the fascist party had, by law, priority in hiring. The recognised unions represented by law all employers and employees of the category, whether members or not (Article 5, paragraph 1); consequently collective agreements concluded by them had effects similar to the law, i.e., they were binding on all members of the category.

341. Consistently with the authoritarian ideology and practice of the fascist regime, employers and employees were forbidden to resort to industrial conflict, all strikes and lock-outs being considered crimes against the national economy.

342. All labour disputes, whether relating to the application of an existing collective agreement or arising out of the request for new conditions of work (Article 13), if not settled peacefully by the parties, had to be submitted to a special section of the Courts of Appeal (composed of professional judges and of 'experts') functioning as a labour court. The decisions of the court – in fact very limited in number had the same binding effects as collective agreements and had to be taken, in case of disputes over rights, according to the general civil law rules governing the interpretation of contracts, when related to new conditions of work, on equity, balancing the interests of the employees with those of the employers and safeguarding, in any case, the superior interests of national production (Article 16, paragraph 1).

343. The system inaugurated by the Act of 1926 was completed by an Act of 1934, which created the 'corporations', public institutions which were part of the central administration of the state (one for each large sector of the economy). They were composed of representatives of employers and employees, empowered to regulate through authoritative orders not only collective labour relations but all economic activities, to foster in a harmonious way the superior interest of national production. The corporations were intended to mark the evolution of the regime from the original 'liberalistic' attitude towards a tighter management of the economy; but in fact they had little opportunity to operate. The rigid machinery of authorisation, set up by law, prevented completely the theoretically proclaimed possibility of self-determination by the producer, and caused a growing paralysis of a system dominated by the intermingled apparatus of the fascist party and of the fascist unions.

344. After the fall of fascism (25 July 1943) a decree of the Badoglio government (9 August 1943) abolished the corporations and all other institutions of the 'corporative' phase of the regime, but maintained as such, the structure and legal status of fascist labour unions, putting them under forced administration and coopting as leaders men of the anti-fascist resistance. This ambiguous situation, corresponded to the attitude, relatively widespread and present also in the constituency of 1947, that some basic feature of the fascist regime (the legal recognition of trade unions, their unity, the extension of collective bargaining) should be maintained, only making unions democratic. The ambiguity ended only when an order of the allied military government (No. 28 of 1944) and then Act 23 No. 369, November 1944, dissolved fascist unions, liquidated their patrimony and proclaimed full trade union freedom. Article 23 of Act No. 369, in order to guarantee a minimum of protection to the workers (particularly to the non-organised) kept in force all collective agreements concluded under the fascist regime 'apart from subsequent modifications'.

§2. The Protection of Trade Union Freedom

I. Article 39 of the Italian Constitution

345. Trade union freedom has been solemnly proclaimed as a fundamental principle of Italian industrial relations by Article 39 of the Constitution (1948), declaring that 'labour union organisation is free'. This norm is, first of all, a confirmation of the more general principle of freedom of association sanctioned by Article 18 of the same Constitution, the confirmation being necessary to mark beyond any doubt the distinction between present practice and that of the fascist regime. In this respect, trade union freedom has traditionally been held to imply the right of individuals to organise, to join a union without any condition required by law, to resign from it, to choose among different unions and to refuse to belong to any union (negative freedom). But it implies, moreover, a constitutional prohibition on the state from interfering in internal union affairs, e.g., predetermining by law their aims and models of organisation, defining areas of union jurisdiction (which, on the other hand, can be and is done by the legislator for other associations). The only condition explicitly required by Article 39 of unions asking for recognition – but considered applicable to all unions, even the non-recognised – is that union constitution and bylaws be inspired by the principle of internal democracy. Nonetheless other conditions, such as a minimum number or percentage of members, have been, more or less legitimately, derived from the second part of Article 39 as conditions of recognition and unions are required to acquire the status of 'most representative union'.

346. The constitutional guarantee applies to the workers, who are the direct beneficiaries of trade union freedom: it refers to all types of workers, including public employees, atypical workers and also independent and associate workers (Const. Court n. 171/1996). But it also applies to labour organisations themselves, meaning any association, coalition or organisation (also different from associations) of employees, whether temporary or permanent, connected or not with the established trade unions, for the purpose of promoting the collective interests of the members pertaining to their working and, more broadly, social conditions. The guarantee applies as well, although indirectly, to employers (who – differently from workers, can be, as individuals, parties to collective agreements and industrial conflict) and to their organisations operating for the purpose of promoting common interests related to industrial relations. The recognition of this employers' freedom does not imply that their activity – collective bargaining and lock-out – is protected and qualified by law in the same way as similar labour union activity.

347. Legitimate aims of labour organisations, and of strikes, can be not only of an 'economic' but also of social and, broadly speaking, political character. To identify the workers organisations' beneficiaries of the constitutional guarantee and of the connected freedoms sanctioned by ordinary legislation, it is decisive to look not only at their goals, but at the type of action used to promote them, particularly collective bargaining and strike action, which are the qualifying signs of labour unions. In this respect a major problem has been posed by some categories of public employees for which strike action is considered illegal or excluded by the interested parties, because of the particular nature of their functions, especially magistrates and police employees.

348. For the latter, freedom to organise for collective purposes was explicitly denied by Decree 205, 24 April 1945. But Article 9 of ILO Convention No. 87, ratified by Italy (Act No. 367, 23 March 1958), combined with the general principle of Article 2 of the same convention, and with Article 39 of the Italian Constitution, implies that armed forces and police are guaranteed this freedom unless the legislator specifically limits it. The limits have been set only for armed forces (Act 66/2010). After much discussion, a reform of the entire police system was approved by Act No. 121 of 1981. The Act explicitly recognised to all police guards the right to organise for collective purposes. It also profoundly changed the traditional military organisation, hierarchy and status of the corps, closely aligning the basic regulations of police employees – working conditions, recruitment, promotion – with those of most civil servants. A system of collective bargaining has also been recognised that is partly similar to those of other public employees although with some restrictions, in particular short of the right to strike (*see* below).

Act 46/2022 recognises the right to associate and to bargain also to armed forces, following the decision of the Constitutional Court 120/2018 which declared unconstitutional the prohibition to form unions provided by the previous legislation.

349. Wide consensus exists on the fact that police employees and armed forces should not have the right to strike: implicitly so, Decision No. 31 of 1969 of the Italian Constitutional Court and now explicity for armed forces Act 46/2021. The lack of, and/or the renunciation to exercise the right to strike does not exclude the character of trade unions – although somehow atypical – to the organisations of these workers, and the rights and freedom connected with this character. These organisations, like those of magistrates, exist and strive to improve working conditions of their members, through bargaining, although often informal, which in fact influences public power in enacting the rules governing their employment relations.

Moreover, they can exert pressure different from that of the strike to attain their goals due to their peculiar position, e.g., by influencing public opinion and using the solidarity of the rest of the labour movement.

350. The title of trade union should not be granted to organisations instituted by law for some professional workers (lawyers, physicians, etc.), not only because these are not subordinate workers but because the law entrusts these organisations with the (only) power to control admission to the profession and its code of ethics, giving such workers a monopoly in this respect. Such a monopoly position would be unconstitutional and against Article 39, if it referred to a trade union. In practice, these organisations often operate as unions, organising their members particularly to put pressure on public authorities to receive higher tariffs for services rendered (e.g., for medical services rendered under the social and public health system).

351. Trade union freedom, being a constitutional principle, operates basically as a guarantee of the individual's and of the organisation's rights vis-à-vis the state. But again, like many constitutional principles, it also applies to the relationship between individuals and between private organisations. This aspect is particularly important for trade union freedom, because its major limitations can now occur not by the initiative of the state, at least of a democratic state, but only in the course of the employer-employee relations. In spite of that, the private and personal effects of the rights defined in Article 39 were not in fact recognised by the courts or by many legal authors until the principle of trade union freedom was confirmed and specified by the so-called Statute of Workers' Rights (Act No. 300 of 30 May 1970).

II. International Legislation

352. The Italian legislator had ratified long before 1970 the basic international legislation concerning trade union freedom. Act No. 367, 23 March 1958 ratified Convention No. 87 (1948) of the ILO, concerning the application of the principles of the right to organise and to bargain collectively with respect to the individual employment relation. Italy has also ratified (Act No. 848, 4 August 1955) the European Convention on Human Rights (1950), whose Article 11 directs states to guarantee the individual's right to organise collectively, and the European Social Charter of 1961 (Act No. 929, 3 July 1965), which not only confirms the principle of trade union freedom (Article 5) but also recognises the right to bargain collectively and, although with limits, the right to strike (Article 6), which is not considered in the above-mentioned international legislation.

A few European documents have recognised these basic rights: the Social Charter (1989), which, however, has no legal value, then the Charter of Fundamental Rights approved in Nice (December 2000: Articles 12 and 28), the Lisbon Treaty (2009), which recognises to the preamble on basic rights the same legal value as the provisions of the Treaty and lately the Pillar of social rights (approved on 17 November 2017) which reaffirms the most important social principles and the basic rights of employees.

Following the guidelines of the Pillar of Social Rights the European Commission has approved quite a few directives on social and labour issues (*see* above, paragraph 58).

These international and European sources of law provide for some sort of institutionalised control on the implementation of their principles by the ratifying states. Within the ILO this control is entrusted to the investigation and control commission and to the committee on trade union freedom; by the European Convention to a Commission on Human Rights and, in the ultimate instance, to the European Court of Human Rights.

353. Two further sources must be mentioned: the International Agreement on Economic, Social and Cultural Rights prepared within the United Nations in 1966, which directs states, among other things, to guarantee both trade union freedom and the right to strike (Article 8); the EEC Regulation of 15 October 1968, enacted in accordance with Articles 48 and 49 of the Treaty of Rome, deals with the equality of rights with regards to trade union membership and activities:

A worker who is a national of a Member State shall enjoy equality of treatment as regards membership of trade unions and the exercise of rights attaching thereto, including the right to vote; but he may be excluded from taking part in the management of bodies governed by public law and from holding an office governed by public law (e.g., having a seat in the labour court). Furthermore, he shall be eligible for workers' representative bodies in the undertaking (Article 8, Title 2).

This international legislation – on which further details can be found in other monographs – has traditionally not been very effective in Italy because of the limited attention paid to it by the interested parties (public authorities, lawyers and the social partners themselves) and, most important, because it lacks sanctions and control apparatus sufficiently adequate to force its application.

354. The limited or non-effectiveness on employers-employee relations of both Article 39, paragraph 1, of the Italian Constitution and of its international specifications and integrations contributes to explaining why the Italian legislator felt the need to intervene explicitly in 1970 in this matter and to devote to trade union freedom Title 2 of the Statute of Workers' Right.

§3. Trade Union Freedom Protection by the Statute of Workers' Rights

355. Title 2 of Act No. 300 of 1970 is the basic source of protection of trade union freedom in Italy. The same principles apply also to public employees, as explicitly stated by Act 29/1993 and Act 59/1997. Article 14 reaffirms for 'all workers, the right to form trade unions, to join them and to take part in union activity', underlining – in polemic against the so far prevailing interpretation of Article 39 of the Constitution – that this right can be exercised 'within working places'. Article 15 declared null so-called discriminatory acts, i.e., any act or agreement intended:

(a) to subordinate the employment of a worker to the condition that he belongs or does not belong to a trade union or that he ceases to belong to it;
(b) to dismiss a worker, discriminate against him in the assignment of jobs or in job classifications, in transfers, in disciplinary sanctions, or to otherwise prejudice him because of his union affiliation or activity or his participation in a strike.

The explicit protection from anti-strike discrimination is the most important innovation introduced by Act No. 300 to Article 1 of ILO Convention No. 98, by which Article 15 is inspired. The same dispositions are extended by Article 15 (last paragraph) to acts or agreements discriminatory because of political and religious motives; subsequently the same rule has been applied to all discrimination for sex, race, ethnic reasons (Act 903/1977). The principle of non-discrimination has been further extended and generalised by Decree 216/2003 implementing EU Directive 78/2000. The formula used by letter (b) of Article 15 of Act 300 ('otherwise prejudice') is appropriately very broad so as to cover a variety of acts (different from those expressly mentioned), not identifiable a priori in their content, but in fact capable of limiting trade union freedom.

356. The discriminatory acts indicated under point (a) – due to the difficulty of application and the minimal effect of the sanction of nullity – are also punished, according to Article 38 of the law, with a fine from EUR 154 to EUR 1,549 or with imprisonment from fifteen days to one year (for the most serious offences, the fine and imprisonment are amalgamated). In fact, no case has been reported of penal sanctions issued for violation of this provision. The ordinary action of nullity provided for by Article 15 has been rarely used. Most frequently, the discriminatory acts have been sanctioned and removed using the special emergency procedure of Article 28 of Act No. 300, which gives the judge (now the *tribunale*) the power to issue cease and desist orders in any case of anti-union activity on the part of the employer; this procedure is faster than ordinary action and more effective because any violation of the judge's order is itself penally sanctioned (*see* below paragraphs 444 ff.).

357. Anti-union discrimination can be engineered by the employer not only through acts detrimental to some of his employees, but also by distributing benefits to them in such a way as to influence the exercise of their union freedom. This last case is countered by Article 16, which prohibits the employer from granting any collective economic benefit which is discriminatory on account of the motives indicated in Article 15; the judge is empowered to order the employer to pay into a public pension fund a sum equal to the amount of benefits paid for a maximum period of one year, on the demand of the workers discriminated against or by the unions indicated by them (a type of sanction quite new in Italian law).

358. The discriminatory practice of this kind most often used in the past has been that of the so-called anti-strike bonuses, i.e., sums paid by the employer in addition to regular wages to workers who abstained from striking. The scope of Article 16 embraces all economically valuable benefits, even those not directly monetary (e.g., extra vacations, promotions, more compatible working positions).

Such benefits are prohibited not only if designed to discourage but also to encourage union affiliation or activity, because Article 16 refers generally to the motives of Article 15, whose point (a) explicitly mentions the protection of negative trade union freedom.

359. Article 17, again reproducing a principle asserted in ILO Convention No. 98, prohibits 'employers and their associations from organising or supporting by any means, financial or other, trade unions'. Employers and their associations violating this norm can be ordered by the judge at first instance to cease and desist from any illegal interference with union freedom, according to the procedure provided for in Article 28 of the Act; in the most serious cases the judge can order the dissolution (disestablishment) of the dominated (the so-called yellow) union. The limits to the applicability of these provisions may not be easy to set: in principle, only those employers' attitudes or initiatives which, taking into account all circumstances of the case, tend to and are likely to influence union behaviour and to impair the genuineness of union representativeness should be held illegal, not those forms of union-management cooperation arrived at through genuine collective bargaining. Employers' financial contributions to funds for social, educational purposes and the like, set up by agreement, must, for example, be considered legal, even if administered by a majority of union or workers' representatives. These funds are included in the provision of Article 10 of the Act, according to which 'cultural, recreational and assistant activities promoted within the enterprise are run by bodies composed of a majority or workers' representatives'. Also legal are the payment of wages for union officers or delegates carrying out union activity during working time (a minimum time off from work paid by the employer is provided for by Article 23 of the Act); check-off clauses and practices (provided for by Article 26, 2nd paragraph of the Act, and now agreed upon in most sectors of the economy).

360. Similarly, the mere fact that management shows itself willing to consider the bargaining proposals of one union more favourably than another, without granting the former any specific privilege, cannot be held illegal. In practice, very few cases have been brought to court under Article 17; the evidence for illegal interference has proved difficult to find and has succeeded only in respect of the most blatant circumstances: the direct participation of foreman or supervisor in organising workers' delegates or representatives outside and against unions affiliated to the major confederations, or tampering with union delegate elections.

§4. Negative Trade Union Freedom

361. As it has already been suggested, trade union freedom includes the right of individuals not to join any union; and this right is 'absolute', i.e., protected against interference by any subject not only the employers and employers' associations but also union members and unions themselves. This conclusion can be clearly drawn from Article 15 of Act No. 300, but has always been taken for granted in Italy, as deriving from Article 39, 1st paragraph of the Constitution. In fact, these aspects of trade union freedom have never posed serious problems in Italy, due mainly to the historical features of Italian industrial relations. The weakness of Italian unions has given, until recent times, absolute priority to the defence of positive trade union freedom of all workers vis-à-vis the employers, making less relevant – or even non-feasible – the problem of discrimination by the unions themselves.

362. At plant level, moreover, unions have been, until the late 1960s, absent as such and the works committees, as now in the case of the shop delegates, have been elected by all workers, whether union members or not. This corresponds to the basic attitude and philosophy of the Italian trade union movement, i.e., that it should represent the interest of the working class (Marxist) or of the 'category' (Catholics) and not merely of the affiliated workers. Such an attitude, combined with the competition existing among the three major confederations, which basically could not afford to refuse new members, has guaranteed workers a substantial freedom of choice. This is true de facto because at law, a worker refused membership by a union has, strictly speaking, no redress. Such a situation explains also why the whole issue of internal union justice and of individual guarantees within the unions has never been practically relevant in Italy.

363. For similar reasons, both historic and ideal, the various forms of union security clauses and restrictive practices of negative union freedom, which have given rise to troublesome debates in other countries, have always been virtually unknown in Italian labour relations. In any case, it is unanimously held that Article 15 of Act No. 300 has confirmed the illegality of union security clauses (such as closed shop, union shop, maintenance of membership and the like), and of restrictive practices not formalised by agreement, such as blacklisting and boycotting of non-union members. The same conclusion is true, although doubts have been expressed by certain authors, of more indirect practices intended to induce workers to join a union, such as benefits reserved for trade union members, which were agreed upon in a very few cases in the late 1960s. No distinction between direct and indirect pressure to join a union, or distinction based on the intensity of pressure (i.e., the amount of benefits) is authorised by the combined provisions of Articles 15 and 16 of Act No. 300. The nullity of such clauses implies that the benefits paid by employers to union members can be claimed back as being without consideration.

364. More subtle is the case in which these collective benefits are subordinate to the condition that workers pay at least some contributions to the bargaining union for the advantages rendered through bargaining. The answer is controversial and not tested in practice. This condition might be illegal as being against Articles 15 and 16, but it is difficult in practice – as the experience of other countries proves – to distinguish between sheer financial contributions to union bargaining services and a more general support for all union goals and policies, which the non-members may not (want to) share. The result of admitting 'free riders' is counterbalanced by the need to guarantee a maximum of pluralism and spontaneity within the labour movement, and to avoid union bureaucratisation. Experience seems to prove that all these restrictive practices increase union responsibility vis-à-vis the employer and their feeling of security to the detriment of their responsiveness towards the workers.

This is the basic argument for protecting negative trade union freedom even in the framework or the law, such as Act No. 300, which is entirely designed to promote union growth and collective bargaining.

A somewhat different but related issue concerns the implementation of collective agreements signed by some unions and refused by others (*see* below).

365. Negative freedom is recognised, fundamentally not only in favour of non-union members but also members of a union, protecting them from pressures to abandon it in order eventually to join or form another union, and to guarantee the same members the right of dissent to the point of leaving the union and organising in a different way. The promotion of union organisation and collective bargaining cannot be made so absolute as to annul the basic right to self-determination of the workers, who are, after all, the chief beneficiaries of and participants in union freedom. On the other hand, the protection of negative freedom is not directed only towards the unions, because always exerted with the interested help of the employer, who becomes the main 'ally' in infra-union or inter-union conflict.

366. Negative freedom is not recognised and protected on the same level as positive freedom, because the latter is fostered by Act No. 300 through a series of privileges and limits on employers' powers in favour of union activities within the enterprise. Negative freedom is not regarded as being violated by those clauses, not infrequent in our collective agreements, which fix for non-union members a price higher than that for members for services which are not directly related to their position in the individual employment relation: in particular a special price, for receiving a copy of a collective agreement which is paid through a system similar to check-off. These services can be refused by non-members without any prejudice to their working position.

367. The principle of trade union freedom does not imply in fact complete equality between the various unions, although it might be in theory. Special status and powers are recognised by Article 39, Constitution, second paragraph, to registered unions: in the absence of implementation of this provision, a privileged status is now recognised on the part of the most representative unions (*see* below paragraphs 412 ff.).

368. A controversial issue connected with the equality of treatment and trade union freedom has been posed in Italy by cases in which the employer discriminated between unions in collective bargaining, bargaining separately with some unions or granting to one certain contractual benefits (paid time off work for union delegates, etc.). As has already been indicated, this practice is not per se in violation of Article 17 of Act No. 300. In fact, the guarantees of Article 39 of the Constitution and of Act No. 300 of 1970 do not imply in general (for the private sector) a duty on the employer to bargain with any union (*see* paragraphs 425 ff.). The employer can, therefore, legitimately bargain separately or agree with some unions only on certain points (with a single limit of Article 17 of Act No. 300).

This conclusion is, however, contradicted by some court decisions, including some of the Supreme Court (not fully consistent). While confirming that the employer is not obliged to bargain, he must do so with all unions on equal grounds, provided they are representative unions (*see* paragraphs 350 ff.). An important consequence drawn is that bilateral joint committees which have been set up through collective bargaining in some (particularly public) sectors – and having major functions (such as hiring systems, monitoring promotions, discipline, labour market administration) – must include representatives of all representative unions and cannot discriminate against some. The question has arisen most frequently in cases where the employer bargains with the three major confederations (CGIL, CISL, UIL) and with Confederazione Italiana Sindacati Nazionali Lavoratori (CISNAL; the neofascist confederation: *see* paragraph 322) or CISAL, given the fact that the former three traditionally refuse to sit at the same bargaining table with the latter. The court's decisions mentioned above may force the employers into an almost impossible impasse situation. In fact, inviting CISNAL or CISAL to join the same bargaining table may cause the three major confederations to quit. It must be underlined that in 1996 CISNAL changed its name to UGL claiming to be an organisation no longer linked with the fascist doctrine which inspired CISNAL activity over many decades in the post-war period. The Supreme Court has also held that the employer, while being allowed to simply refuse to bargain with the unions, cannot legitimately bypass them and deal directly with employees. Such behaviour would contradict the basic purpose of Act No. 300, and Article 19 in particular, which is to promote unions as the natural counterpart of the employer within the enterprise.

369. A decision of the Const. Court (231/2013) which declared unconstitutional Article 19, co. 1, lett. *b* of Act 300/1970 (*see* below) stated that the employer cannot refuse admission to the bargaining table a union which is actually representative of the enterprise. The decision seems to imply in this case a duty to bargain (*see* below paragraph 420). But the Court does not specify how to identify the Unions with which the employer has to bargain, because, as the court admits, the criteria of representativeness must be determined by the legislator. These criteria have been fixed for the public service (Decree 396/1997, now Decree 165/2001, Article 43 1°co.). For the private sector the legislator so far has abstained from any intervention, leaving the ground to the self-regulation from social parties (*see* below).

Chapter 2. The Trade Unions and the Employers' Associations

§1. Organisation and Structure of Trade Unions

I. The Trade Unions

370. As can be seen in Table 2, the degree of unionisation in Italy during the post-war period has fluctuated, being unequally distributed in different sectors of the economy and on the whole relatively low. The fairly high number of members acquired by the united CGIL immediately after the war (often linked to the union by a general political tie rather than by a clear organisational relationship) sharply decreased after the split of 1948 and throughout the 1950s. While a slight increase at the beginning of the 1960s proved temporary, more stable growth began in 1968–1969 on the wave of the struggle of that period, with the significant help of the legislature (Act No. 300 of 1970) and of the introduction in most collective agreements of check-offs, which have also strengthened union organisation and finances. Unionisation reached its peak (in relative terms) in 1977–1978, with over 50% for the three major confederations and probably over 55% including independent unions, an unprecedented figure in Italian history.

The degree of unionisation in agriculture hit a maximum of 99.8% during the 1970s, due to a quasi-monopolistic power acquired by trade unions – and recognised by legislation – in the control of the local labour market (public employment and unemployment lists). Unionisation in the public services has also been traditionally higher than in manufacturing and it has continued to grow in the last years, due, among other things, to the wider recognition of collective bargaining (Act No. 93 of 1983, Act 297/1993 and then Act 59/1997), totalling 53% in 1982.

Unionisation in both manufacturing and the private services began to decline percentage-wise after 1978. Now the trend seems to have stabilised. Total union membership in absolute terms has not decreased also because of the vast recruitment of retired employees, a traditional practice of Italian Unions. The federation of retired employees increased rapidly its membership. In 2018 CGIL declared 2,995,354 members (around half of the total members), CISL 2,201,864 (almost half), UIL 574,865. In 2018 CGIL declared 2,651,890 members, CISL 1,711,576 and UIL 571,066 members (Table 4).

Table 4 The Degree of Unionisation CGIL-CISL-UIL (Number of Members '000)

Year	*CGIL*	*CISL*	*UIL*	*TOTAL*
2005	5,617.8	4,287.5	1,784.1	11,689.5
2010	5,634,229	4,542,354	2,184,911	12,361,494
2011	5,684,964	4,485,383	2,196,442	12,366,789
2012	5,712,642	4,442,750	2,206,181	12,361,573
2013	5,639,097	4,378,629	2,216,443	12,234,160

Year	*CGIL*	*CISL*	*UIL*	*TOTAL*
2014	5,616,340	4,302,352	2,222,665	12,141,367
2017	5,199,730	4,040,873	2,256,074	11,496,677
2018	5,438,700	4,050,680	2,273,321	11,762,701
2021	5,000,000	4,076,033	2,309,970	11,386,003

Upper managerial employees (*dirigenti*) have traditionally organised separately from other employees (*see* above paragraph 76), which they are entitled to do according to the general principles of Article 39, 1st paragraph of the Italian Constitution and Articles 14 and 19 of Act No. 300 of 1970. Middle and low management (first and second-line supervisors) have also begun to create various associations of their own; although these associations claim officially not to be trade unions, they are meant to promote common interests which are not felt to be adequately represented by the major confederations (CGIL-CISL-UIL) (*see* above paragraph 74).

371. In 1943 Italian workers rebuilt democratic unionism, organising in a single unitary confederation: the Italian General Confederation of Labour (CGIL), which grouped together all the major components (political and cultural) of the Italian labour movement. The end of post-war cooperation among the various political parties of the coalition, the ousting by Christian Democrats of the communists and socialists from the government (1947), and the international tension of the cold war, caused growing difficulties within the CGIL, which brought about its split in 1948. Since then, Italian organised labour has been divided into three major confederations, namely, in order of magnitude, the CGIL, grouping communist and socialist workers, mostly the former; the Italian Confederation of Workers' Union, CISL, grouping traditionally Catholic workers and linked to the Christian Democratic party; it has included a considerable number of workers politically not committed, and groups connected with parties both of the centre-right and centre-left coalition; and the Italian Workers' Union, UIL (grouping socialists, in a clear majority until the collapse of the Socialist party in 1992, Social Democrats and Republicans).

372. In 2021 CGIL declared 5,000.000 members, CISL 4,076,033, UIL 2,309,970. Of less but growing importance is CISNAL (originally a Neofascist confederation, which has acquired greater autonomy and changed its name to UGL). A few strong independent unions exist mainly in public service, particularly in schools, railways, etc.; quite a few independent unions are grouped in a confederation. CISAL claims 1 million members (350,000 in industry and over 350,000 in public service). CONFSAL is another confederation of some autonomous unions, strong particularly in the schools. Forms of independent 'radical' union (COBAS, CUB, COMU), have been active particularly in some sectors of the public service (post, schools, railways) using extreme protest and bargaining action, often in opposition to the major confederations. Indeed, many factors and difficulties seem to be contributing to the decline and then stagnation in union initiatives and power. Unrest is growing not only among the white-collar workers and a lower management who feel punished by the egalitarian policy of the three major confederations, but also among large sectors of the traditional rank and file.

Particularly difficult is the organisation of the different kinds of atypical workers which have grown in number (*see* above). The major confederations are trying to organise these workers through specialised sectorial associations: NIDIL for CGIL, ALAI for CISL, CpO for UIL. It must be noticed that all the data on unions' affiliation are based on unilateral declarations of the same unions. Consequently they are far from certain, particularly those submitted by some small or independent organisations.

373. During the 1950s, the relations between CGIL, CISL and UIL, particularly the former and the second, consisted of bitter polemic and competition, reflecting the political division of the country and an ideological struggle within the labour movement, with CISL and UIL claiming to be the only representatives of free and democratic unionism and CGIL the only true defendant of the working class. Since the beginning of the 1960s, the tensions have begun to ease, and political and ideological controversies to be pushed into the background, if not abandoned. The three confederations began to practise a close 'unity of action' bargaining and conflict. This practice was consolidated after 1968–1969, under the impulse of an unprecedented rank and file militancy and union activity which led to new unitary union representative bodies at the plant level.

374. The three confederations seemed on the verge of a merger in 1971, when their general governing bodies, fixed a definite time for it (the end of 1972, beginning of 1973). The decision proved to be pre-mature. Resistance to its pursuit in fact redeveloped within CISL and UIL, due to complex factors. The traditional fear of dominance of organised labour by the communists, and the diffidence towards the capacity of CGIL to act independently of the Communist party, regained ground within these two unions.

375. In fact, the long-standing drive towards greater autonomy from the political parties has been for a long time scarcely successful in the three confederations. Moreover, the various components of the labour movements have traditionally different views, not on ultimate goals, which are stated similarly in a rather general way in union charters, but on the concrete role of organised labour in society, on its relations to the parties and the state, on how to obtain and shape social democracy, etc.

376. In the face of the postponement of organic unity, the three major confederations signed in 1972 an agreement creating the so-called Federation CGIL-CISL-UIL. The metalworkers even went beyond the equal representation formula, operating under a single denomination (FLM: Federation of Metal Mechanic Workers) and deciding in a more unitary way on all major union policies. The slowing down of the process towards unity during the 1980s caused growing difficulties within the Federation. These difficulties reached their height during the controversy over the slowing down of the escalator clause (1983–1984). A government decree on this issue was bitterly opposed through political strikes organised by CGIL and in Parliament by the Communist party. After these events, the Federation was officially declared 'dead'.

After this acute crisis, 'unity of action' among the three confederations has regained ground both in bargaining with employers and in concertation with government. But the relations among these confederations in collective bargaining and even more in social concertation, remain influenced by the political scenario, in particular by the coalition in power. The social pacts of 1993, 1996, and again of 2007 were signed jointly by the major confederations. The pact of July 2002 on labour policies has been signed with the centre-right government by CISL, UIL and UGL, but opposed by CGIL (*see* below). The same division among the confederations again under a centre-right government has been reproduced in the conclusion of the agreement of January 2009 concerning the reorganisation of the collective bargaining structure (*see* below), and recently in the positions on government policies: CGIl and UIL proclaimed strike action against the governments led by Draghi and by Meloni, which was not joined by CISL.

377. At the international level, CGIL, CISL and UIL are affiliated with the International Confederation of Free Trade Unions (ICFTU). At the end of the 1970s, CGIL joined the European Confederation of Free Trade Unions (ETUC), to which CISL and UIL belonged from the beginning. Major industrial unions are members of the international industrial organisations.

378. Italian trade unions are complex organisations, structured on a double line of organisation: so-called vertical and horizontal lines, converging at the top in the confederation. Vertical structures (the national unions, called federations, and their provincial, regional, and local sections), organise all workers of the same branch of the economy. This is of variable latitude, usually including different sectors, e.g., the metal mechanic unions organise six major sectors (steel, auto-aeronautic, shipbuilding, general mechanics, foundries, electro-mechanics and electronics), the chemical unions also organise the rubber and pharmaceutical sections, the textile unions, the garment industry.

The trend is towards simplifying union structure, through amalgamations, in the public sector where it has traditionally been most fragmented but recently also in the private economy. The number of 'vertical' unions affiliated with the major confederations has been reduced from 36–37 to 12–16. This reduction, for example, has created one single union for school employees, one for transport workers, and one for the public service.

379. Italian unions have never been organised on a craft or occupational basis, apart from a few limited cases: some independent unions within the public service (school, railway, postal service unions) and the confederation of managerial employees. Jurisdictional disputes have also been very rare in Italian history, for the same reason and, if arising, are handled by the executive and jurisdictional bodies of the national union interested and /or by the Confederation. In the last year, however, the representativeness of the major confederation has been threatened by the diffusion of autonomous unions and associations characterised by often opposite ideological orientation, but linked to specific trades and occupations: not only in the public sector but also in quite a few areas of services. They are strongly linked to sectoral interests and effectively criticise the confederation for being too concerned with general problems.

380. The national unions, although affiliated to the Confederation and bound to follow its basic principles and directives, are independent organisms, with their own structure, and powers to discharge all essential union functions. The provincial trade unions, affiliated to the nationals, have also a fairly large amount of autonomy and in fact have been since the sixties, the basic structure of vertical unions; provided with financial autonomy, they are in charge of all union activities of the category in the province, under national supervision (recruiting new members, collecting dues, coordinating company-wide and plant-wide bargaining, or even handling it directly). In 1979–1980 a major organisational reform was decided by the three major confederations aimed at strengthening and reassessing their structures (in addition to regrouping vertical unions, *see* paragraph 326). The regional union structures have been strengthened, both politically and financially, so as to parallel the growing impact of the regional governments on many social and economic matters. The role of these structures remains in these areas and not directly in bargaining, because there is no regional bargaining level. Union and workers' representative structures at the plant level will be discussed below.

381. Horizontal structures aggregate all workers and/or vertical structures in each geographic areas: national (named confederations) regional, provincial and sometimes local (at decentralised levels they are called chambers of labour by CGIL and UIL, *unioni*, i.e., unions of unions, by CISL). Horizontal structures have been traditionally very important in Italy (probably more than in any other European country), due to many factors: the late development of Italian industry and the fragmented character of the labour market, the traditionally high level of unemployment, the political orientation of the Italian labour movement, particularly of CGIL, giving great importance to the unity of the working class, of which the chambers of labour have traditionally been a symbol, and to the pursuit of general goals by the unions.

This importance decreased in the sixties, with the development of national unions, particularly in the industrial sector, but it is still considerable, especially within CGIL.

382. Horizontal structures are in charge of the representation of the general 'political' and social interests of the labour movement in their area of competence, taking all necessary action vis-à-vis the public authorities and institutions, in the field of social reforms and the like, coordinating bargaining policies and actions of the different affiliated unions, particularly on points of common interest.

Table 5 Trade Unions Structures

Confederations			*Sectoral Federations – National*			
	Metal Mechanics	*Chemical*	*Commerce*	*Others*		
National	Fiom	Filcea	Filcams			
	>>>	CGIL	Fim	Flerica	Fisascat	
		CISL UIL	Uillm	Uilcid	Uiltucs	
			Regional Organisations			
			Metalmechanics	Chemical	Commerce	Others
		Regional	Fiom	Filcea	Filcams	
Horizontal organisations	>>>	Chambers of labour	Fim Uillm	Flerica Uilcid	Fisascat Uiltucs	
			Territorial Organisations			
			Metalmechanics	Chemical	Commerce	Others
	>>>	Provinces	Fiom	Filcea	Filcams	
			Fim	Flerica	Fisascat	
			Uillm	Uilcid	Uiltucs	
			Plant Representations			
			RSA, RSU,			

This scheme is basically similar for CGIL, CISL and UIL: the main difference is that CISL and UIL are confederations of unions and, particularly the former, leave more autonomy to their affiliated unions than CGIL, whereas CGIL is a confederation of workers, traditionally more centralised.

383. In Italy there is no legislation regulating the administration and functioning of the trade unions. Their internal structure, determined by their own constitutions and bylaws, follows patterns common to most associations; given the complexity and dimensions of the unions, their assemblies are composed of delegates of the members, elected in varying proportions, step by step from the local structures to the national unions and to the confederations. Conventions are called (involving all the structures), as a rule every four years, to decide (or ratify) the general lines of union policies. Each convention elects the governing body of the union, variously named (general council or directive committee), which in turn elects a more restricted executive board and a variable number of secretaries. The latter have the responsibility to take day-to-day decisions and run union activity, with the help of full-time officers, hired and paid by the union although a growing number of union delegates is now paid by employers.

384. Most secretaries – apart from small unions or sections – are also full-timers relieved of all other professional activities and paid by the union. The position of union officers – being hired – is different from that of union secretaries and delegates elected in the various governing bodies which are the only politically responsible organs with respect to the rank and file. The apparatus of union officers, however, plays an important role in running union affairs and also in shaping its policies.

385. In Italy union dues have been traditionally low, and not even regularly paid, this being not a minor sign of the loose character of the workers' affiliation and cause of the unions' organisational instability. The diffusion of check-off since the end of the 1960s has contributed significantly to an increase in dues and to making their payment more regular. Most national unions have obtained, through collective agreement, annual dues fixed in percentage to wages. For the industrial sectors the percentage tends to be 1% of the monthly wage, including basic wage rate and cost of living allowance. For the agricultural sector the percentage varies in different provinces and is lower. In the public service annual dues are on average 0.80% of the monthly wage for most categories. But these percentages are only approximate and adapted by the same organisations, according to the needs of the various sectors and territories (and with tacit understanding among the three confederations). In addition to annual dues, a fixed sum is paid for the union card (in CGIL is EUR 3).

The distribution of the dues among the various structures of the organisation is variable in the three confederations and according to the categories. On average horizontal structures receive 20% of dues (25% in CGIL); the sum is there divided among the three territorial levels (provincial, regional, national confederations). The vertical categories get the remaining percentage (75%–80%).

A popular referendum, organised in 1995 by some political groups, has abrogated Article 26 of the Workers' Statute and Article 4 of Act 29/1993 which legally endorsed check-off respectively in the private and public sector. This result seemed to indicate a general loss of popular support for the trade unions. The impact of the referendum on the private sector has been, however, scarce, because check-off has continued to be possible according to the national collective agreements existing in almost all sectors. But no right to check off can be exerted in those enterprises which are not bound by collective agreements.

In the public service a framework agreement signed between all the unions and the government agency representing the public employers (Agenzia per la rappresentanza Negoziale delle Pubbliche Amministrazioni (ARAN)) in December 1995, has confirmed the possibility of check-off and also the freedom of choice by the individual employees (with periodic control of their adhesion to payments).

II. Present Difficulties and Prospects

386. During the last decades in Italy, like in most developed countries, trade unions have been confronted with serious challenges. Some observers have been inclined to forecast a future of vertical decline of unions leading to deunionised societies, where labour relations will be (again) governed by market individualism and there will be less and less room for organised collective actions. Many indicators of union crisis are visible: the decline of union membership and density, and reduced capacity to mobilise industrial conflict, both reported in many countries; declining 'appeal' of union ideals to the public opinion; union retrenchment in defensive posture whereas the employers are often regaining the initiative in industrial relations. Different factors contribute to union difficulties: accelerated international competition and technological innovations; recurrent periods of economic difficulties, particularly in the crisis of 2008 and now 2020–2021, changes in the composition of the labour force (increased participation of women, higher average education of workers, diffusion of atypical and irregular work, etc.).

However, the forecasts of decline for the labour movement which have attracted much attention particularly during the 1980s, have been in part reshaped. The impact of the factors indicated above has not cancelled the role of the unions in social and economic life; membership has stabilised in some countries and collective action remains important, in others the decline is more visible and but it has reduced the role of traditional unions, increased the competition by new sectoral or professional groups, and by the employers themselves.

At the workplace level, union difficulties have been related to the reduced scope of economic bargaining, also due to the critical conditions of many enterprises during the years of the crisis. The reopening of economic margins in same enterprises has not been sufficient to solve the problems; often it has fostered centrifugal trends rather than reinforced the basis of union power within the enterprises. Centrifugal pressures have favoured new forms of enterprises – unionism or individualism and have fostered divergences between workplace organisations and national unions even in countries, like Italy, with strong central traditions. On the other hand, management innovative practices in human resources and the increased pressure for greater employee involvement in the joint handling of matters such as industrial restructuring, organisation and technological innovation productivity shares, have found plant union representatives ill equipped to react to the difficulties of collective bargaining.

387. Comparative research indicates that the various type of unions have showed a different capacity to adjust to the representation crisis according to some key variables. The most widely considered are the mix of centralisation-decentralisation of the industrial relation system and in particular of collective bargaining; the capacity of unions to influence and establish alliances with political actors; more in general the scope of their initiatives with respect both to the employers and the political systems. In this respect some characters of Italian unions (middle centralisation, broad range of objectives, alliance with political parties) might help them to react to the present difficulties. Major obstacles are the ideological rivalries, too informal organisation of workplace, life and action, uncertainty in fully adopting the participative model of industrial relations, and political tensions.

The economic crisis that began in 2008 which has affected the global scenario has had a negative effect on the conditions of employment and on the labour markets: with the return of mass unemployment, growing uncertainty and precariousness of employment, risks of poverty among large sectors of the population even in rich countries. The recovery of the economy after the crisis of 2008 and again after the Covid pandemic of 2020, and the war in Ucraina, has been significant also in Italy but not sufficient to stabilize the scenario of the economy and change the negative prospects for the union's activities.

388. Structural factors such as the pressure of globalisation, and of new digital technologies, are posing serious challenges to the capacity of organised labour to represent its constituencies, the traditional workforce and even more the growing number of atypical workers. The future prospects of industrial relations will depend on the capacity of the unions to counteract these trends by renewing their representative strategies and forms of collective action. But the unions' initiative is, at best weak; it may not be sufficient to redress the balance of power unless it is sustained by public power and possibly by some kind of tripartite action between them and the social parties. Restoring this balance of power and guaranteeing the basic conditions for a social compromise is important – in my opinion – in order to tackle the roots of the social and economic crisis and their consequences.

389. As has already been pointed out, Italian labour unions have traditionally organised mainly at a territorial level and were absent at the plant or company level. This was true before fascism, during the regime and after World War II, until the late 1960s.

390. Within the enterprise, personnel were traditionally represented only by 'works committees' (*commissioni interne*), bodies directly elected by all employees irrespective of their trade union membership. Their first establishment and regulations go back to the early 1900s: a fundamental agreement was signed in 1906 between the Italian Federation of Metalworkers (FIOM) and Itala (the original FIAT). Works committees, which had been developing in most large industrial firms up to 1922, were dissolved by fascism (Agreement of Palazzo Vidoni 1922 and Act of 1926 already quoted) and substituted in 1939 by the so-called fiduciaries, a fiction of workers' representatives. After the fall of fascism, the first pre-occupation of the newly rebuilt CGIL was to re-establish the committees through an agreement concluded with the industrial employers' association (2 September 1943). Since then the works committees have always been regulated by collective inter confederal agreements (for the industrial sector: 7 August 1947, then 8 May 1953 and 18 April 1966, still formally in force but no longer implemented; separate agreements of similar content regulated the committees in the commercial and banking sectors). Attempts to recognise the works committees by law – made especially in the fifties by the CGIL – have always failed, also due to opposition by CISL.

391. According to these agreements, the works committees were elected (and always have been) by all the employees of each plant, through secret ballot, on the basis of lists, separate for blue- and white-collar workers, with a rigidly proportional system. In practice members have been elected, in the very large majority of cases, on the basis of lists put forward by the major trade unions.

392. The general competence of the works committees was to 'contribute to keeping normal relations between the workers and management of the enterprise with respect to the regular development of production, in a spirit of co-operation and mutual understanding' (Article 3, paragraph 1, Agreement 1966). Bargaining powers were explicitly excluded by the agreement and reserved to the unions themselves. Nevertheless, works committees played a decisive role in labour relations at plant level during the 1950s and until the middle 1960s, going beyond their official powers, acting as workers' 'advocates' in the daily problems of working life, practising a sort of informal bargaining with management (more or less effective according to the circumstances). In the course of time they came to be viewed with decreasing favour by the trade unions.

393. During the 1960s CISL, followed by the two other confederations, tried to launch a new representative structure, the union plant branch (*sezione sindacale aziendale*), a direct expression of the union and composed of all members of the union within the enterprise. These attempts, which ran alongside the unions' efforts to decentralise bargaining to the plant level, almost completely failed and the union plant branches remained by and large on paper, apart from a few major industrial plants in the most unionised categories.
At the end of the 1960s, both the works committees and the union plant branches proved incapable of meeting the strong demand to participate and to exercise bargaining power coming from the rank and file. The works committees progressively disappeared almost everywhere. Attempts to revive the union plant branches have been made by those national unions which were most opposed to the new forms of 'delegates'. They had some success outside the industrial sectors (commerce, agriculture, public services).

394. The first 'delegates' appeared in 1968–1969 in some large plants in northern Italy on the initiative of workers or groups organised outside the unions, and were sometimes extremely polemical against them, accusing them of having lost touch with the rank and file. But they have been incorporated into the unions, generalised on the initiative of the major confederations, which managed to regain control of this movement, recognising the potentialities of the delegates as a new representative formula. Generally speaking their structural characteristics, which differentiate them from both works committees and union plant branches, are that each delegate is an employee of the firm elected by a group of fellow workers who share a similar working position; the election is generally held during a meeting of the group (Article 20, Act No. 300), without any predetermined list, irrespective of union affiliation; the delegate is directly responsible to the single group of workers and generally can be removed at any time. All delegates of the plant or of the enterprise form the 'delegate council' or 'factory council' (*consiglio di fabbrica*), which in major firms elects an executive committee and less frequently, a secretary from among its members.

Differently from both works committees and union plant branches, the delegates and their council have been recognised by the major confederations as their representative structures at the plant level, and given the competence to exercise all major union functions, including actual collective bargaining (*see* the Agreement of 1972 which created the Federation CGIL-CISL-UIL and subsequent confederal regulations, agreements of 31 May 2013, 10 January 2014 and lately March 2018 (*see* below). The confederal directives, however, have been fully implemented only by the industrial unions, and have been resisted by other unions more favourable to the 'pure' associative model of union plant branches. Even in industrial unions the competence to bargain and to decide strike action has been usually not granted to the single delegates, but to the delegate councils, or to their executive committee, which can be more easily controlled by external union officers, the delegates remaining competent to handle grievances in first instance, and to act as a liaison between the rank and file and the council.

395. Delegates and their councils have been, and still are where they exist, the beneficiaries of the rights recognised by Title 3 of Act No. 300 (*see* below paragraphs 362 ff.). They became the main representative bodies at the plant level, in the industrial sector, combining, for the first time in Italian labour history, the dual nature of the workers' representative at the workplace and of the representative of the external union, similar to shop stewards in Britain.

396. Union control over the delegates and councils has usually been fairly secure (a large majority of the delegates are union members). The recurrent tensions between the three confederations are often felt within the unitary structure of the delegates; these tensions make it more difficult for them to keep the balance between the dual aspects of their nature.

Proposals have been repeatedly advanced by the trade union themselves, but also by political parties, to introduce more precise rules for the election and functioning of plant union representatives as a part of wider proposals to improve democratic procedures within the unions.

But these proposals have never been put into practice. It is unlikely that we shall see the formal development in Italy of a double representative structure, as has happened in France, Germany or Spain, or the total disappearance of an elective system for all workers such as that of the delegates or workers councils. The attempt of the unions has been to look for some type of mixed system whereby the plant representatives are partly elected by the workers and partly designated by the trade union organisations operating within the firm. After a few local experiments, this mixed model has been endorsed in a general agreement among CGIL-CISL-UIL (March 1991) which has been subsequently adopted with modification by the interconfederal agreement of 23 July 1993 and of December 1993, signed also by the major employers' association, beginning with Confindustria. The unit are representatives (RSU) – this is the name given to the new model – have been consequently recognised as the general workers and union representatives at the plant unit and firm level.

397. Two major points have remained, however, critical until recently. A delicate balance was envisaged between the representatives which are elected by the workers (two-thirds) – and consequently should report only to them – and the part which has been reserved to the unions as such (one-third). This second part was held essential, particularly by minority unions, to guarantee their identity and in general some responsiveness of the RSU to union organisation: for this reason it is also held essential by the employers' association. However, the reserved quota of one-third has been objected to – particularly within CGIL – as being scarcely democratic (or even unconstitutional if the mixed model were to be adopted by legislation). In fact it has been cancelled by the agreement of 10 January 2014 (*see* paragraph 389). Second, the RSU is not recognised as sole bargaining agents at the plant level, but should bargain only jointly with the traditional union representatives – precisely because of their ambiguous nature and 'unsafe' responsiveness. The employers themselves insist that plant bargaining, being linked to national bargaining, should be conducted by agents responsible to the national unions (i.e., the territorial unions and not the RSU).

398. A legislative definition of these issues derives from Decree 396/1997, modified by Decree 165/2001 (Article 43) for public service. The Acts have regulated the system of collective representation at the workplace, distinguishing more clearly than in the private sector between the union representatives (RSA) and the unit representatives elected by all workers (RSU). Moreover, they have set out some basic criteria for ascertaining union representativeness. This definition is important because it has been agreed upon by trade unions and has been considered a possible pattern for the private sector.

In fact this has been the case in the various attempts made by the three major labour confederations to regulate the matter. Their efforts have brought to subsequent agreements, by the major unions confederations and Confindustria on 28 June 2011, 31 May 2013, 10 January 2014, and 9 March 2018, which confirms the commitment of the parties to respect some basic rules of industrial relations and to guarantee the cohesion of the system.

The agreement of 2014 seems to clarify the critical points mentioned above. The RSU are endorsed as the only representative body at the plant level with full bargaining powers and the signing unions renounce to set up separate RSA representations. However these latter structures are still present in some sectors and areas. All the members of RSU are to be elected by the employees. Similar rules are provided in other agreements signed by the peak organisations of others sectors, e.g., the agreement of 16 November 2015, between the major unions' confederations and Confcommercio (employers' confederation of the commerce and service sectors).

The one-third of members previously reserved to the unions has been abolished. The unions are entitled however to present lists for the RSU elections, according the rules to be defined at the level of the individual sectors, by the affiliate vertical federations. Following these rules the votes received by the unions in the RSU elections are the essential base for ascertaining their representativeness (*see* below).

The rules consolidated in the confederal agreement of 2014 are not fully operating. Moreover they are binding only on the signatory associations, and consequently do not cover the entire economy.

The need a legislative intervention remains acute, ever more so after by the recent decision of the Constitutional Court (231/2013) on the criteria of unions' representativeness (*see* below).

§2. The Employers' Associations

399. Employers' associations reproduce by and large the same dual structure of the unions, being historically a response to workers' organisations. Some peculiarities are nonetheless significant. Private employers are grouped not in a single but in three confederations, one for each major branch of the economy: industry (*Confindustria*), commerce (*Confcommercio*), agriculture (*Confagricoltura*). A separate confederation (*Confapi*) organises small-medium size industrial firms, in competition with Confindustria, but it is in significant in industrial relations apart from in some areas of the country.

Artisans are also represented by separate confederations: Confartigianato and CNA being the two largest. The Confindustria is the most powerful employers' association: according to the latest figures (2022), it represents 151.000 firms with 5,382,382 employees.

400. State-owned and controlled undertakings disaffiliated from the industrial confederation of private employers in 1957, following the directive of Act 22 December 1956, No. 1589, which was held by the Italian Constitutional Court not to be in violation of the employers' freedom to organise, and formed two separate organisations: ASAP, grouping all petrochemical public undertakings, and INTERSIND, grouping all remaining public undertakings, which covered all the main industrial sectors and some in large-size commercial distribution. ASAP has also become an association which has been extended to all the main industrial sectors, representing, for the most part, large firms. Enterprises represented by INTERSIND (again mainly large ones) came to employ about 500,000 workers.

The trend towards privatisation of state-controlled enterprises and convergence in industrial relations policies has made the separate representation of these organisations less and less significant. ASAP was merged with Confindustria in 1994 and INTERSIND has also joined Confindustria, where it keeps some organisational identity. Following the 'privatisation' of public service (Act 29/1993, *see* above) and the consequent legalisation of collective agreements in this sector, public administrations are represented at the bargaining table by a specialised public agency (ARAN).

401. The private employers' confederations are complex organisations, like their labour counterparts. The confederation of industrial employers is composed of many national unions (federations), each covering a large branch of the industry: e.g., the Federation of Metal-mechanical Employers has much the same jurisdiction as the Federation of Metal-mechanical Workers, and so it is with the Federation of Textile Employers. The Confederation has also decentralised horizontal structures with provincial industrial associations (106) and regional ones (18). Until 1970 the Confindustria acted directly as the bargaining agent at the national level (particularly for the pattern-setting metal-working industry), consistent with the centralised structure of this organisation and of collective bargaining in Italy.

Since then national industry associations have been given greater authority in developing bargaining strategies in order to meet the growing strength of industrial unions and more dynamic and decentralised bargaining trends. This is particularly true for the major national federations, those of the metalworking (*Federmeccanica*, founded in 1971), textile and garment (*Federtessile*, founded in 1975) and chemical employers (one of the oldest and most autonomous). The Confindustria still plays an all important role in handling bargaining issues of general concern (*see* paragraphs 416 ff.) or in giving guidelines acting as the common representative of the employers vis-à-vis the political system. Provincial associations maintain a key role in guiding bargaining action at the enterprise level, in assisting individual firms during the administration of agreements and the relative disputes, and in providing a wide range of technical services in social and economic matters.

402. Unlike the case of trade unions, the individual employer may affiliate with the provincial industrial association and not with the federation of his category (which happens not infrequently) or (less frequently) vice versa. Moreover, national federations do not have, in most cases, independent provincial or local sections. These two factors weaken the vertical structure vis-à-vis the provincial horizontal associations, which are, with the confederations, the core of the employers' organisations. The majority of powers and activities (from legal and economic advice to members, to the actual collective bargaining) have been traditionally vested in horizontal structures. In any case, employers' associations as such, maintain a somewhat looser character than labour unions, because the individual employers particularly the major companies keep a fairly large degree of independence in shaping their bargaining policies and can directly influence national bargaining.

The recent activism of employers in industrial relations is more the work of individual employers, particularly of large firms, than of employers' associations. Also, for this reason, such activism often lacks uniform direction, apart from the general aim of promoting more flexible industrial relations and human resource management, corresponding to the demands of increased international competitiveness.

The possibility of establishing employment relationships without trade unions is not considered realistic a part from certain sectors of small industry and in high-tech firms. Elsewhere management policy seems to wave between attempts to involve the unions in forms of worker participation (emblematically expressed in the so-called IRI protocol of 1982) and attempts to restrict in an 'opportunist' way the influence of the unions and the area covered by collective industrial relations.

Recently some large firms have taken a course of action in decentralised bargaining openly different from that advocated by their associations (Confindustria in the first place) to the point of revoking their participation in the association (FIAT being the clearest case).

A final remark is necessary concerning both collective actors. They can hardly play a significant role in the shaping of a European social dimension if they remain organised on a national basis and if their European representatives (CES, UNICE) continue to lack significant bargaining power, as they still do even after the Maastricht Social Protocol of December 1992.

§3. Legal Status of Trade Unions and Employers' Associations

403. Italian trade unions and employers' associations are non-recognised de facto associations, therefore lacking legal personality. In fact, Article 39, 2nd part, of the Italian Constitution provides for the registration of trade unions, and employers' associations, and the consequent recognition of their legal personality, as a prerequisite to allowing them the power to conclude collective agreements 'generally' binding, that is, on all employees and employers operating within the scope of the bargaining unit. This constitutional provision, however, has remained a dead letter, because the legislation required to implement it was never passed. This is for a number of reasons: trade unions came to fear that the registration procedure could open the way to state interference in internal union affairs, much greater than that intended by the framers of the Constitution, especially with an unfriendly government, as in the fifties. According to Article 39, the public authorities granting recognition had, apparently, only to ascertain the existence of the conditions required by the norm (democratic charter, minimum number of affiliates) not to control the merits of unions' representativeness or internal functioning. The diffidence of the unions, however, was well-founded and fostered by a Bill prepared by the government in 1952 to implement Article 39, very restrictive of trade unions' freedom.

404. Minority confederations, particularly CISL, were also afraid that the procedure provided for in Article 39, involving proportional representation of each union at one bargaining table, would have given the CGIL an absolute control of the (necessarily unitary) bargaining process, and would have prevented any practical possibility of separate bargaining at different levels (on which CISL relied in the 1950s to break the monopoly and bargaining models of CGIL).

Moreover, the advantages granted by Article 39, which motivated the (initial) favour by CGIL (in particular, the 'generally' binding effects of collective agreements) became, as time passed, less and less valuable with respect to the above-mentioned hazards.

405. The second part of Article 39 was modelled on the bargaining structure predominant in 1947, based almost exclusively on national industry-wide agreements and, due to the weakness of the workers on the labour market, gave high priority to the extensions of these agreements to the non-organised. The development of bargaining at plant level since 1960 has strengthened the position of the unions in the undertaking and so has pushed the question of general applicability into the background. In 1959 the government enacted a law under which the collective agreements then in force were incorporated into special statutes, thus receiving legal sanctions and becoming generally binding: a result similar to that provided for in Article 39, although transitory, which further reduced the pressure for the implementation of Article 39. The same result had, since the early 1950s, been partially guaranteed with regard to minimum wage by the prevailing court interpretation of Article 36 (*see* below paragraphs 582 ff.).

406. Finally, with the increasing unionisation, collective agreements managed to cover, without legal help, a large part of the interested regular workers, particularly in the industrial sector, and in the most advanced areas of the country.

The obsolescence of Article 39, 2nd part, has become more widely recognised and indirectly confirmed by the Statute of Workers' Rights (Act No. 300 of 1970), which takes for granted the status of unions as non-recognised organisations. This situation, whereby unions live, and are felt to live, largely outside any legal interference, corresponds to a basic diffidence and scepticism, common to other legislatures, towards union recognition and regulation as a suitable means of stabilising and controlling industrial relations. As such, it is a basic element of that sort of economic laissez-faire which has characterised the evolution of Italian labour relations in the post-war period, and to which we will return.

In recent years various reasons (the growing tension among different unions, their crisis of representativeness and the need to control bargaining behaviour) have, however, provided the basis for a possible reappraisal of the problem of union regulation. The implementation of the directives of Article 39 – as they are – is still regarded as out of the question by most observers. Attention is focused on different approaches: improving basic democracy procedures within the trade union by way of self-regulation or possibly with legislative support. Only unions accepting minimum standards should be eligible for certain benefits and recognised as legally representative.

407. As private non-recognised associations, trade unions and employers' associations fall, in general, under the provisions of Articles 36, 37, 38 of the Italian Civil Code governing the matter. They cannot, even if they requested it, obtain recognition and legal personality – like other private associations – according to Articles 12ff. of the Civil Code, because the recognition procedure of Article 39 Constitution is considered mandatory (in fact trade unions are not interested, since recognition under Articles 12ff. would imply even tighter control than under Article 39 Constitution). Article 36 states that the administration and functioning of non-recognised association is regulated by agreements between the members (i.e., by the associations' constitution and by-laws) (1st paragraph), and that the association shall be represented in legal proceedings by the president or director (2nd paragraph). In case of non-performance of obligations entered into by persons representing the association, creditors may exert their rights on the social fund and jointly on the personal patrimony of the persons who have acted in the name of the association (Article 38) (i.e., not of all members).

Union constitutions and bylaws have full competence in regulating the internal life of the organisation and have been almost completely exempted from any public and judicial control even in case of grievances brought by members claiming unjustified treatment; cases of judicial redress are absolutely exceptional.

408. Although lacking legal personality, trade unions and employers' associations have limited relevance as entities distinguished by their individual members. The main differences from recognised associations are the regime of responsibility for the non-performance of the social fund, and the lack of publicity concerning the acts and financial resources of non-recognised associations, which in fact makes it more difficult to recover damages from them or to exert other monetary rights.

409. There is no doubt that unions and employers' associations can conclude collective agreements legally enforceable by them, as far as the obligatory part is concerned, although the courts have tended in the past to interpret rather restrictively the provision of Article 36, 2nd paragraph, Civil Code, recognising for de facto associations a limited capacity to act before the courts. In practice, there have been no cases reported of unions being sued for failure to perform obligations under a collective agreement, and only one case of a union suing an employers' association (for failure to submit certain grievances and to recognise appropriate decisional powers with respect to a grievance committee set up by a national collective agreement).

410. The normative part of the collective agreement, on the other hand, cannot be enforced by the trade unions, because, according to the prevailing (but questionable) opinion, it entails rights only on the individual workers covered by the agreement and can therefore be enforced only on their initiative. The trial capacity of trade unions has been recognised beyond any doubt by Article 28 of Act No. 300 of 1970, which enables them to sue in their name the employers in any case of anti-union activity (*see* below paragraphs 444 ff.).

§4. The Most Representative Organisations

411. Articles 36–38 of the Civil Code do not exhaust the legal status of the trade unions and employers' associations. Special norms define the status of re-presentative or of most representative organisations, which is relevant to the acquisition of certain privileges stated by law, apart from a few of them, which are recognised with respect to trade unions for the mere fact of being active and organised at the national level (e.g., Article 28 of Act No. 300 of 1970).

412. The most important of these privileges are:

(a) The rights to designate representatives in public organs and institutions, particularly of an administrative nature (boards of directors in social security institutions, tripartite commissions operating within public employment offices, Act No. 264 of 1949 and Articles 33–34 of Act No. 300 of 1970 Act 469/1997 on regional and provincial tripartite commissions for consultation and concertation on labour policies; tripartite commissions to conciliate labour disputes on rights, Act No. 553 of 1973 and Act 183/2010; tripartite commissions for control of homework, Act No. 877 of 1973; National Council for Economics and Labour, regulated by Act No. 936 of 1986). Recently tripartite commissions competent on labour market policies and training have been set up by regional laws; commissions to control the regularisation of irregular work, commissions for the certification of atypical labour contracts (*see* above).

(b) A series of rights granted in order to promote union activity at the plant level by Title 3 of Act No. 300 of 1970.

413. The requirements necessary for recognition as a representative or most representative organisations have varied according to the different fields, and are stated partly by law and partly by administrative practice, and are in any case subject to discretionary interpretation by the courts. Traditionally the following requirements have been taken into account jointly: the number of members, resulting from common knowledge; balanced presence of the organisation in the various branches of the economy, in case of a confederation; national dimension of the organisation; active participation in collective bargaining and in the handling of labour disputes (*see* e.g., Act No. 902 of 18 November 1977).

414. A very important provision referring to the notion of most representative unions is Article 19 of Act No. 300 of 1970, which includes in it:

(a) Unions affiliated to the confederations most representative at the national level, referring, therefore, the notion to the confederation as such, not to the affiliated unions (abrogated by a referendum in 1995, *see* below).
(b) Unions not affiliated to the aforementioned confederations (independent unions), which have signed national or provincial agreements applied in the productive unit (where the rights provided for by Act No. 300 are to be exercised).

The Constitutional Court (decision 231/2013), has decided that in order to implement this requirement the simple fact of adhering to an agreement is not sufficient; effective participation in the bargaining process is necessary.

The first requirement excludes the notion any organisation is active only at the company or plant level. However, the notion of representativeness has become controversial. On one side, its 'expansion' has reduced its selective capacity and allowed the recognition of the various rights connected to it to an increasing number of organisations, often of weak representativeness, particularly in the public service. This 'inflation' of collective actors is seen with concern by the employers, as well as by the government, which has tried to introduce more precise limits to the notion in the public sector (including a minimum percentage of members and votes to the unions) and by the Constitutional Court (which has denied the status of most representative union to the associations of cadres by arguing that they cannot be considered confederations in so far as they organise only one professional category of employers and therefore cannot benefit from letter (a) of Article 19 of Act 300).

415. These controversies have been dramatised by two popular referendums, organised in 1995 and aimed at abrogating Article 19. The most sweeping of them, which asked for the abrogation of the whole norm, was not approved; the second, which wanted to repeal only letter (a) of Article 19, got a majority of the vote. The consequences of these results are rather complex. The plant representatives of the three major confederations – RSU or other – remain legally untouched – because via letter (b) they still are considered representative, since they are usually signatory to national collective agreements applied to the productive unit; consequently they enjoy the same rights of Title 3 of Act 300 as before. The abrogation of letter (a) has caused problems to the representatives of those unions which are not signatories of agreements applied in the enterprise (some independent national unions or some sectoral unions affiliated to CISNAL, now UGL, and CISAL), particularly because the courts do not hold sufficient the mere formal signature of the collective agreements but require an active participation to its formation; and the agreement must regulate thoroughly some important area of labour relations (*see* below the decision 231/2013 of the Constitutional Court).

416. But even apart from the legal consequences, the result of the referendum has underlined the need to revise the concept and relevance of union representativeness. Decree 396 of 1997 and Decree 165/2001 have given a precise definition of it in the public service – where indeed it is particularly necessary because only representative unions can be admitted by public administration to collective bargaining. Mixed criteria have been accepted following the compromise solution already experimented in practice: representative unions are those which get an average of 5% between votes in elections and members adhering to the same unions. In this way the two main criteria of representativeness sustained by the major historical ideologies of trade unions – CISL on one side and CGIL-UIL on the other – have been combined. This solution, agreed upon by the major unions, has reduced the 'inflation' of representativeness; but even so seven to eight unions are usually recognised as representatives in the public service and in some sectors like transport at the local level even.

A similar rule has been adopted by the social parties for the private sector in the agreement of 10 January 2014, which is a sort of unified text on this matter and has been confirmed by the agreement of 9 March 2018. The representativeness for the purpose of bargaining at the national level is recognised by the unions which reach the 5% measured on an average between the quota of members (on the total union members) and the votes in the elections of the RSU.

The agreement reached between the major unions confederations and *Confcommercio* (commerce and service sectors) on 16 November 2015, fixes the criteria in slightly different terms: number of members and number of votes (but without quotas), plus number of labour disputes and of unemployment issues handled.

These agreements might serve as a basis for a general definition of representativeness. Proposals to this extent have been repeatedly presented to Parliament; but no solution was adopted due to disagreement among the major unions in which the government has been so far unwilling to mediate.

A protocol has been signed between the National Institute of Social Security (INPS) and the Ministry of Labour which establishes a procedure to collective from all the firms the number of employees affiliated to the various unions.

This procedure could allow to have certified data of union membership (which so far were only based on the declarations of the interested organisation). But it has not yet been fully implemented.

417. Even in the absence of an organic reform some evolution of the concept of representativeness has, however, occurred. On the one hand greater emphasis is being given, following the 1995 referendum, to the unions' effective influence within the workplace vis-à-vis the mere connection with external most representative confederations (where representativeness is indirectly presumed). The former aspect, effective influence is decisive for workplace bargaining issues and unions' rights; the latter remains relevant for general issues, i.e., whenever the law delegates to the unions the right to participate in public bodies or to negotiate over specific matters. Recently the concept of 'comparatively most representative union' has been introduced by several Acts (Act 196/1997, Decree 61/2000, Act 30/2003). The reasoning and content of this new, indeed odd, concept are far from clear. Apparently it aims at reinforcing the weak selectiveness of the original concept of representativeness by specifying that some powers are reserved by the law only to the unions which can be considered most representative relative to the others (still representative); in practice to the major confederations.[1]

In addition Act 389/1989 has provided that the wages fixed by the collective agreements signed by the most representative unions and employers associations are a necessary basis to calculate social security contributions. Moreover the content of the same agreements must be respected by the enterprises as a condition to receive various kinds of public incentives and benefits (*see* below).

1. A parallel referendum abrogated Art. 47 of Act 29 of 1993 which regulates the most representative unions in the public service.

Chapter 3. Institutionalised Relations Between Employers and Trade Unions: Legal Support for Trade Union Activities at Plant Level

§1. Trade Union Rights

418. A major set of rules concerning trade unions rights, and indirectly defining their legal status vis-à-vis the employers, is laid down by the Title 3 of the Statute of Workers' Rights (Act No. 300/1970). This Act, which is the fundamental source of law governing collective labour relations, has marked a profound change of attitude in the Italian legislature towards organised labour, with regard both to the constitutional approach of Article 39 and to the substantial 'abstentionism' seen during the 1950s and 1960s. Following an idea which had been receiving growing consensus during these years. Act No. 300 intervenes not in order to regulate unions as such at the national level but in order to promote their presence and action effectively at the plant level.

419. The focus of the Act is no longer on union recognition and the extension of collective agreements, but on some basic rights which are granted to the unions and to the workers as prerequisites to the promotion of union activity and collective bargaining within the place of work, beyond a certain size, impinging on management prerogatives. The Act supports union activity at plant level on the assumption – common to quite a few modern labour legislators – that strengthening it is a major contribution to the fostering of institutionalised bilateral relations between organised labour and employers. In 1970 there was a concern to reinforce the position of the major labour confederations (CGIL, CISL and UIL) vis-à-vis not only a managerial class reluctant to recognise their right to operate and bargain within the undertakings but also vis-à-vis the strong pressure exerted by the rank and file in the wave of strikes of 1968–1969, which had threatened to elude any kind of control.

420. In fact most of the rights provided for in Title 3 of the Act are granted to the most representative unions as indicated above (the four major confederations, plus certain established independent unions), or better to the plant representative structures affiliated to them, as provided for by Article 19 (*see* above paragraph 394), with the explicit exclusion of organisations operating only at plant or company level, in particular the radical extra- or anti-union groups mentioned above.

421. The constitutional legitimacy of this selective choice has been questioned as being against trade union freedom and equality of treatment, because it discriminates between different unions, favouring the established and bigger ones to the detriment of the smallest and most recent. The Italian Constitutional Court (in 1974), however, has rejected this objection, upholding the distinction made in Article 19 as being 'rationally founded', and therefore not contrary to the principle of equality of union freedom. According to the court, it is proper to recognise the major rights of Title 3 only with respect to unions capable of representing workers effectively and genuinely, in order to avoid fragmentation in the labour movement and in order not to encourage the proliferation of small groups, which, particularly if limited to the company level, can easily become victims of a narrow conception of union representation or, worse, of employers' manipulation. On the other hand, these rights can be readily acquired by any organisation, through bargaining with the employers, or, according to the law, as soon as they become representative. Moreover, Act No. 300 guarantees (at least) some basic freedoms of action within the places of work to the workers as such, and therefore also to non-representative groups so as to enable them to organise and strengthen their positions: the general freedom of opinion and of union activity sanctioned by Articles 1 and 14; the right to strike; the right to collect dues and make propaganda and recruit members sanctioned by Article 26, 1st paragraph; protection against employers' discriminatory acts, in Articles 15 and 16. The constitutional legitimacy of Article 19 has been confirmed in different aspects by subsequent court decisions (334/1988; 492/1995; 244/1996; 345/1996).

The Court has further specified (Decision No. 30 of 1990) its position by deciding that only the most representative unions are entitled to the rights of the Title 3 and that collective agreements extending these rights to other plant representatives are null and void.

The importance of Article 19 in order to identify the plant union representatives and the beneficiaries of the rights of Title 3, with the specifications indicated above (paragraph 361) remained decisive even after the referendum of 1995. But the abrogation by the referendum of letter (a) has altered the balance of the norm and motivated a decision of the constitutional court (231/2013), to declare lett (b) partially unconstitutional (*see* above). The case was brought to the court after the refusal of FIAT to recognise the rights of title III and to admit to the bargaining table the metalworkers union (FIOM), which is in fact very active in the enterprise but has refused to sign agreements applied in FIAT.

As a consequence the norm is 'corrected' so that the rights of title III must be recognised not simply to unions which are signatory of agreements applied in the unit but only to those which actively participate in bargaining. The decision does not give more specific and positive criteria to define the union representativeness, particularly in cases where no collective agreement is applied in the firm. According to the Court positive criteria may be fixed only by legislator.

422. Article 19 does not define any fixed model of organisation for the unions and the workers within the plant: it requires only that any representative organ be formed democratically 'at the initiative of the workers' (no minimum number being fixed) and be somehow connected with the most representative unions, as indicated. Article 19, therefore, and the related rights of Title 3, apply to all types of representative organs which the most representative unions have created or recognised at plant level (not only the union plant committees of delegates) insofar as the most representative unions recognise them as their representative structure at plant level, which is the case in most industrial unions (*see* above paragraphs 337 ff.). These rights have been recognised to the RSU not only in the private but also in the public sector. Decree 396 of 1997 modified by Decree 165/2001 (Articles 42 and 50) grants preferential rights indeed both to RSA and RSU, leaving to collective agreements the specific definition and distribution of these rights. In fact, besides an exclusive access to collective bargaining, these representative bodies are entitled to time off and leave of absence for union activities, proportionally to their representativeness, taking into consideration also the territorial diffusion and the weight of organising in the given area.

423. It is not relevant, on the other hand, that delegates (and also RSU) are elected also by non-union members, and may themselves be non-members. Article 19 and Title 3 do not apply instead – with the exception of Article 22 – to works committees, which have never been recognised as full union representative bodies (*see* above paragraph 340) by the major Italian confederations: the legislature itself, in Act No. 300, clearly chooses to disregard them as beneficiaries of these privileges.

424. The leaders of these union structures are entitled to a minimum number of hours off work, paid by the employer, variable according to the size of the production unit in which they operate. Article 23 grants this right to:

(a) union leaders for each representative union in units involving up to 200 workers, belonging to the category for which the union is organised;
(b) one leader for each representative union each 300 or fraction of 300 workers (belonging to the category as above);
(c) one leader for each representative union each 500 or fraction of 500 workers in larger units, in addition to the minimum number fixed under (b).

The minimum number of hours paid by the employer, which can be increased by collective agreements (like the number of union leaders), shall not be less than eight hours monthly in firms mentioned in (a). This paid time-off is granted to union leaders for any activity included in their mandate, on the single condition that they give written notice to the employer, as a rule, twenty-four hours in advance, through their representative plant structure.

425. Article 24 grants, furthermore, the right to some leaders to take time off work, without pay, for a minimum of eight days a year, in order to participate in collective bargaining or in union conferences, similarly on condition that they give written notice to the employer, three days in advance, through their representative structure. The notion of union leader is furthermore not determined by Act No. 300 and may also apply to workers exercising a temporary union office, provided that they are indicated as such by the most representative union. Infact the definition of the notion is left to the decision of the Union to which the worker belongs. In practice, possible disputes concerning the identification of these beneficiaries are resolved most often by collective agreements, which do not fix a number of hours for each leader, as the Act does, but provide for a total sum of yearly hours at the disposal of the union representative structure, which can then indicate from time to time the specific worker entitled to use them (apart from any previous qualification).

The tensions among the major unions have created difficulties in the application of these clauses, i.e., in the distribution of time off work, the problem is whether to distribute it equally among the three unions (as Act 300 does) or in proportion to their members.

426. Finally, Act No. 300 grants to union leaders a special protection – in addition to the general protection granted to all workers by Articles 15, 16 and 28 – against discriminatory dismissals and transfers. Article 18 (4th, 5th and 6th paragraphs) provided that in case of dismissal of such union representatives, and also of members of and candidates for the works committee, on joint demand by them and their union, the *pretore* (judge of first instance) can order, at any stage of the proceedings, the immediate reinstatement of the employee, if he believes that the elements of proof produced by the employer to justify the dismissal are irrelevant or insufficient. The employer who does not obey the order of reinstatement, in addition to the wages due to the employee according to the 2nd paragraph of Article 18 (*see* above paragraph 234), must pay a sum equal to those wages to the public old age pension fund (a special sanction like that provided for in Article 16). These special accelerated precautionary proceedings have been used only rarely, because the procedure set up by Article 28 has proved as fast and even more effective in protecting these employees from discriminatory dismissals.

427. Article 22 provides that union representatives of Article 19, members of and candidates for works committees, can be transferred from the productive unit in which they work only if a *nihil obstat* is given by the relative union, and that such special protection – like that against dismissals – applies to candidates for elections to the works committee, until the third month thereafter, and for all others until the year following the cessation of their term of office. The legislature has presumed that a discriminatory intention is always present in the order of transfer by the employer – meaning transfer to any location, even temporary, of such union officers from their normal place or work (plant, but also department) or single job position as impairing their capacity adequately to represent the workers and perform their office. In the absence of the *nihil obstat* the order of transfer is not valid and the employee is not obliged to obey it.

This protection has been extended by national collective agreements: first, by making it applicable to all union delegates, and not only to the representatives covered by Article 19 (so defeating also certain restrictive interpretations of Article 22, which limited its protection to a number of union representatives equal to that provided for in Article 23); second, by requiring the *nihil obstat* also for cases of dismissal of union delegates (a provision already contained in the interconfederal agreement of 18 April 1966, on the constitution and functioning of the works committees).

428. Other special rights promoting union activity at plant level are contained in Title 3. Article 20, 1st paragraph provides that: ‘workers have the right to meet together in the productive unit in which they work, outside working time, and within working time, up to a maximum of ten hours a year for which they will receive regular pay. Better conditions can be provided for in collective agreements.’ The right to meet could be drawn in principle by Article 1 of Act No. 300 of 1970, which confirms that workers have the right to freely express their opinions within the workplace, according to the principles set out in the Constitution and in the same Act No. 300. A special discipline, however, like that of Article 20, was felt necessary to guarantee the concrete exercise of this particular way of expressing opinions collectively, imposing on the employer the obligation to cooperate positively, i.e., putting at the disposal of workers appropriate rooms and services within the plant in order to make meetings possible and paying the minimum number of hours. For this reason, in order to fall under the discipline of Article 20, meetings must observe certain conditions set out by Article 20 itself and they must be called by union representatives provided for in Article 19 (jointly or separately) or by the RSU (Unitary Representatives) with an agenda containing 'matters of union interest or related to labour' and notice of the meeting must be given to the employer. The expression 'matters of union interest or related to labour' (which is used also in Articles 21 and 25) is purposely broad, and includes not only working conditions within the single plant, and national bargaining problems but also broad social and economic issues, falling within the interests and goals of organised labour. The limits of the notion, not easily definable, indeed, can be drawn, by and large, by the indications elaborated by the Italian Constitutional Court with respect to strike action (*see* below paragraphs 594 ff, 501 ff.).

429. Meetings called without obeying the conditions indicated by Article 20 are legitimate according to, and within the limits of, Article 1 of Act No. 300. If held during working time, they can be protected as a particular form of strike. Article 20 sanctions, finally, the fact that meetings can concern all the workers of the unit or only part of them and can be attended by officers, not employees of the firm, of the most representative unions who have created the representative organ of Article 19, on the single condition that notice must be given in advance to the employer. The employer or his executive staff, instead, cannot participate in the meetings, unless invited.

430. The right sanctioned by Article 20 has proved very important not only in initiating a democratic debate among the workers but also in helping unions to organise new plants, allowing union officers to do so from the inside instead of from the outside: as a matter of fact, a series of general meetings – which can be called even by a small group of union representatives within the unit – is the first generally rather effective step towards a process of organisation.

431. Collective agreements also regulate the matter, enlarging the benefits (e.g., the number of hours) or, more frequently, specifying the conditions for the exercise of the right, e.g., the guarantees of certain minimum safeguards for production and safety, a period of advance notice (the validity of some of those clauses has been questioned, as being more restrictive of the right than Article 20 itself).

432. According to Article 21, the employer must allow the holding of a referendum, within the enterprise and outside working time, among all the employees, or part of them. The referendum shall concern matters of union interest, or related to labour, and shall be called by all the representative union structures of Article 19. The latter condition is required in order to avoid the proliferation of referenda as a means of competition between unions. The practice of referendum has been almost unknown in the Italian labour tradition. The unions, particularly the CISL, while recognising the need to improve democratic procedures, and decision-making processes, fear that the risks of its use (above all oversimplification of issues) will far outweigh its actual capacity to increase rank and file participation in union life. But the attitude is changing. In the last years a few referenda have been promoted by the union in cases of serious splits among themselves and/or among union territorial leadership and plant delegates, particularly on accepting management plans for industrial restructuring and for the approval of controversial collective agreements (enterprise wide and also national). The results of these referenda have been often uncertain and on occasion negative for the unions, which has not contributed to increasing the favour towards a strengthening or legislative regulation of this system. According to the prevailing opinion the negative result of the referendum has only political and not legal effects, consequently it does not invalidates collective agreements.

A common occurrence has been the use of mass consultation by employees on major issues of negotiation with the government. The techniques of consultation – indeed rather rudimentary – amounted to something midway between a referendum and an assembly meeting.

The recurrent tensions among the major confederations have had consequences also on the use of referendum, e.g., CGIL and some industrial unions adhering to it (the metalworkers in particular) have reacted to agreements signed separately by CISL and UIL by challenging their validity and opportunity also by way of a referendum among the interested workers, which has been refused by CISL and UIL; relevant cases have been the confederal agreement on fixed-term contracts (*see* above) the metalworkers' agreement of 2003 and of 2009, and the confederal agreement of January 2009 on the collective bargaining structure (*see* below paragraph 482).

433. The matter has been regulated by consensus among the three major unions and Confindustria in the confederal agreement of 10 January 2014. These agreements admit the use of the referendum under certain conditions, for the validation both of national agreements (*see* below). For the effectiveness of enterprise-level agreements the confederations consider sufficient the approval by the majority of the RSU, because they are elected by all the employees. The agreement concluded by the RSA are considered effective if they are approved by RSA representing a majority of unions members present in the enterprise. But in this case the agreement must be submitted to a referendum, if so is demanded by one union-signatory to the January 2014 agreement, or by the least 30% of the employees.

The referendum is considered valid if 50%+1 of entitled employees participate, and the enterprise agreement is rejected with the majority of those actually voting.

Similar rules are fixed in the agreement of 16 November 2015, for the Commerce and tertiary sectors: a major difference is that the enterprise level agreement must be approved by the RSU, not alone, but 'in accordance with the local or national unions organisation (which want to keep some control on the representatives elected in the enterprise).

A special kind of referendum is provided by Article 14 of Act 146 of 1990, as modified by Act 83/2000, at the initiative of the Commission for the strike action in essential services, in case of serious dissent among workers or unions over the minimum standards of services to be guaranteed during the strike (*see* below paragraphs 580 ff.

434. Indeed, the controversy over the use of referendum and other forms of workers' consultation reflects the general issue of union internal democracy and representativeness.

Italian unions have traditionally underestimated the importance of formalised rules of internal democracy. While this was to some degree inevitable in the context of strong political militancy and organisational growth of the 1950s and 1960s – it has become more and more counterproductive in the mature and less 'heroic' environment of the last decades. The lack of clear rules in this respect does not contribute to improve an image of trade unions which is somehow losing 'glamour' (if not deteriorated) with respect to public opinion in general and to the more sophisticated and demanding groups of employees.

A remedy for this situation can hardly be found with simple shortcuts, it implies a long search for both direct and representative channels of democratic expression at the various levels of the union organisation.

435. Article 25 grants to union representatives (provided for by Article 19) the right to post up publications, texts and bulletins concerning matters of union interest or related to labour, in places which the employer must put at their disposal within the unit and located where they are accessible to all the workers. The right was one of the first to be provided for by collective agreements since the early 1960s. The law recognised it more effectively, however, free from any limitation (as existed in the first agreements), such as the duty to submit the materials to be published to the employer. The employer has now no direct control over their content, even when it could amount to a crime; apart, of course, from the possibility to resort to the judiciary.

436. According to Article 27, in units occupying at least 200 workers, the employer must put permanently at the disposal of the union representatives (provided for by Article 19), for their activity, a common room, adequate to their needs, within the unit or in its immediate neighbourhood. In units with fewer than 200 employees, the room must be put at the disposal of union representatives, not permanently, but when they demand it their meetings.

During the lockdown caused by COVID the unions have exercised the right to meet according to Article 20 in telematic forms.

According to courts decisions this practice is legitimated, but it is up to the unions plant representatives to organise the meetings with no obligation of the employer to collaborate.

The use of electronic devices has become common also for the exercise of other collective rights such as that of posting up publications in electronic billboards (Article 25) and also of communicating with the workers, including the possibility of using firm intranets with management consent.

The exercise of these rights is regulated by some collective agreements.

437. Article 26, 1st paragraph, recognises the workers' right to collect dues, make propaganda and recruit members for their organisations within the places of work 'without prejudice to the regular activity of the plant'. As has already been indicated, this norm, being a specific application of Articles 1 and 14 of Act No. 300, is of benefit to all workers, and therefore all their organisations: not only unions other than the most representative but also political parties. This is the principal occasion in which Act No. 300, mainly intended to support trade unions, takes into account, and sanctions, at least a basic activity of proselytism by political parties within the productive unit.

438. The second and third paragraph return to the promotion of trade unions. The former provides that the trade unions have the right to collect dues through a check-off system, according to the rules stated by the collective agreements, which must guarantee to workers the secrecy of their trade union choice (i.e., that the employer does not know the union to which each worker pays his dues). This provision is a logical development of Article 15 of the law, outlawing discriminatory acts because of union affiliation (by the employer and by the unions themselves) and of Article 8, which forbids the employer to make investigations into political, religious and trade union opinions of the workers, as well as any circumstance not relevant to their professional attitudes.

The third paragraph of Article 26 provides that, in the absence of collective agreements, the individual employee can claim the check-off dues in favour of the trade union indicated (in which case the need for secrecy is disregarded). The second and third paragraphs of the norm have been abrogated in 1995 by a popular referendum, but check-off has continued to be possible according to collective agreements (*see* above paragraph 335).

439. Finally, Article 30 provides for a paid leave of absence, according to collective agreement regulations, in favour of members of the governing bodies, provincial and national, of the most representative unions; Articles 31–32 for non-paid leave of absence in favour of workers elected to public functions (members of national and regional parliaments, mayors, etc.) and to union offices at the provincial and national level for the length of their mandate and with full social security protection.

440. The provision of Title 3, like those of Article 18, Act No. 300, does not apply, differently from the rest of the law, to all firms, but only to 'each productive unit' (i.e., plant, office, branch or independent workshop) employing more than 15 workers, in industry, and more than 5 in agriculture. It applies also to smaller units of the same firms located in the same municipality, if the sum of their employees reaches the numbers indicated. Employees have to be understood as any persons engaged by an individual labour contract or apprenticeship contract.

The legislature has judged it unwise to grant the above-mentioned unions' rights in the smallest productive units – where union activity is simple or non-existent. This limitation, which cuts off from the possible benefits of the law a considerable number of workers, given the highly fragmented structure of the Italian economy, has been considered constitutionally legitimate and not unduly discriminatory by the Constitutional Court (1975).

441. Another important limitation was fixed by Article 37, which provides that the norms of Act No. 300 apply to employees of public institutions only to the extent that 'the matter is not regulated otherwise by specific norms'. This has been interpreted as excluding almost completely the applicability of Act No. 300 to public service because special norms regulating the matter otherwise have been found in most sectors of public employment and because, on the other hand, employees of public institutions do not include, according to prevailing courts opinion, state employees. But most principles of Titles 2 and 3 have been progressively extended to public employees (state employees included) by way of collective bargaining and subsequently by Act No. 93 of 1993, Act No. 59 of 1997 and Decree 165/2001. These Acts confirm the applicability of the same principles to all public employees. Article 28 of Act 300 has had for a long time a special regulation and has been made fully applicable only by Act 83/2000 (Article 4) (*see* below paragraphs 444 ff.).

442. Since 1970 the delegates and their councils have been the chief representative bodies operating at the level of the enterprise or establishment, their position as representatives of employees and union and as bargaining agents has been indirectly but clearly supported by the rights and powers granted to them by Act No. 300 of 1970. Delegates' councils, usually with the assistance of external unions, have had almost exclusive competence to handle relations with the employer, through bargaining and in the administration of the collective agreement. The same position has been taken by the new form of representation, RSU, since it has been recognised as the main representative body at local level. This is true not only for the private but also for public sector (Decree 369/1997 and Decree 165/2001). Specialised forms of employee representation at the plant and local level are recognised by the law in the matters of health and safety. Act 81/2008 provides that they be elected by the employees or designated within the RSA and RSU.

The prevailing legislative approach has left little room for any form of joint body (joint committees and the like) including both unions 'and employers' representatives: these forms have been traditionally seen with great diffidence by Italian unions, which have always found unilateral representation and collective bargaining the most effective means of promoting workers' interests and of governing industrial relations. In recent years a change of attitude has been reported (*see* Chapter 5).

§2. Repression of Employers' Anti-union Activity

443. A key provision enforcing the principles of Title 3 of Act No. 300, and, more generally, all the norms protecting trade union freedom and activity, is Article 28. This article provides that 'whenever the employer indulges in behaviour designed to deny or to limit the exercise of trade union freedom and union activity, as well as the right to strike, the local organs of the national trade unions interested can demand that the *pretore* (judge of first instance) of the place where the act has been carried out issue an order to cease from the behaviour and to cancel its effects. The *pretore*, now the Tribunale, must convene the parties within two days (the term is not compulsory and is in fact not respected) and acquire basic information; his decision (decree) is immediately effective and can be opposed by resorting to the same Tribunal (the same jurisdiction but not the same person), but remains effective until the Tribunal's decision. The employer who does not obey the order issued by the judge is punished according to Article 650 of the Penal Code (imprisonment up to three months or a fine up to 206 euro).'

444. Article 28 has been the most widely used provision of Act No. 300: there were thousands of cases particularly in the first period (subsequently the number has decreased). The unions have resorted to it in order to question the lawfulness of a wide range of employers' actions suspected of limiting their activity and workers' freedom, most frequently when they were too weak to counteract the employers' illegal behaviour by direct action, but also in cases of intense industrial conflict, as further support for collective pressure. This frequent use of the law has marked a change of attitude both by the unions, traditionally very reluctant in Italy, and sceptical towards judicial intervention in collective labour relations, and by the courts, which have been called to decide the most delicate aspects of employer-union relations, an area until that time quite beyond their knowledge. Recently Article 28 has been often used by unions to exclude from collective negotiations or dissent from agreements concluded between employers and other unions.

445. Some reasons for this success can be found within the norm itself and its fundamental characteristics: the rapidity of the proceedings (the average length ranges from one to two months, an unprecedented record with respect to the traditional slowness of Italian labour courts); the right of action given directly to the unions (the individual worker affected by discrimination being easily dissuaded from suing the employer for obvious reasons); the penal sanction for non-compliance with the judge's order (a sanction new in Italian law, aimed at enforcing indirectly employer's behaviour, which could not be a ready object of specific performance, according to the general rules of civil procedure); the broad definition of anti-union activity, similar to that of Article 15, which covers all sorts of acts in fact capable of limiting workers' and unions' rights (these acts cannot in fact be predetermined analytically).

446. The prevailing opinion, endorsed by the Supreme Court, has held Article 28 applicable not only in cases of employers' conduct attacking the unions directly and violating their rights or powers recognised by specific provisions of Act No.

300, e.g., refusal of meetings within the firm called following the conditions of Article 20, transfers of union leaders without the *nihil obstat* of Article 22, etc., but also in cases of reprisal measures taken immediately against individual workers, whenever they strike indirectly at the rights of the unions and prejudice their position within the firm, e.g., dismissals, transfers or other discriminatory acts against workers because of their union militancy.

It is relevant, on the other hand, that such dismissals, transfers or other acts are considered elsewhere, in particular by Articles 15 and 18 of the same Act No. 300, which empower the worker dismissed, transferred or discriminated against, to take individual action. Such discriminatory acts violate both individual and collective rights (they are unlawful in both respects) and it is therefore understandable that the system provides two distinct corrective steps to protect each of them: Article 28 may be (and often has been) used by the union to defend its rights as an autonomous entity independently of steps taken by the aggrieved worker (under Article 15 or 18).

It has been controversial whether Article 28 can be used in case of violation of union rights deriving not by the law but by collective agreements. Act 146/1990, regulating strikes in essential services, has resolved the issue positively, but only in case of violation falling within the scope of the Act agreements with an employer exercising executive service). This partial legislative indication should support a positive answer to the issue in general.

A special case of unfair practice is provided by Act 428/1990 (Article 47) and Act 18/2001 which declares Article 28 applicable in case of violation of information procedures concerning the transfer of enterprises.

447. In public service, Act 29/1993 – settling a long-lasting legal controversy – makes Article 28 applicable in case of violation of union rights in a strict sense; violations of individual rights (*see* above paragraph 388) remain justifiable before administrative tribunals (like all public service cases) even though with a special accelerated procedure. But this distinction has been temporary: Article 4 of Act 83/2000 and Act 165/2001 provide that unfair labour practices fall under the same jurisdiction of civil courts, like all private employment disputes.

According to the majority opinion the employer has no duty to bargain with the unions, but the decision of the Constitutional Court 231/2013 may be interpreted to imply that the employer cannot refuse to admit to the bargaining table representative unions as defined by the law. Moreover the courts have considered it an unfair practice to bargain directly with the employees or with non-union representatives; some decisions, but not all, have also considered it unfair to discriminate among the various unions. However, the employers can legitimately apply agreements concluded only with some unions to all employees, including members of the dissenting unions.

448. The only condition set by Article 28 is that the union has to prove that the employer's behaviour under the circumstances affects union rights and powers. There is no need to prove positive intention to violate union rights or bad faith: the employer has to prove that he had a justifiable reason legitimating his behaviour (e.g., just cause for dismissals). In fact, the burden of proof on the unions has not been so difficult to meet as expected from past experience, because courts have made wide use of de facto presumptions.

449. The constitutional legitimacy of Article 28 has been questioned on two main grounds: because it grants the right to sue only to national unions (and not to other unions or collective groups, nor to the individual aggrieved workers); and because it forbids any act of the employer against the right to strike, without stating the limits of lawful strike. The Constitutional Court, however, rejected both objections in 1974 (and subsequently in 1988 and 1995): the first for much the same reason given for the rejection of objections to Article 19, i.e., because it is reasonable, and not unjustly discriminatory, to recognise the most effective action provided for by Article 28 only to the established and nationally representative union (and because the aggrieved worker is, in any case, free to bring ordinary action under Articles 15 and 18 of Act No. 300). The second objection has been rejected by denying the assumption on which it stands, i.e., stating that strike action is protected against employers' reprisals only if within the limits derived from a long-established interpretation by the courts of the notion of a legal strike.

Chapter 4. Collective Bargaining

§1. Historical Evolution of Collective Bargaining

450. Collective bargaining is the cardinal element in the administration of industrial relations and the main source of regulation of the employment relationship. This fundamental role of collective bargaining with respect to other means of regulating industrial relations, including legislation, has been affirmed for a long time by Italian unions, and to some extent by employers, but has become effective only in the process of time. Collective bargaining scope, structure and procedures have been evolving radically since World War II, due to many economic, political and ideological factors.

451. In the late 1940s and early 1950s, virtually all sectors of the economy and all branches of industry were covered by national collective agreements, one for each 'occupational category'; negotiated by the trade unions, which generally all signed the same agreements, and the employers' associations. A major role, however, was played by the so-called interconfederal agreement, a type of agreement unknown in many countries, which aims at the uniform regulation of given institutions in one whole sector of the economy (industry, agriculture, services, public service). Provincial agreements were very rare, concluded for a limited range of questions of minor importance, mainly in the building and mining industry. Company or plant bargaining was practically non-existent, due to the absence of unions at that level, although some questions concerning working conditions in the enterprise were informally negotiated by works committees.

452. The resulting bargaining system was highly centralised, parallel to a more general trend in Italy, surviving from the past, whereby all decisions on major aspects of public life were characterised by centralisation. Interconfederal agreements regulated all matters of major importance: the regional differences in the minimum wage, the 'sliding scale' mechanism (namely the automatic adjustment of wages to changes in the cost of living), works committees, collective and individual dismissals and up to 1954 went so far as to fix wage rates in industry (later on these began to be bargained at the level of each branch of industry). Moreover, industry-wide bargaining was coordinated and controlled by the confederations.

453. Finally, due to the relative weakness of the national unions in that period, national agreements were reviewed only at long intervals and had little effect in ameliorating working conditions, e.g., the average wage increases guaranteed to industrial workers during the 1950s by the sliding scale mechanism have been higher than those acquired through national industry-wide bargaining.

454. Industry-wide bargaining acquired growing importance between 1954 and 1960–1962, though remaining on the whole rather static (wage increases being much lower than productivity increases). It often covered – as in the case of the metalwork industry – an extremely wide field. For this reason it proved incapable of meeting the substantial technical and economic differences between the various sectors, and even more so between the various enterprises concerned, limiting itself to fixing minimum wage rates and conditions of work, not real ones, much in the same way as the law might do. A basic principle inherent in this system of national bargaining was the exclusion of negotiations at lower levels. This did not imply that individual employers could not unilaterally offer their staff better conditions. In fact, they took ample advantage of the possibility to do so: wage drift became very high in the 1950s, due to the progressive drying up of the labour supply.

455. The centralised system was quite acceptable to the employers because it allowed their associations tight control on bargaining activities and freed the simple employer from direct contact with the unions, while giving him ample leeway to influence his employees outside union channels. On the union side, it corresponded to the – initially well-founded – need to unite scarce forces in order to guarantee uniform minimum conditions of work to an impoverished, fragmented and still mostly agricultural working class, privileging the weak sectors thereof with respect to the elite. But with the passage of time this choice proved less and less rewarding for organised labour; it caused the confederations (all of them) to lose influence rapidly with the elite and in general the growing industrial population, while not enabling them to guarantee a satisfactory defence of the underprivileged.

456. Major changes of direction began to occur in the late 1950s, which marked a transition from exclusive national bargaining to a new system, called ‘articulated bargaining’, and introduced formally by a series of agreements in 1962–1963. This transition was spurred on by various factors. The accelerated economic and occupational growth bettered the unions’ position in the labour market, and relieved the workers from the long-lasting fear of unemployment, increasing their inclination and capacity to strike. The parallel technological renovation of Italian industry profoundly altered the basic conditions of employment (incentives, job classification, etc.) in different ways according to various sectors and firms, causing many clauses of national agreements to fall into obsolescence.

457. Finally, there was a growing acceptance, by the major enterprises, of collective bargaining as an essential means of stabilising industrial relations vis-à-vis the social and economic tensions of the period. This new attitude, was promoted particularly by state-owned or controlled enterprises, which disaffiliated in that period from the associations with private industry, following a directive from the government.

458. The need for change was felt, although with some delay, by the major confederations and their affiliated industrial unions; first, by CISL and UIL, more sensitive to the problems of industrial society and exposed to the free bargaining philosophy imported from other Western countries, but then also by CGIL, which, abandoning a too dogmatic and ‘political’ approach to industrial relations, came to see the advantages of the new method of bargaining for keeping up with the rhythm of the industrial evolution and getting growing power within the ‘capitalist system’.

459. The formal recognition of 'articulated' bargaining came with the 'protocol' agreement of 5 July 1962, on bargaining levels and procedures in the metalwork industry, signed with the organisations of state-controlled undertakings, under the auspices of the Ministry of Labour for the first time actively intervening in the dispute with a pro-labour attitude. This protocol served as a model for private employers and was later extended to virtually all branches of industry.

460. The basic feature of the model was to sanction a bargaining system rather peculiar to Italian industrial relations, based on different levels coordinated through a more or less precise distribution of competence. The national industry-wide agreements, were the barycentre of the system setting the general conditions of work for the various sectors of the industry (in the metal work industry there were six).

Plant-level bargaining was strictly dependent and had to conform to the principles set in the national agreement. It is required to fix, beyond the matters delegated to lower levels, the procedure to be followed, the bargaining agents (which are the provincial unions, not the unions' plant locals, and the provincial employers' associations) and, in the case of productivity bonuses, the date of the negotiation and the maximum and minimum amounts. In exchange for the legitimisation of decentralised bargaining, the employers received on the side of the union a commitment, written in the national agreement, not to strike for the time and over the questions covered by the agreement.

§2. The Structure of Collective Bargaining During the 1960s and the 1970s

461. The model of bargaining structure inaugurated in 1962–1963, while opening up new possibilities for union action at the plant level, was clearly preoccupied with controlling and limiting bargaining decentralisation. This control functioned in the short run but became more difficult in subsequent times.

The wave of strikes of 1968–1969, spurred by a labour market newly favourable to labour and led by a revived working class, sanctioned the end of articulated bargaining. In the major industrial agreements signed in 1969, the unions refused to renew the no-strike clauses and the tight distribution of competence which characterised the agreements of 1962.

462. The main consequence of this was, and has been until 1993 (paragraph 416) for most industrial categories, that bargaining can develop free from any contractual limitation: i.e., any matter can be bargained at any level and at any time; at the shop level even matters already dealt with in the national agreement can be negotiated. Coordination between the different levels of bargaining and industrial peace for the duration of the (various) agreements were not guaranteed by any bilateral obligation, but rested on opportunist judgments made by the bargaining agents themselves (and on the capacity of the central organisation to control decentralised initiatives). This bargaining structure reflected the relatively low level of institutionalisation of collective labour relations in Italy.

463. Since 1969, in fact, there has been an unprecedented development in bargaining, especially at the plant and company level; agreements at this level are counted in the thousands every year, and are accompanied by a close network of informal bargaining down to the single shop or department. Plant- or company-wide bargaining is no longer merely integrative with respect to national agreements, but often anticipates results which are generalised later by the latter. This has been the case for many of the major innovations in bargaining matters, i.e., the trend towards equality of treatment between blue- and white-collar workers, the new system of workers' classification, and some union rights (later recognised also by Act No. 300 of 1970).

464. In spite of the growth of plant bargaining, national agreements have continued to maintain their important role, providing a uniform platform of treatment for all employees of the sector in question, most relevant to the high number of small and very small firms, which make up the Italian industrial structure, where plant bargaining is less widespread and effective. The reduced effectiveness of plant bargaining in small firms accounts for the persistent wage differentials between employees of enterprises of different dimensions.

465. The change of bargaining structure described above has been accompanied by a similar innovation in bargaining practice and results. Wage increases agreed upon at national and plant levels have become conspicuous since 1969 and, in a few years, have brought average Italian industrial salaries close to European levels. They have been equal for all employees, regardless of their job and basic wage rates (whereas up to 1969 they were in a percentage relationship with the basic wages). This egalitarian policy of Italian unions caused a relative reduction in wage differentials between jobs, traditionally rather high in Italy. After 1984 they started to reopen.

466. The scope of bargaining, again mainly under the impulse of enterprise bargaining, has been extended from merely economic matters to potentially all aspects of labour relations, which can in fact be appropriately dealt with only within the undertaking: organisation of work, content of jobs, workloads, sub-contracting, control of overtime and, more recently, information and control of management investment policies.

§3. Trends Towards Centralisation (1975–1984)

467. In this period the dynamics of collective bargaining, especially of wage increases, posed dramatically the problem of the competitiveness of the Italian economy.

468. The attempts to rebuild some forms of tangible coordination between the three levels of bargaining (through no-strike clauses or similar obligatory clauses) have been of uneven effectiveness due to stubborn union resistance. But a tendency emerged towards the centralisation of bargaining, not so much through formal clauses as through de facto concentration of the major powers of decision at the confederal level.

469. At the inter-confederal level matters such as the following have been regulated since the mid-1970s: the guarantee of wages to workers in case of lay-off or reduction of working hours for economic reasons (agreed upon in 1974 and then converted into law: *see* above paragraphs 202 ff.), the functioning of the 'sliding scale' mechanism, which was considerably strengthened (in 1975), so as to guarantee an automatic wage increased nearly equal to the cost of living increases, particularly for low-paid workers.

470. Even though the unions have repeatedly refused to set formally a maximum to wage bargaining at the plant level (as proposed by employers and the government), wage claims have become more strictly controlled than in the past and are lower than the automatic wage increases due to the sliding scale. In fact, the emphasis of both national and plant bargaining since the mid-1970s has been in part shifting away from economic goals (wage increases) to the so-called qualitative objectives (conditions of work and quality of life, work organisation, labour mobility, organisational guarantees, etc.). The trend towards recentralisation of bargaining and towards a more moderate evolution of labour costs – to keep them in line with the European average – has been favoured by the government (*see* below paragraphs 415 ff.).

471. The most significant examples of the growing initiative of the confederations are the framework agreements which have succeeded one after the other between 1977 and 1984. First there was the agreement of 26 January 1977, which aimed at revising the structure of wages, cutting down the indirect element of labour costs, exceptionally high in Italy (in particular automatic wage increases due to seniority, and seniority allowances), at correcting the abnormal effects of the sliding scale mechanisms in force in some sectors, so as to bring them in line with the general interconfederal agreement of 1975, at favouring better and more flexible organisation of work.

472. This effort was in part successful insofar as it helped to control inflation (this had reached a peak of nearly 20% in 1977 and subsequently slowed down to 15%) by reducing wage indexation and stabilising economic and social relations in the short run. But it came to an end fairly soon for two basic reasons: the benefits expected by the parties, in particular the trade unions, did not completely materialise (unemployment kept growing: 8% in 1979, 9% in 1982). The Communist party, excluded from the National Unity government, ceased its support to the policy of social agreement, thereby influencing the CGIL in the same direction and weakening the trust of other unions in the 'political trade-off' which is usually implied in social pacts of this kind.

473. After a long period of impasse a wide-ranging agreement was signed on 22 January 1983, this time with the formal participation of the executive. The unions accepted a slowing down of indexation (18%: paragraph 158), a maximum wage ceiling for the next national bargaining round, plus an 18-month wage freeze on plant bargaining (which they had never done before) and, lastly, control on the same level of bargaining with the prohibition of renegotiating issues already defined at the national level and the promise to provide for more formal grievance procedures (possibly including arbitration) directed at preventing microconflicts. These concessions were compensated by the state with fiscal benefits plus family allowance increases; with a series of measures envisaged to promote youth employment, to enhance union participation in labour market policies and to promote workers' participation in capital raising through a Solidarity Fund (*see* paragraph 489). The employers agreed to start negotiations on the major national agreements – which they had blocked for over a year. In exchange the state renewed social security benefit reductions and the union ensured greater labour flexibility, better control of industrial conflict, plant bargaining and absenteeism. The government committed itself to implement a series of legislative measures, indicated above, and to hold tariffs and administered prices within limits compatible with the maximum caps of inflation envisaged in the agreement: 13% in 1983, 10% in 1984, 7% in 1985.

474. This agreement was signed in a direction similar to that pursued by other countries, particularly of central and northern Europe. In fact, many observers pointed out that it was showing some characteristics of concerted economy or of 'neocorporatist' systems: centralisation of industrial relations, tripartite agreement with an active government role and marginalisation of Parliament; union involvement in economic decisions, especially regarding policy; growing institutionalisation and proceduralisation of collective relations.

For a period of time the agreement helped to contain the instability of industrial relations. But its greatest effect was to 'fiscalise' the social conflict, i.e., to reduce its effects at the public expense, while the ambitious project to reform the fundamental traits of industrial relations through concerted stabilisation policies did not make substantial progress.

475. Reactions of the major confederations to this 'deal' were mixed: the Communists of CGIL refused to accept the package; the other two confederations – CISL and UIL – plus the socialist minority of CGIL, accepted it. Lacking consensus of all the unions, the socialist led Craxi government issued a series of decrees containing some of the main points of the agreement accepted by CISL and UIL and all the employers' associations: maximum ceiling on indexation for six months (*see* paragraph 195); further liberalisation of hiring (paragraphs 131 ff.); confirmed support to work-training contracts (paragraphs 116 ff.); the so-called solidarity contracts (paragraphs 241); framework regulation of part-time working (paragraphs 101 ff.). The troublesome events of 1984–1985 confirmed difficulties in implementing corporatist solutions or concerted stabilisation policies in Italy.

§4. Bipolarism and Stabilisation: The Social Pact of 1993

476. Since the mid-1980s, the trends have been again ambivalent and exposed to contrasting pressures.

Strong pressure first came on decentralisation of bargaining. Decentralisation reflects a general economic trend, encouraged by the new technologies with flexible forms of production. It often appeared to be stimulated by initiatives on the part of the employers, the opposite of what happened during the years 1968–1975. Also in this respect, however, the trend towards decentralisation has always been controlled by the centre. Even the employers' associations have recognised the persisting importance of the national collective agreement as an element of stability for the system.

477. An important contribution to the coordination of the bargaining system came from the tripartite agreement of 23 July 1993 – a major step in the Italian experience of social pacts. The parts of the 1993 agreement which are explicitly devoted to collective bargaining include the following provisions: the rate of increase in nominal wages is to be determined through periodic tripartite consultations and must be consistent with the government's macroeconomic predictions as stated in its yearly budget and in line with anticipated inflation. The structure of collective bargaining is modified so that those clauses of the national collective agreements that govern hiring and firing practices, job classifications, career trajectories, etc., are to be negotiated every four years, whereas wage clauses will be renewed every two years.

Bargaining will take place at both the industry and company (or territorial, in the case of small companies) levels. However, company and territorial bargaining can take place (every four years) only on issues not already regulated by the national contract. Moreover, wage increases deriving from company-level bargaining are to be financed through productivity increases or performance improvements – i.e., exclusively measured after these criteria.

Finally, the agreement of July 1993 contains provisions for a comprehensive reform of the unions' plant-level organisational structures (the so-called *rappresentanze sindacali unitarie RSU*) aimed at relaunching internal democracy and grass-roots participation (*see* above paragraph 345). Bargaining power at decentralised company level are recognised to new unions structures (RSU) jointly with the territorial unions. The aim is twofold: to make the agents responsive to the members but, at the same time, to keep them under the control of union officers, responsive in turn to the national unions, and consequently to the national level of bargaining. It is important to notice that this bargaining, according to the July agreements, is applicable not only to the private sector but also to the public service (where centrifugal pressures are traditionally high and have caused in the past abrupt and uncontrolled wage dispersion).

The regulations agreed upon in July 1993 have succeeded in stablising for the first time the Italian bargaining system. The following national bargaining rounds (1994, 1996, 2001) respected the directive of the accord by keeping wage increases – for the first biennium –within the limits of planned inflation (3.5% in 1994 – 2.5% in 1996 – 2.0% in 1997). Company-wide bargaining, even though it has not been so closely linked to productivity as was indicated in the pact of 1993, has been restricted for the same period to issues not covered by national bargaining.

§5. Collective Bargaining in the Years 2000: More Decentralisation?

478. The stabilisation of industrial relations promoted by the 1993 agreement has been exceptional in the Italian history; and short-lived because it was soon, again exposed to tensions. Some tension are of political origin and come from the relationship between the centre-right government, in power from 2001 to 2006 and from 2008 to 2011, and the unions, particularly the leftist confederation CGIL.

But pressures come also from the changing economic conditions, in particular from increased global competition and the economic crisis began in 2008. This has created serious difficulties for the Italian economy which is less and less protected by institutional factors, such as a competitive use of devaluation of the currency, which is no longer possible within the EU.

The major trend of the collective bargaining system has been towards decentralisation. Employers took the lead in requesting greater decentralisation of the collective bargaining structure than that agreed in 1993. The aim was to acquire more flexibility in wages and in work organisation at the enterprise level. The unions' reactions have been different. While CGIL refused to introduce major changes in the existing bargaining structure, CISL and UIL agreed on the need to give greater importance to decentralised bargaining; but they too claimed that the change should not alter the role of national collective agreements in setting minimum standards, particularly for the employees of small firms which are the majority of the Italian economy.

On the other hand the same unions argued that a greater importance could be recognised for enterprise bargaining only on the condition that this bargaining be promoted and extended by public powers; now it operates only in a minority of Italian firms while in small firms union representatives are usually absent. According to the same unions territorial bargaining should be promoted in the areas characterised by a majority of small firms where enterprise bargaining is impracticable.

479. Attempts by the social parties to agree on a reform of the collective bargaining system have been reiterated in recent years. A framework agreement was reached on 22 January 2009 among all the employers' associations and CISL, UIL, UGL in spite of the dissenting opinion of CGIL. New agreements have been signed, this time also by CGIL, on 28 June 2011, specified in 31 May 2013 in 10 January 2014, and lately in 9 March 2018.

The national agreements maintain the central role of setting standards common to all the employees of a given sector, but a greater importance is recognised for decentralised bargaining. This trend has been favoured by the legislator: directly by Article 8 of Act 148, 2011, which empowers decentralised agreements to derogate in a wide range of issues to national agreements, and also to legal norms; and indirectly by Article 51 of Decree 81/2016 (below paragraph 483).

480. An innovation concerns the criteria to determine wage increases. Instead of corresponding to the anticipated rate of inflation (as in 1993) the 2009 agreement provides that they should follow a provisional index based on consumer prices as harmonised at the European level, minus imported energy prices. The index will be defined by an independent body and last for four years. Divergences between the provisional and the actual inflation will be ascertained bilaterally at confederal level. This innovation is meant to give a more certain basis to wage negotiations, since the old criteria were too subject to political influence.

The parties agree to reduce the number of national agreements, which has progressively grown (over 400 agreements) at this time, and lately over 800, calculated by the archives of National Council for Economy and Labour (CNEL). Furthermore the accord of January 2009, followed by the agreements of May 2013 and 10 January 2014, states that decentralised bargaining may concern only the matters delegated by the national level or by the law with elsewhere, according to the principle *ne bis in idem* (not twice on the same issue). Wages must be calculated exclusively on the basis of actual performances and of the results of the interested units.

These provisions are intended to specify and strengthen a rule which was already present in the 1993 social pact, but which was widely derogated in two directions: (1) the wages negotiated at decentralised level were scarcely connected with productivity and tended to simply increase the national remuneration. (2) national bargaining went beyond the official role to protect wages from inflation and tried to 'capture' also part of productivity gains – whatever they were in each sector. The argument of the unions was that decentralised bargaining was possible only in a minority of enterprises, 25%–30% according to the sectors and areas. In order to meet this argument the parties agree that wage increases, in the form of lump sum may be negotiated to compensate employees, mainly in small firms, who do not receive any remuneration beyond that granted by national bargaining. The diffusion of decentralised bargaining was to be favoured by initiative of the parties and by public incentives, reduction of taxes and social security contributions on wages.

481. On the other hand this level of bargaining is allowed to modify the economic and normative condition agreed upon nationally in cases of economic crisis or in order to promote new economic initiatives. This is another innovation with respect to the traditional rule whereby decentralised agreements could only improve the terms bargained nationally: and is intended to be another incentive to the diffusion of these agreements.

The interconfederal agreements of 28 June 2011, this time signed by the major unions' confederations, including CGIL, confirmed the rule that decentralised bargaining can modify national agreements within the limits and the procedures fixed by the same agreement. In any case union plant representatives can conclude agreements modifying the content of national agreements in the following matters: worktime, work organisation and work execution (a rather wide term).

The agreement of 10 January 2014, assembling previous regulations, reaffirms this relationship between national and decentralised bargaining and provides that company-wide agreements signed according to its rules by the plant representativeness are binding for all the signatory parties (similar rules are fixed in the agreement of 16 November 2015, for the commerce and tertiary sectors).

These agreements confirm the intention of the social parties to favour bargaining decentralisation but to keep it under central control. Such a control is legally weak, because, according to the courts, decentralised agreements are valid also if concluded beyond the limits stated by central agreements. Its practical effectiveness will depend on the capacity of central unions to guarantee respect for the limits by their local affiliates.

482. The legislator has not intervened directly in regulating the structure of collective bargaining, which is considered a matter for the social parties. But Article 51 Decree 81/2015 has indirectly influenced the question by providing that when the legislator delegates to collective agreements powers to regulated some matters these powers may be exercised by both national and company-wide agreements. This rule recognises to decentralised agreements the same legal status as that of national agreement and consequently also the power to derogate to the conditions bargained nationally.

483. The unions' request to have recognised a territorial level of bargaining has not been accepted by the employers. The accord of January 2009, and the further specification in the agreements of 2013 and 2014, indicate more certain procedures for the renewal of the agreements, to be held every three years (*see* below) and for the settlement of disputes concerning the implementation of the accord (via conciliation and arbitration). The agreements also commit the parties to refrain from conflict during these procedures and specify that the national contracts will indicate the sanctions for behaviours contrary to the implementation of the contract.

The agreements of June 2011, May 2013, and January 2014 have provided that the agreements containing no strike clauses, are binding only for the union representatives belonging to the parties signatory to the agreement and not for the individual employees, thereby refusing judicial opinions on the issue (*see* below).

It is worth notice that national bargaining rounds in the fallowing years have by and large respected the guidelines agreed upon in 2009 with some adaptation, particularly on wage increases; and the final agreements, have been signed also by the unions adhering to CGIL. The low inflation of recent years has reduced the impact of the rules present in many national agreements which linked the periodic wage increases to the consumer price index. The link however is never automatic but subject to ex ante or ex post verification.

Some innovations have been introduced by the national agreements for the metalworking industry of November 2016 and of February 2021. The wage increases agreed at firm level are 'absorbed' by the subsequent national wages increases while previously they were always granted to all employees covered by the agreement and consequently summed up to the national wages.

The innovation aims at reducing the burden on national bargaining rounds and to leave more room to decentralised agreements. Moreover these metalworking agreements have reduced the increase in monetary wages, and compensated with a contribution of the firms to supplementary health insurance, and with the right of employees to a number of hours for personal education and training.

The rapid increase of inflation in 2021—2022 linked to international tensions and the energy crisis has contributed to greatly reduce, both the income of the population and the real wages of workers, whose dynamics in recent years has been rather low.Italian trade unions, recalling past experiences of the effects of wage – prices spiral, have so far adopted a policy of wage moderation.

Recent provisions of the government, lately the budget law for 2023 (Act 97/2022), have reduced social security contributions on wages, with the aim of increasing the net take home pay.

But the pressure of the unions is growing to agree on some system of wage indexation more protective than the present which links wages to the cost of living, excluding the impact of imported goods (which now influence great part of the inflation).

§6. Collective Bargaining and Public Powers

484. While up to the 1960s the Italian collective bargaining system developed, by and large, free from state intervention, the following decades have shown signs of a more active role of public powers. The changing orientation of different Italian governments which have been in office in the years has not contributed to the consistency of labour policies.

485. A major example of a supportive attitude of the legislature towards union activity is the Statute of Workers' Rights of 1970.

Secondly, beginning with the renewal of the main national agreements of 1969, mediation by the Ministry of Labour has been of growing and sometimes decisive importance for the solution of major labour disputes. Increasing initiative has also been taken by the peripheral offices of the Ministry (regional and provincial labour offices), and, in some cases, by regional governments. Public mediation has abandoned the traditionally (and officially) neutral approach of the 1960s. During the 1970s it has pursued the same goal as Act No. 300, i.e., to promote trade unions as bargaining agents at all levels. More recently it has taken a more balanced position.

At the same time the role of the Labour Ministry in the pursuance of public interest has grown, e.g., it was decisive in promoting the 1983–1984 trilateral bargaining rounds and in social agreements of the following decades (1993, 1996, 2002, 2007). The impact and the direction of ministerial interventions vary according to the political coalitions governing the country.

A major weakness of ministerial mediation is that it operates informally, lacking precise legal regulations or any consistent policy to coordinate the various interventions between them and the general public labour policy of the government. The central and peripheral organisations of the Ministry of Labour, furthermore, are hardly equipped with technical staff capable of meeting the growing need for mediatory intervention; and nor are the offices of the regions.

486. Between 1976 and 1984 growing economic difficulties, inflation and heavy increases in labour costs caused an unprecedent government intervention to restrict collective bargaining, through certain anti-inflation measures, in part similar to those enacted in other countries. An initial and temporary measure (Act No. 699/1976) aimed at reducing the effectiveness of the sliding scale mechanism, by imposing a partial forced saving of sliding scale increases, which were to be paid not in cash but in public certificates of credit.

487. A second measure, Act No. 91 of 31 March 1977, intervened in two major directions: first, by subtracting the seniority allowance from the influence of the cost of living increases (*see* above paragraph 258); secondly, by stating that no wage increase dependent on the cost of living could be calculated in terms which were more favourable to the workers than those fixed by the sliding scale mechanism agreed upon for the industrial sector (*see* paragraph 414). Both these interventions represented an exceptional deviation from the tradition of the Italian labour law insofar as they set maximum limits to the bargaining capacities of the collective parties. Up to then the basic principles had been that legal norms could always be improved in favour of workers by collective agreements. Some doubts have been raised that the provisions of Act No. 91 go against the constitutional principles of Article 39 (freedom of collective bargaining), Article 36 (sufficient and proportionate wage), Article 3 (equality of treatment). But the Constitutional Court rejected all these constitutional objections (Decision No. 142 of 1980, No. 697 of 1988; and partially different No. 124 of 1991).

488. A further government intervention in collective bargaining occurred in 1984 following the breakdown in tripartite negotiations. The deviation from traditional 'abstentionism' was much greater since the 1984 decree did not have the full consensus of the labour movement (as it did in 1977), and it impinged directly on a major object of bargaining such as wage indexation. For these reasons the decrees have not only been bitterly opposed in Parliament by the Communist party but they have also been attacked on constitutional grounds. This time the strongest argument was infringement of collective freedom of action (Article 39) due to the lack of unanimous union consensus in the government decision. Here again the Constitutional Court rejected all the objections (Decision 34 of 1985).

489. In the same period the confederations played an important role, fully recognised by the Constitutional Court, as political counterparts to the government, to some extent replacing the too cautious initiatives of the political parties. They put long-term pressure on the government to obtain certain social reforms, of which the country was badly in need: the public health system, better public housing programmes, public transportation, school reform, a public policy for the development of southern Italy, so as to redress the most serious imbalance in Italian society, etc.. But the results of this political bargaining with the public powers have been uneven, and variable overtime.

490. During the 1980s the wave of 'liberalism', the growing international competition and the consequent need to increase the efficiency and flexibility have influenced also the system of industrial relations. These elements have spurred quite a few elements of deregulation and have favoured decentralisation of the bargaining structure.

The 'regulatory' role of the state in labour matters has been gradually reducedits importance as an authoritative partner in the government of industrial relations. This role has become more difficult to play, for the same reasons which make more difficult the attempts to regulate centrally labour relations in the post-industrial or 'service' society. Some of these difficulties are common to most advanced countries. They are tied to the economic crisis and hence to the reduced resources for distribution among the social parties by the state; to the growing international competitiveness which reduces the margins of manoeuvrability of national states in stabilising industrial relations, irrespective of government political orientation. They are enhanced by the differentiation in the social composition of the labour force in technologically advanced societies, which increases the competition among different, often small and variable, groups and reduces union representative and control power.

Other obstacles lie in the Italian political and institutional system: the instability of public powers, due to the frequent changes in government coalition and policies, an inefficient public administration unable to implement the policies bargained among the social parties; and the recurrent tensions among political parties which has continued, although in a different way, after the collapse of the Christian Democrat and Socialist parties on the one side, and the transformation of the Communist party into a social democratic party on the other.

491. In spite of these difficulties the search for some sort of concertation, throughout the 1990s, and in recent years has continued. The practice of concertation has been successful in producing a series of tripartite social pacts: even though the nature and content of these pacts a major result of social concertation has been the tripartite agreement of 1993, which contains a wide range of reform commitments (*see* above paragraph 450): abolition of the escalator clause (*see* above), rationalisation and privatisation of public service employment relations, a first reform of the pension system, a tax reform aimed at eliminating various inequalities and reducing tax evasion, procedure directed to stabilise labour relations and to regulate the bargaining structure. In exchange for wage moderation, the accord institutionalised the participation of unions to periodic consultation about all major issues of labour policies and vocational training. Another important social accord was signed in 1996, which has been largely transferred in Act 196 of 1997 reforming labour market regulations, and one in December 1998, which, however, remained largely on paper due to the subsequent political crisis of the centre-left government.

The coming to power of the centre-right government in 2001 has made more difficult the relations with the unions, in particular with the left wing confederation CGIL. The government declared that it was unwilling to follow the previous practice of concertation, which was considered to be too dependent on the search for unanimous consensus (particularly hard to find with CGIL). Consequently it has proceeded to what it called 'social dialogue' with the aim of reducing the length of consultations and of looking for agreement with those 'willing to agree'. In practice this decision has led to a series of separate agreements only with CISL, UIL, UGL while CGIL took a negative attitude, arguing that the government proposals were totally unacceptable.

492. A social pact was signed in July 2002 by government with these unions, without CGIL, and with the employers' associations. The main contents were: a commitment – largely implemented in Act 30 of 2003 – to introduce new regulations on atypical contracts and to increase labour market flexibility, including a tentative liberalisation of the law on individual dismissals (Article 18 of the Workers Statute: *see* above); the promise to reform the law on salary integration to increase unemployment benefits and to reinforce the measures for promoting employment and economic growth, particularly in the depressed areas of the country.

The coming to power of a centre-left government in 2006, prompted a return to the practice of 'unitary' concertation which led to a new agreement signed by all the major confederations, including CGIL. This agreement is mainly directed to redress some controversial measures approved by the preceding government on labour flexibility, and on retirement age while confirming the commitment to reform employment benefits and to promote employment and economic growth.

The following centre-right government faced the same tensions with the unions, particularly with CGIL, experienced in the past.

The adoption of sheer liberalisation policies, against union consensus, has proved difficult for the centre-right government, due to the strong opposition both of the labour movement and of the centre-left parties (but also due to the divisions internal to the centre-right coalition).

In 2011–2012 the 'technical' government led by Mario Monti, former EU commissioner, has not followed the traditional concertation procedures, and has adopted mainly informal consultation and social dialogue in the shaping of major reforms, such as that of old age pensions, and of the labour market (*see* above). The subsequent government, led by Enrico Letta, based on a grand coalition, between the two major parties, exceptional in the Italian tradition, adopted the same line of action as that of its predecessor. The premier Matteo Renzi who has been in office between 2013 and 2016, has repeatedly expressed the view that the labour reforms should be neither restrained by unions' opposition nor slowed down by lengthy concertation procedures. In fact the major reforms of his governments have been passed often disregarding unions' opinion.

The coalition governments of 2018_2019 and 2020 have continued to pay uneven attention to the relations with the social parties, and to involve them in actual concertation on major economic and social policies.

It remains to be seen what will be the policy of the right-wing government which took office in October 2022.

§7. The Legal Status and Procedure of Collective Bargaining

I. Generalities

493. The traditional feature in the Italian bargaining system is its lack of any specific legal provisions for the bargaining procedure, scope and content and, in general, for the conduct of the parties to the negotiation and application of collective agreements, with the exception of provisions of civil law concerning contracts in general. This feature has been only partially changed by recent legislation.

494. A specific regulation is indeed provided for in Article 39 of the Italian Constitution, making collective agreements generally binding. The power to conclude agreements thus effective is reserved by Article 39 for the registered trade unions, provided that they form a 'unitary representative organ', whereby each union is represented proportionally to its membership. The agreement reached through this organ is automatically binding on all employers and employees operating within the scope of the bargaining unit, this being a major difference from the situation in neighbouring countries, such as France and Germany, where collective agreements may be extended through a subsequent act of public authority.

495. The political reasons which prevented the implementation of Article 39 have already been mentioned. In addition to these, other technical difficulties were inherent in the procedure itself. The formation of unitary representative organs presupposes a precise determination of the membership of the various unions, which was not easily attainable in the past; the various proposals submitted in the 1950s designed to solve this problem did not meet with the consent of the trade unions, which, on the one hand, did not trust each other and, on the other hand, were suspicious, as they have always been, of any state control of their internal organisation. This difficulty partly explains why the legislature has progressively shifted from the constitutional project of treating unions, for bargaining purposes, in strict proportion to their membership, to the idea of granting privileges, not directly in bargaining but indirectly in collective action, to all the most representative unions. This notion of representativeness can, in fact, be defined in a simpler, although more approximate, way, through a set of mainly external indicators, without interfering directly in internal union affairs.

496. A further difficulty would have been to determine, by an act of authority, the exact scope of the bargaining unit, thereby again interfering with the freedom of the union to organise. The definition of the bargaining unit must be necessarily authoritative and observed by all collective agents, if collective agreements are to be 'generally' binding, while it can be left to the social partners themselves, if the agreements bind only the affiliated members, as they still do at present.

497. The lack of any legal provision for collective bargaining has become a major characteristic of Italian industrial relations, as the pressure to implement Article 39 of the Constitution has declined. While originally it stemmed rather from a number of inertia factors, or from mainly tactical motives, it has come with the passage of time to be recognised by the trade unions, and to a large extent by management and the public authorities, as the most suitable means of promoting effective bargaining and improved relations between social partners. This is an attitude which marks a drastic transformation in a country where the prevalent traditions and ideologies favoured the establishment of union action within a well-defined legal framework.

498. Free from legal schemes and regulations, collective bargaining has been able to adapt to the radical changes in economic and technological conditions which have come about in the post-war period. In particular, the non-implementation of the rigid procedure provided for by Article 39, modelled exclusively on national bargaining and chiefly concerned with the extension of collective agreements, has facilitated the decentralisation of bargaining, so as to abandon completely the model presupposed by the writers of the Constitution.

499. The Statute of Workers' Rights (Act No. 300 of 1970) has confirmed the attitude developed among the social partners in the preceding years. The law has consciously renounced the regulation of collective bargaining, and, indeed, even the direct promotion of the bargaining procedure, limiting itself, instead, to the granting of certain right to the unions at plant level as a prerequisite to actual bargaining, i.e., as an indirect support for the unions' bargaining power (*see* above).

500. The notion of the 'most representative unions', on the other hand, has never been applied to collective bargaining so as to define the bargaining agent; this is true only in the public sector (Act No. 93 of 1983 and Act No. 29 of 1993). This fact reduces the 'discriminatory' or selective impact of the notion. The proposal, advanced during the preparation of Act No. 300, to sanction by law a general duty on the part of the employers to bargain in good faith has been refused. The reason for this was declared explicitly, namely that such a duty would have implied, as the experience of other countries proved, some sort of legal regulation of bargaining agents and of bargaining units, a feature which at that time was not acceptable to the social partners and which was deemed inadvisable by the government.

501. At present a duty to bargain may be inferred implicitly from certain provisions of Act No. 300, or from other Acts, but limited to specific matters: health and safety at work (Article 9), social services within the enterprise (Article 11), the number at workers required to guarantee minimum essential services in case of strike (Article 29), conditions and times for the enterprise to ask for guaranteed wage integration in case of economic difficulty. An endorsement of the duty to bargain may be inferred by the decision of the Constitutional Court 231/2013 mentioned above.

502. This collective laissez-faire has fostered only to a limited extent the growth of rules of self-discipline dictated by collective agreements instead of by law.

Instead this lack of rules has been a factor of instability and of unpredictability in industrial relations, particularly in the recent years when the scenario of industrial relations has become more and more turbulent and the capacity of both unions and employers association to control the labour market has been weakened. The risk of this lack of definite rules has been repeatedly denounced by employers and by the government and by the unions themselves. . It can be said that the instrumental part of Article 39 has been 'historically' eliminated, instead the parties' have introduced consensual regulations of bargaining structures, through various interconfederal agreements which have attempted to establish in Italy an institutionalised bargaining system (*see* below paragraphs 454–456).

But in spite of commitments by the same parties, these agreements have been scarcely effective and often openly disregarded both by minority unions and by dissident employer's associations. For this reason the need to regulate these issue, beginning with the criteria of social parties representatives, and the effects of collective agreements has been recognised by a growing members of experts and by the parties themselves. Quite a few bills have been proposal and discussed in Parliament; but so far with no result.

II. Types of Collective Agreement

503. In principle, four types of collective agreement are recognised by Italian law, the last being the only one fully operative. (a) The collective agreements concluded under the fascist regime, which have been kept in force by Article 43 of Act No. 369, 23 November 1944, 'apart from subsequent modification'. The incidental provision of Article 43, after much discussions has been interpreted as legitimating not only modifications by agreements generally 'binding' (such as the corporative agreements) and modifications more favourable to the workers (Article 2077, Civil Code), but any modification introduced by any subsequent collective agreements. The practical relevance of corporative agreements has been rapidly decreasing and is now confined to marginal categories of workers, not covered by any other agreements, and to a very narrow range of items.

504. The collective agreements, generally binding, concluded according to Article 39 of the Italian Constitution, which are not operative in practice due to the lack of legislation implementing the constitutional provision.

505. The collective agreements incorporated in special statutes under Act No. 741, 14 July 1959, thus becoming generally binding in an indirect fashion. Act No. 741 was intended to meet the need recognised by Article 39, namely to guarantee also to non-unionised employees the minimum protection of collective agreements, but following a different procedure, so as to avoid the impasse of the implementation of Article 39. The mechanism provided for in Act No. 741 differs formally from that of Article 39, since the general effects were not attributed to the collective agreements themselves but to governmental decrees. It somewhat resembled the procedures of extension established in other European countries such as France and Germany, the major difference being that the Italian government had no powers of discretion and thus incorporated all existing agreements deposited by one of the stipulated associations, with the limit that the incorporated provisions could not be contrary to the imperative legal norms (Article 5) (the control in this latter matter being exerted by the judiciary). A further limit is that only the normative and not the obligatory parts of agreements could be legitimately incorporated into decrees; this limit derives from the spirit and, indeed, the very title of Act No. 741, which refers to the guarantee of 'minimum economic and normative treatment'. As a consequence, the Constitutional Court declared illegitimate, for example, the incorporation and extension of parts of agreements providing for grievance procedures.

506. Following the directions of Act No. 741, the government issued about 1,000 decrees, each one incorporating the clauses of a collective agreement: the Act allowed the incorporation not only of national agreements but also of provincial agreements, on certain conditions.

In 1960, another and similar Act was passed (No. 1027), renewing the powers of the governments to incorporate collective agreements. This attempt to make permanent the system inaugurated by Act No. 741, however, was struck down by the Constitutional Court (Decision No. 106, 1962). The Court upheld the constitutionality of Act No. 741, while recognising that it practically amounted to an extension of collective agreements outside the procedure prescribed by Article 39, because it aimed at granting minimum protection to workers as a *transitional* remedy to the lack of implementation of Article 39 itself. For the same reason the renewal of powers granted to the government by Act No. 1027 was held unconstitutional, being considered to alter the temporary character of the extension. As a consequence of this, all the decrees incorporating agreements concluded after 3 October 1959 became void, and thus many important categories of worker (metalworkers, mineworkers, telephone workers, etc.) could not benefit from the minimum standards of treatment guaranteed by Act No. 741. The large number of collective agreements which received the force of law in 1959 were effective in providing a minimum legal standard, which new collective bargaining could take as a starting point. This effectiveness, however, decreased with time, as the new bargaining improved the collective discipline of most sectors of the working population and devaluation made rapidly insufficient the minimum wages fixed by the decrees issued in 1959–1960.

507. The only fully operative collective agreements are those concluded according to the general principles of civil law concerning contracts (however with, important integrations). The major consequence of the 'common or private' legal status of Italian collective agreements is that they are binding only on the parties to the agreements (trade unions, employers' associations or individual employers) and, in principle, on the individual employers and workers belonging to the associations that have negotiated them. These effects however are extended with different techniques beyond the sphere of the signatory parties. The extension is favoured by legislation and by the courts both for the national and enterprise-wide agreements, although in different ways for the two types of agreements (*see* below). A major distinction – although not exclusive – as to the binding effects of collective agreements is between their normative and their obligatory aspects. These two distinct aspects correspond also to the diverse contents and functions of the agreements.

508. The normative part of the collective agreement contains norms which regulate the content and conditions of the individual relations of employment. The majority of collective agreement stipulations (e.g., those related to wages, benefits, cost of living allowances, job classification, working-time, holidays, and, in part, the protection of union officers) belongs to this part. The content and format of these clauses, like the entire agreement in general, are not predetermined by law but are left to the contractual autonomy of the parties, the single limitations being that collective stipulations contrary to imperative legal norms are null and void, unless they provide for economic and normative conditions more favourable to the employees.

509. The legal justification for the normative effects of the collective agreements has been widely discussed in Italy. Traditionally, it is held that the parties to the agreement are enabled to bind not themselves but their affiliates, namely employees and eventually employers (in the case of national or provincial agreements), because they have received the power to represent them through an ad hoc mandate or, as a rule, through the very act of affiliation to the organisation. In fact, this theory does not fully explain the binding effects of the normative part as they are unanimously recognised in the Italian system. Italian courts always held applicable to private law collective agreements the principle of Article 2077, Civil Code (in spite of its having been enacted for corporative agreements), according to which the clauses of an individual labour contract, whether preceding or subsequent, contrary to those of a collective agreement binding the employers and employees concerned 'are de jure superseded by the latter, unless they contain special conditions more favourable to the workers'.

510. This conclusion of Italian jurisprudence, although often criticised by legal scholars, has been indirectly supported by the legislature which, in Act No. 533 of 1973, regulating the settlement of labour grievances, has implicitly confirmed the binding effect of the collective agreement as stipulated in private law.

511. According to the prevailing court opinion, Article 2077 concerns only the effects of collective agreements on individual employment conditions, and does not regulate the relation between collective agreements of upper levels (national) and those of lower levels (company-wide). The coordination between the different bargaining levels, and the control of decentralised bargaining, rests only on the clauses agreed upon by the parties, with no legal support. Similar clauses have been included in the inter confederal agreements of 2009 and of 2013–2014 (*see* above paragraph 45); and in the agreement of 16 November 2015, for the Commerce and tertiary sectors.

Act. 148/2011 has intervened directly in the matter by stating that decentralised agreements – called proximity agreements – can derogate also *in pejus* both to legal provisions and to the conditions stated in national agreements.

512. Another controversial problem has arisen as to how to determine when the conditions laid down in the individual contract of employment are more favourable than those resulting from collective agreement stipulations. In the past, Italian courts were inclined to decide the issue after comparing the individual clauses of the two contracts. More recently, they have tended to consider the entire discipline concerning a certain matter (e.g., overtime, vacations, etc.) and to judge prevalent the one which, as a whole, is most favourable to the employees.

513. The opinion traditionally prevalent in Italian courts holds that in order to be bound by the normative part of a collective agreement both employees and employers must, in principle, be members of the participating organisations. In practice, however, it is highly improbable that an employer bound by a collective agreement, as a member of the employers' association participating the agreement, or having concluded or accepted it himself, would apply it only to unionised workers: this would indirectly favour unionisation. But this conclusion is not easily applicable to agreements – particularly company-wide – containing restrictive or pejorative clauses: e.g., on the choice of employees to be laid off; on women's night work. The legislator has intervened in some cases by implicitly recognising the generally binding effect (mostly) to company-wide agreements – if adopted following the principle of majority (lately Act 8 of Act 148/2011).

The courts tend to recognise general effectiveness to these agreements (*see* below 506).

According to a widespread opinion this de facto conclusion can also be supported legally, either by Article 15 of Act No. 300 of 1970, which forbids any discriminatory act of the employer on the grounds of union activity or affiliation, or better on the basis of the principle of equality of treatment, which can be derived from Article 36 of the Italian Constitution, as operating at least with respect to a single employer.

Recently the issue has been debated from a different perspective, with respect to collective agreements signed by some unions, in particular CISL and UIL, separately from others, in particular CGIL, a practice almost unknown in the past because the three major confederations used to bargain together vis-à-vis the employers (and also the government).

According to prevailing opinion and to the general civil law principles the agreement is fully valid even though signed only by some of the representative unions. A majority representation is requested only for collective agreements which are generally binding according to Article 39 of the constitution and for those operating in the public service (because the majority rule is explicitly provided by Article 43(3) of Decree 156/2001). No similar rule exists or can be derived for collective agreements concluded according to the rules of civil law.

But in the inter-confederal agreements of 2013 and 2014 (similarly in the agreement of 16 November 2015 for the commerce and tertiary sectors) the social parties have endorsed the majority rule for the first time explicitly as a requisite of the validity and effectiveness of both national and company wide agreements. This commitment is important but is legally binding only on the signatory parties because the inter confederal agreements of 2013–2014 like any other collective agreements, have the status of private law contracts. The employer who has concluded an agreement with the signatory unions and who is bound by it cannot apply it only to the members of the signatory unions excluding the members of the non-signatory one, for much the same reasons as indicated above. A different conclusion has sometimes been reached for restrictive or pejorative clauses of the agreement which could not be forced on the members of the dissenting unions. But here another rule might operate, whereby the various clauses of an agreement cannot be taken separately one from the other; consequently the acceptance, implicit or explicit, of a given agreement also implies the acceptance of restrictive clauses.

514. An employer whose affiliation to an organisation stipulating the agreement terms remains bound by the agreement throughout its duration. The same is true for the employer who takes over, as a result of a total or partial transfer, the enterprise of an employer bound by the agreement.

515. A collective agreement can be applicable to, and have normative effects upon, the content of the individual labour relationship similarly when the employer, although not bound to, adheres either explicitly to the agreement, for example stating his adherence in the letters of hire to his employees, or implicitly, by means of a uniform and continuous application of its stipulations to his employees.

516. The burden of proof as to the applicability of the agreement rests on the plaintiff employee, and may not be easy to realise since there is no publicity system regarding employers' association membership. In order partially to alleviate this burden, it is held by the Italian courts that if the employer does not object in time during the court proceedings that he is not a member of an organisation bound by the agreement, then the objection cannot be made subsequently and the applicability of the agreement is considered proven.

517. We have seen how the pressure for the extension of collective agreements has been traditionally high in Italy. The major initiative to meet this pressure, in the absence of implementation of Article 39 of the Constitution, and apart from the transitional remedy of Act No. 741, has been taken by the judiciary by means of a rather 'bold' interpretation of Article 36 of the Constitution, combined with Article 2099 of the Civil Code, first adopted in the early 1950s and becoming rapidly established thereafter. According to this opinion Article 36, which grants to the worker the right to a wage proportional to the quantity and quality of his work, and in any case sufficient to guarantee himself and his family a free and dignified life, is immediately operative and binding between employers and employees. In fact, Article 36 has been the first constitutional norm to be accorded such a binding effect between private parties by the courts. As a consequence of this, the clauses of any individual contract of employment fixing a wage contrary to Article 36, i.e., insufficient or non-proportional, are null and void.

518. A second assumption – indeed, logically and legally highly questionable – is that the nullity of the clauses fixing the wage can be made equivalent to their absence: this assumption legitimates the applicability of Article 2099, Civil Code according to which, in the absence of an agreement between the parties to an individual labour contract at a given wage, this can be fixed by the judge on equity, taking into account the opinion of the union concerned. The judge empowered to fix the wage in the individual case may refer to the amounts stipulated in the collective agreements applicable to the category to which the employer and the worker belong, or to a 'similar' category, although the employer and the worker are not bound by it.

519. As a consequence of this interpretation, private collective agreements have become indirectly applicable also beyond their 'natural' sphere of influence, as a guideline for the judge in determining the indefinite constitutional notion of 'proportional and sufficient' wage. In fact, this guideline is not considered binding, nor the only indicator for the judge, but it has been followed to a large extent, although always subject to discretional modification by the judiciary. Such an application of Article 36 differs from the extension of the collective agreement and lacks its effectiveness for various reasons: because it is limited to the wage clause of the agreements and is subject to judicial discretion (which has generally been used to reduce the collective wage in the individual case). Moreover, the violation of the collective wage cannot generally be redressed (as in the case of extension) and can only be questioned by the individual worker by means of individual proceedings (generally initiated at the termination of the labour relationship). It has, in any case, at least in correcting the most blatant cases of low salaries, been rather successful, particularly in non-industrial areas and in small units and for marginal workers.

520. Another means of indirectly extending the effects of private collective agreements, in certain cases, is provided for by Article 36 of Act No. 300 of 1970. This provision obliges the state and all public bodies to include in all contracts for the execution of public works, and in all financial subsidies to entrepreneurs, a clause explicitly requiring the beneficiary or the executor to apply to his employees conditions not inferior to those contained in the collective agreements of the appropriate bargaining unit and area. The violation of this clause brings about a sanction by the public administration, including the possible revocation of the benefit and, in the most serious cases or in cases of a second violation, the exclusion of the offender from any further concession or benefits or from any execution of public works. A further pressure to extend the effects of the national agreements comes from the legislation which reduces social security contributions in certain areas and conditions: this benefit is granted only to those firms which apply standards not lower than those bargained with the most representative unions (e.g., Act No. 89 of 1991; Act No. 214 of 1992). This rule concern the application of national agreements, which are considered to be setting basic standards of wages and working conditions. Article 10 of Act 30/2003 also requires the application of territorial agreements as a condition for receiving these benefits (the condition applies to some sectors which have a majority of very small firms such as commerce, tourism, artisan work).

521. In recent years the legislator has repeatedly favoured in one way or another the extension of collective agreements to all employees concerned – more often to all employees of the company. In certain cases the extension concerned areas in which collective agreements were granted the power to modify legal norms, particularly to deregulate certain labour regulations: e.g., decide terms and conditions of the use of audio-visual equipment and of employee searches (Articles 4 and 6 of Act No. 300; paragraphs 127–128); forbid particularly heavy work for women otherwise allowed (Articles 1–5, Act No. 903 of 1977; paragraph 163); state conditions of solidarity contracts (paragraphs 183 and 230); define the remuneration to be counted for the seniority allowance (Act 297/1982, paragraph 232); regulate the use of vacations (Article 66/2003), define the limits of temporary work (Act 276/2003) and the conditions of fixed-term contracts (Act 99/2013). Similar general effects of collective agreements were indirectly provided by Act 92/2012 which indicated that the compensation due to continuous collaborators cannot be inferior to the wages fixed by national agreements. The norm however has been abrogated together with the regulations of these collaborators by Decree 81/2015.

In other cases, the agreements produce generally binding effects as a part of a more complex administrative procedure: e.g., agreements on lay-offs and on mobility (rotation, criteria for the selection of employees, Act 223/1991; agreements on fixed-term contracts (Decree 368/2001) on part-time regulation, Act 863/1984 and now Decree 276/2003; enterprise transfer, Act 428/1990, Article 47).

Another example has been introduced by Act No. 146 of 1990 which grants the collective agreements the power to determine the minimum standards of service during the strike in essential public utilities (*see* paragraph 588).

Courts have also supported this trend of recognising general effects, particularly in company-wide agreements, even though containing restrictive clauses, e.g., concerning lay-offs or (*see* paragraph 441) the organisation of working time. Often they have declared that these agreements can bind individual employees, regardless of their union affiliation, arguing from the representative character of the unions, or from the 'indivisibility' of collective interests of employees within the company (Cassation, 2 May 1990, No. 3607). But they have hardly gone so far as to impose the agreements also on members of dissenting unions, because this has been considered contrary to union freedom and pluralism (Cassation, 13 January 1993, No. 289). An indirect extension seems to derive from Article 50 of Act 50/2016 on public tenders – which provides that tender must include social clauses aimed at promoting employment stability and at directing the successful bidders of the contract to apply to the employees the collective agreements of the relevant sector. But *see* above the limitation deriving from the connection between the various clauses of the agreement.

A further example of legislative recognition of collective agreements' peculiar effects is the regulation provided by various Acts (196/1997, 488/1999, Acts 383/2001, 210/2002) of the so-called *contratti di riallineamento* (contracts of wage realignment). These agreements are intended to promote the 'legalisation' or 'regularisation' of black market wages. They allow companies observing them a period of time (four to five years) to gradually comply with minimum bargained national wages and social security contributions related to them.

522. On the whole, however, the problem of guaranteeing the minimum protection of collective agreements to non-unionised workers is still open. In recent years it has been regaining new urgency, due to the great number of workers employed in the smallest productive units and outside the firm (homeworking). Precise and comprehensive surveys are not available, but partial estimates indicate that between 20 and 30% of industrial workers are outside the coverage of collective agreements, mostly in this marginal areas of the economy.

More over in some it these sectors collective agreements are being signed by unions and employers association of scarce representativeness which provide wages and works conditions below decent standards.

The passage of a law concerning the extension of collective agreements even though advocated by the social pacts (those of 1993 and again of 2007–2009), remains doubtful due to the persistent impasse over Article 39 of the Constitution.

But the constitutional court has held compatible with the constitution the extension of the wage provisions of collective agreements, based on Article 36 of the constitution; the case concerned a similar extension provided by Act 142/2011 on workers' cooperatives. This solution has been endorsed by the major unions which prefer it with respect to a law on minimum wage.

A possible alternative measure to protect marginal workers could be some kind of minimum wage, whose introduction in Italy is discussed (*see* above paragraph 195).

523. Apart from certain scholarly efforts to advocate an indirect extension of collective agreements by means of generalising the jurisdiction of Article 36 of the Constitution to include the entire normative part of the agreement, others are proposing the enactment of a legal minimum wage which would guarantee basic protection to the weakest sector of the labour market, while leaving collective bargaining to operate on its own to control wages in the remaining areas of the working population. A legal minimum wage has been imposed by Act 92/2012 for collaborators working on projects (*see* above). A similar indication was contained in Act 183/2014. But the government has so far renounced the implement this indication, postponing the decision to consultations with the Unions.

524. The normative effects considered so far concern the collective agreement vis-à-vis the individual labour contract. The relationship between collective agreements and the law follows different rules. In principle collective agreements can modify the law only *in melius* and not *in pejus*, i.e., can provide only terms more favourable to the employees. Exceptions have been, however, introduced in both directions. The legislator has sometimes authorised collective agreements to derogate *in pejus* (for the worse) to imperative norms, or better to deregulate totally or partially some areas of labour law considered to be too rigid; the task has been given to collective agreements, and not performed directly by the law itself, because the social parties could be usefully involved in it and decide more appropriately according to their evaluations and the circumstances. A general provision to this extent has been introduced by Act 148/2011 (Article 8), which empowers decentralised agreements (local and enterprise wide) to derogate to a wide range of legal norms on working time, control on new technologies, job classification, and in general terms and conditions of employment and of national collective agreements on the following conditions: that the agreements be concluded by most representative unions, be sustained by a majority consensus (the reference is to be interpreted to a criteria of the confederal agreement of 18 June 2011 and of 31 May 2013) and be finalised to favour employment, competitiveness, the handling of productive crisis. The agreements concluded according to Article 8 have binding effects for all employees concerned. The norm is the clearest case of legal support to the extensions of the effects of collective agreements and also to their derogatory powers. Article 8 has been criticised for giving these collective agreements a too-swiping power amounting to subverting the traditional supremacy of the law.

In practice the possibility recognised by Article 8 to derogate from legal and collective standards has been used with caution by the parties, mainly in case of serious enterprise difficulties to overcome the crisis and preserve employment.

Less frequently, indeed exceptionally, the law has fixed maximum limits to collective wage bargaining: *see* the legislation connected with income policy in the 1970s and 1980s.

525. The obligatory part of the collective agreement lays down obligations between the contracting parties. A traditional classification, derived from German jurisprudence, distinguishes three types of obligation: the duty to implement the agreement; the duty to influence the members of the organisation(s) participating in the agreement in order to apply its normative part; the peace obligation.

526. The legal significance and autonomy of the first duty has been questioned by Italian scholars. The duty of implementation is so much of the essence of the agreement (of any agreement) that it coincides with its minimum legal content: to stipulate an obligation means to assume the duty to implement it. However, there has been no speculation in Italy as to the duty of fair representation, as a rule of conduct of the collective parties in the administration of the agreement. This is due to the fact that the most serious problems dealt with under this heading in other countries do not arise in Italy: for example, the right to sue or to bring grievances under the normative part of the agreement being granted to the individual worker.

527. The duty to exert influence is connatural to the agreement and requires that the parties use whatever means they have at their disposal reasonably to induce their members to live up to the agreement: for example, not to sign individual contracts which would be contrary to the agreement. It does not imply that they guarantee the behaviour of their members, unless explicitly stated otherwise. This duty, like, more generally, the whole obligatory part, had a (potentially) major relevance during the 1960s in the system of articulated bargaining. But even then it was never tested and sanctioned legally, maintaining predominantly the value of a merely political (or moral) commitment.

528. By far the greatest interest has been devoted in Italy to the peace obligation, i.e., the obligation on the part of the parties involved to abstain from any form of industrial action in order to modify the collective agreement for as long as it remains in force. This opinion has been recurrently advanced by Italian scholars that a relative peace obligation, limited, i.e., to matters covered by the collective agreement, is also a natural effect of the agreement, being essential to its function of maintaining freedom from industrial conflict for a certain period of time. This opinion, however, has never been sustained in the Italian courts and has been largely questioned by Italian legal scholars. The chief objection to it is that the (implicit) peace obligation cannot be derived as a function of the collective agreement identified a priori by the interpreter.

529. The above-mentioned function of guaranteeing industrial peace for a definite period can be recognised only if the parties have declared themselves in agreement with it, i.e., only if the peace obligation is the object of an explicit clause in the agreement. In the absence of such a clause, the collective agreement is to be understood only as settling the existing conflict and not as giving any promise for the future. If this were not so, it would not be understandable why the parties bargain so hard about introducing into the agreement an explicit relative no-strike clause; there are no examples in Italian bargaining practice of absolute no-strike clauses, i.e., related to matters not covered by the agreement (but always within the definite limits of subject matter and time not to nullify the right to strike).

530. (Relative) peace clauses, hardly present in Italian bargaining practice until the 1960s, have become an essential part of the articulated bargaining system. The agreements of 1962 contained most often the duty on the part of the trade unions not to promote industrial action and not to sustain claims designed to modify, change, integrate what had been agreed upon at the various levels of bargaining (the metalworkers' national agreement). Sometimes the duty of the parties to abstain from industrial action before going through the grievance (conciliation) procedure provided for in the national agreement was similarly involved. The practical importance of these factors decreased with the fall of the articulated bargaining system in 1969. The 1983 agreement mentioned above (paragraph 415) reintroduced two important clauses which should probably be considered as having obligatory effects on the parties, i.e., the prohibition from negotiating at plant-level issues already defined at the enterprise level (the so-called clause of specialisation) and an 18-month wage truce. They also imply a peace obligation within the same limits.

Limited no-strike clauses have been introduced during the 1980s in some enterprise agreements, particularly with state-controlled enterprises (IRI, Italstat), subject to a status quo condition and grievance settlement procedure (both parties agree not to change existing conditions nor to resort to individual action before the exhaustion of the procedure).

The attempts to stabilise Italian industrial relations by consensus have achieved an important result also in this respect, with the tripartite accords of July 1992 (which contains an explicit commitment not to negotiate wage increases at plant level during 1993) and of July 1993 – which commits the parties not to resort to multilateral action (strike and also unilateral modification of the status quo by employers) during the bargaining round (three months before and one month after the date of renewal). These commitments so far have been by and large respected by the parties.

531. More specific commitments have been negotiated by the parties in the interconfederal agreements of 2009–2011, of 2013 of January 2014 (and 16 November 2015). These agreements delegate to the national sectorial agreements the task to define procedures to prevent conflicts, to guarantee the actual implementation of all the duties and conditions agreed upon between the parties, and to fix appropriate sanctions in case of violation of these commitments (monetary fines, suspension of trade unions rights and benefits). Moreover in case of behaviour contrary to the agreement the sectorial organisations of both parties, must ask the confederations to set up a conciliation and arbitration committee, composed of representatives of the parties and chaired by an impartial president which will decide the case and the appropriate sanctions in case of violations of the agreement.

The procedures and commitments agreed upon in these agreements are definitely more precise than in the past. But their effects are binding, as in the Italian tradition, only on the signatory parties and not to the individual employees.

532. The legal status and effects of peace clauses have been controversial in Italy. According to a minority opinion, these clauses should be considered null and void as a waiver of the constitutionally guaranteed right to strike. This conclusion is generally refused also by the Italian courts, which object that the clauses contain not an unlawful waiver of the right to strike, but a legitimate restraint on its exercise by the parties involved, in order to achieve the very collective goals (better working conditions, etc.) for which the right to strike itself is recognised.

533. According to the Supreme Court, in the only case decided, peace clauses bind the individual employees, members of the union signing the agreement, not to resort to industrial action, on the same ground as does the normative part of the agreement, i.e., because of the power to represent the members entrusted to the organisations. As a consequence, any strike in violation of the clause is contractually illegal, and legitimates (proportionate) reactions on the part of the aggrieved employer: disciplinary sanctions, including dismissal of the strikers and recovery of damages from them and from the union.

534. Two objections have been advanced with respect to this conclusion, in the opinion of the present writer quite correctly. In fact the same conclusion is not accepted by the social parties themselves, as stated in the last interconfederal agreements. The binding effects of the peace clause cannot be decided a priori or in general, as the court seems inclined to do, but only by way of interpretation of the single clause. The wording of these clauses usually refers only to a duty of the parties to the agreement (e.g., the metalworkers' agreement cited above; the confederal agreements of 2013/2014, and of 16 November 2015) or possibly to the decentralised structures of the same parties: particularly the provincial unions or plant union representatives who might press to improve locally the conditions bargained at the national level. This confirms that the clauses pertaining to the obligatory part of the agreement. It also implies that the peace obligation is violated only if the unions have promoted an illegal strike or have not done all that is in their power, including threatening legal sanctions to restrain their members or their decentralised structures from organising or joining an illegal wild-cat strike. In such cases the consequence of violation would fall not on the strikers but on the unions, i.e., the employer would be entitled to recover damages from them.

535. In the second place, and more radically, it is questionable to admit a peace clause with effects binding the individual members of the unions.

According to an opinion well-rooted in the Italian tradition, the workers themselves are the exclusive beneficiaries of the constitutional right to strike, and therefore the unions cannot avail themselves of it. To grant the unions the power to limit the right of the workers to strike would contradict the basic function of this right, which is to guarantee the effectiveness of workers' self-determination and freedom also vis-à-vis the union organisation.

536. In conclusion, it must be noted that the legal significance of the peace obligation has so far been limited. It has rarely been enforced in court and no cases are known of damages having been recovered from the unions on account of violation. This is due not only to the practical difficulties of achieving such a result but is probably also a further sign of the low degree of institutionalisation of Italian industrial relations and of the lack of faith among the parties as to the possibility of increasing it by way of legal sanctions. The chief value of the peace clauses rests, again, on their corresponding to a political commitment positively evaluated by both parties.

The legal effectiveness of these clauses has been somehow reinforced by the provisions of the July 1993 agreement which provide for an automatic economic sanction in case of violation of the duty to refrain from conflict during the negotiations. According to the agreement, the violation of the parties' commitment will cause the postponement or the anticipation (depending on whether the violation comes from the unions or from the employers) of the so-called vacancy indemnity. This indemnity is an incentive to speed up negotiations; in fact it provides that if the bargaining session lasts over three months or six months after the termination of the previous agreement, the employees will still receive a wage increase equal to respectively 30% or 50% of the expected inflation rate. This provision has been confirmed by the framework agreement of January 2009.

537. To the obligatory part of the agreement belong other clauses: traditionally rather common are institutional clauses, which set up institutions or bodies for the administration of the agreement or for the regulation of the relations between the parties, e.g., the clauses regulating the works committee, those establishing labour grievances committees, the clauses (for the building industry, for artisans, etc.) which set up joint funds to finance fringe benefits and social services in favour of workers of the appropriate category, or lately supplementary pension funds, salary integration, joint bodies for the administration of training and of other labour market matters (*see* above) and the clauses imposing on the employers or employers' associations a duty to re-examine or to negotiate with the unions on certain matters of common interest (this duty appears to operate quite often in practice, but its legal significance has never been tested).

538. The most important national agreements, beginning in the 1970s, and following the EEC directive 2002/14 have introduced clauses obliging the employers or employers' association to inform the territorial unions or the delegates of their programmes of investment and long-term business policies influencing employment and working conditions and, on occasion, to examine these matters in conjunction with the unions. The significance and functionality of these clauses have been much discussed. It is doubtful, for example, whether the latter kind of clause implies a real duty to bargain on the part of the employer (probably not). Most importantly, there are differences of opinion as to whether employers refusing to give (persuasive) information or to examine with the unions the matters provided for by the agreements, can be sued by the union under Article 28 of Act No. 300, on the grounds of committing an anti-union activity. The reasons for an affirmative answer to this are that the rights to information and joint examination seem to be clear union privileges; although of contractual origin, and nothing in Article 28 limits its applicability to legal union privileges. The reasons for a negative answer are that to extend Article 28 to contractual union rights would be beyond the intentions of Act No. 300, and would indirectly sanction the implementation of collective agreements, and thus give the judiciary the power to interfere in very delicate aspects of labour-employer relationships and in the management of the enterprise. The controversy has been partly resolved in the affirmative by Act No. 146 of 1990 (*see* paragraph 517). Article 47 of Act 428/1990 as modified by Act 18/2001, declares Article 28 applicable to the violation by the employer of the information rights of the unions in cases of enterprise transfer.

539. The distinction between the normative and obligatory parts of collective agreements is not exclusive since some clauses contain both normative and obligatory stipulations, whose effects cannot always be readily separated, because they operate together. For example, the clauses regulating conciliation and arbitration procedures in case of individual or mass dismissals (agreements of 1965, *see* above paragraphs 241 ff.), gave rise to obligations between the collective parties as to the handling of grievances, and at the same time governed the individual employment relationship, stating the rights to duties of the individual employer and employee with respect to dismissal.

540. In the absence of legal regulations on the procedure, scope and duration of the collective agreement, these aspects are left to the free determination of the parties, and in practice are handled with a good deal of differentiation, depending on the circumstances. Here it is possible to give some general outlines on the most common practices (in the industrial sector).

541. National collective agreements are usually concluded for a specific period of time, traditionally three years with no reopening clause provided for. The duration was raised to four years by the July 1993 accord; but it has been again reduced to three by the January 2009 agreement with the aim of avoiding or reducing mid-term renegotiations. But this agreement has expired is now variable, mostly four years. Wages and the entire normative part are adapted to the variations in economic and productive conditions once by the sliding scale mechanism, now by plant – and company-wide bargaining, which, especially in a medium- or large-size plant occurred at different intervals: in the 1970s and 1980s often annually; more recently, the pace has slowed down. The general agreement of January 2009 provides that also decentralised agreement will have the duration of three years.

542. Before the termination of the national agreement, more or less close to it according to the circumstances (prior notice required for termination also varies), the unions prepare the claims to be submitted to the employers' association (the so-called platform). More rarely, and only recently, the employers' associations do the same. The various claims are debated in general meetings held at plant level (under Article 20 of Act No. 300), then examined by the territorial (provincial and national) governing bodies of the unions for the final decision and draft of the platform. The interconfederal agreement of 10 January 2014 commits the employer to negotiate on the basis of the platform presented by Unions representing 50% +1 of the category.

543. The claims for national bargaining are often influenced by, and geared to, the result reached in the preceding round of plant bargaining. The claims so decided and transmitted to the employers' associations have often been intended to be 'rigid', i.e., binding quite tightly the committee of union delegates and officers which does the actual bargaining (in plenary meetings or divided into subcommittees for specific matters). But much depends on the circumstances. Recently flexibility has become more common also in this respect. The preparation of the platform, beyond plant level, is done separately by the unions affiliated to the three major confederations, but the final programme is common, and the bargaining delegation itself is unitary. In the last years inter-union tensions have sometimes prevented the presentation of common platform: and the conclusion of 'unitary' agreements. This is particularly the case in the metalworking industry, where the federation FIOM, adhering to CGIL has presented separate platforms in 2003, in 2009 and 2012, and refused to sign the national agreement reached by the other unions with the employers association.

The agreement of 31 May 2013, confirmed in 10 January 2014, has introduced some rules directed to prevent and resolve the cases of intra-union dissent in bargaining at the national level. It states the criteria to identify the unions entitled to bargain, and the application of the majority rule to decide the content of bargaining (never endorsed before). The national agreements signed by unions representing at least 50% +1 of the representatives are binding after a certified consultation of all the employees concerned (a sort of referendum) decided by simple majority. These rules represent an important innovation in the Italian tradition; even though they bind only the signing parties and their affiliates given the private nature of the 2013 agreement.

544. CISNAL and other confederations (CISAL) have been excluded for long time from the actual bargaining by a long-standing practice of CGIL, CISL and UIL, and in fact ended up by signing separately the same agreement stipulated by the former three unions. UGL (formerly CISNAL) and CISAL have recently been involved into the practice of 'social concertation' to the extent that they signed up the two most important trilateral agreements of 23 July 1993, of September 1996, of July 2002 and of January 2009. Some unions other than CGIL, CISL and UIL (e.g., Confsal) are gaining ground as bargaining agents also in industry-wide bargaining.

545. The length of the bargaining process varies, and may be considerable. The practice of striking while bargaining is quite recent in Italy: until 1969, it was practically unknown, the two acts being considered incompatible. Its adoption has contributed to the formation of a more 'compact' and fruitful process of bargaining. The July 1993 accord has attempted to rationalise – here too with some success – the bargaining process, by fixing the timing for presentation of the unions' demands and a cooling-off period of three months before and one month after the expiration of the previous agreement (paragraph 478).

Given the private nature of collective agreements they do not produce effects after their cessation – due to expiration of terms or to advance notice of termination (when the agreement is for an indefinite duration). The effects can continue beyond these limits only when explicitly indicated by the parties themselves. The framework agreements of January 2009 commit the national bargainers to fixed timing and procedures for facilitating a prompt renewed of agreements: in any event the demands for renewal must be presented in due time to allow the beginning of negotiations six months before the expiration of the previous contract. The negotiations completed in 2009 and subsequently by and large respected this timing.

In all major bargaining disputes, a traditional (and increasingly important) factor has been the mediation by the Ministry of Labour or by its peripheral organs (the provincial and regional labour offices), or, less frequently, by regional governments or by the prefects. Mediation may occur either on request of the parties involved or on the initiative of public officials (which the parties are not bound to accept, but which in fact is hardly ever refused).

546. It is customary for the union delegations to report informally to the governing bodies of the unions on the major developments in the negotiations and to submit the tentative draft of the agreement to general meetings of workers in the plants for ratification.

More recently, the referendum has sometimes been preferred to general meetings as a means of verifying the opinion of workers. But the use and the effect of the referendum are controversial among the unions; particularly CISL and UIL have been traditionally opposed to a wide use of it and even more to recognising to the referendum a binding force on union decisions. In fact they have refused to submit to referendum the agreements reached separately from CGIL (*see* above).

But this opposition has been abandoned and the agreement of 31 May 2013, confirmed by the agreement of 10 January 2014 has endorsed a sort of referendum called 'certified consultation' of the workers, as a requisite for the final approval of national collective agreements. A similar provisions is in the interconfederal agreement of 16 November 2015, for the service sectors.

The draft does not usually include a complete renewal of the agreement, but only the modifications to the old agreement. The complete text, resulting from the old agreement together with the new clauses, is prepared later, often after several months. The new agreement generally comes into force at the termination date of this, retroactively, when the negotiations have ended. This practice tends to eliminate any vacancy of collective discipline between two agreements: given the private nature of the existing collective agreements, their effects, both normative and obligatory, do not operate de jure beyond their termination (the so-called ultra-activity is proper to corporative agreements). On the other hand according to the same principles of civil law the existing agreements stipulated for an indefinite period can be terminated unilaterally by giving advance notice.

§8. ENFORCEMENT OF COLLECTIVE AGREEMENTS

547. The legal enforcement of the collective agreement is secured in a way basically similar to that of any private contract. Collective agreements must be interpreted according to the general rules of interpretation of private law contracts (Article 1362 Civil Code) and of those concerning the interpretation of the law. Any question, whether collective or individual, arising out of the interpretation or application of the agreement (dispute of rights), can be brought to an ordinary court by the individual workers and/or employers, if it concerns the normative part, or by the trade unions, employers' associations or individual employers, in the case of a company or plant agreement, if it concerns the obligatory part. The observance of the agreement, however, is secured in the first place by the parties themselves, through a process of grievance solution and continuous bargaining.

548. Conciliation procedures designed to settle disputes on the interpretation and application of the agreement (and of the law), are established by almost all nation-wide collective agreements and follow a more or less standardised pattern. Generally speaking, individual grievances are dealt with in the first instance by representatives of management (from first-line supervisors to personnel directors) together with shop delegates and then factory councils. In the second instance an unsettled grievance is referred for conciliation to officers' provincial unions and of the corresponding territorial employers' associations.

549. The employee who has an individual grievance is almost invariably assisted by a union representative in dealing with it, even though he is not a union member; but assistance during a grievance is one of the most appropriate occasions on which to persuade the employee to join the union. Collective disputes may also be settled at the shop level, particularly if they concern the application of a company agreement; otherwise they are dealt with by the organisation at the provincial level and, in the case of failure, at the national level. The whole procedure is generally followed and established in a rather informal way, although some agreements provide for more detailed steps, such as time limits to submit claims (after which they are foreclosed). Joint interpretation boards, authorised to attempt the settlement of disputes, rather frequent in the 1960s, are now found only in a few sectors (chemical, electrical, telephone), but they are seldom active.

550. The effects of a conciliation agreement following the collective grievance procedure are controversial (*see* above paragraphs 328 ff.). Only the enforcement of corporative collective agreements and of the agreements incorporated in statutes under Act No. 741 of 1959 was controlled by the inspection service of the Ministry of Labour and sanctioned generally by fine.

Chapter 5. Workers' and Union Participation in the Enterprise

551. Italian unions have traditionally regarded collective bargaining as the primary way to govern labour-management relations and to control the position of the workers within the enterprise. Accordingly, they have shown an attitude of strong diffidence towards worker participation in the decision-making bodies of private enterprises and towards any other form of bilateral institution set up to co-determine working conditions in conjunction with management; even though Article 46 of the Italian Constitution states in general terms the right of workers to participate with in the enterprises.

552. The most significant examples of worker participation in the governing bodies of the major industrial enterprises of the country, originated in 1944 in the wake of the Resistance and of the commitment of all anti-fascist parties to make a common effort to rebuild the Italian economy. They did not survive the post-war normalisation of the economy and the breaking down of interparty cooperation, and were progressively eliminated between 1947 and 1948. The few examples of joint committees set up during the 1960s, representing a major concession by Italian unions to the bilateral institutionalisation of collective agreements (in fact, they had limited powers to control their application), had a short and unproductive life, until 1969, when they were eliminated. The works committees never really responded to their original (but ambiguous) function as instruments of labour-management cooperation. When they were not too weak to act independently or to resist management domination, they operated as bargaining agents (abusively), replacing the trade unions.

553. Forms of financial participation the workers, such as profit-sharing or shareholding, had little success in the past. A more favourable attitude has been adopted recently by some large enterprises which have decided, sometime unilaterally in other cases following agreements with the unions, to distribute shares to their employees, either gratuitous or at a price lower than the standard.

The cooperative formula, very widely diffused in the Italian tradition (both Catholic and socialist), was never specifically or predominantly used to foster workers' participation as such. Workers' cooperatives exist and in some areas are significant. But the effectiveness of the self-management that they allow has been uneven depending on the type of governance and on actual practice. On the other hand the links between the trade unions and the cooperative movement have been traditionally influenced by the political parties, in a formal or diplomatic way. Recently these links have been weakened and this has favoured the convergence and unification of the major confederations of cooperatives, which originally were separated following political lines.

554. All forms of co-determination of labour-management relations have met deep-rooted obstacles in Italian political and labour union history. The high level of political ideological conflict, class consciousness in Italian society and in the labour movement, the existence of strong left-wing parties (particularly the Communists) consistently confined to political opposition yet greatly influencing the major workers' confederation; and the very weakness of organised labour (which has kept it away from the enterprise and incapable of influencing the central issues in the management decision-making process) have all resulted in any proposal of even marginal co-determination being long unacceptable to Italian employees. The employers were too conservative to accept any experiment in this direction, or too afraid, with good reason, that in the high-conflict environment of the Italian industry it would hardly be used to stabilise industrial relations without substantial loss of power by the employers, while contributing, in fact, to the strengthening of the counter-union power within the firm.

555. A major exception to this rule has been the public sector, where various forms of joint committee have traditionally been provided with consultative or even deliberative powers concerning many aspects of labour relations, and workers' or unions' representatives have also been present on administrative boards of many public institutions. But these forms of workers' participation are closely linked to the peculiar nature of the employer and of organised labour's tradition in the public service. Their importance has started to decline with Act No. 93 of 1983 which recognised collective bargaining as the prevalent method of determining wages and working conditions in the public sector as well. Act No. 29 of 1993 abolished all the pre-existing forms of co-determination in the public sector, which were considered too pervasive, encroaching on the role of public managers and detrimental to the efficiency of public administration. The Act does not imply a refusal of the participative model; it aims at correcting abuses (which indeed existed); in fact it leaves to the parties themselves to find new ways, more respectful of the role of the parties, to shape participation in the public service. A similar revision has been introduced in the position of union representatives in the public institution administering social security.

556. The modifications in industrial relations that have come about after 1968–1969 have not reduced the central role played by collective bargaining. Nevertheless, the widening of the scope of collective bargaining, to include such matters, traditionally regarded as managerial prerogatives, as manpower planning, work organisation, job security, investment and industrial restructuring, etc., has posed for the trade unions new problems concerning the strategies of private enterprises and their future. Meanwhile, the unions have begun to intervene more and more frequently in major economic decisions of the country, either by way of formal or informal consultation by public powers or through the co-optation of union representatives in a growing number of institutions, not only those administering social security (the most traditional area of union participation) but also those governing the labour industrial restructuring and other major aspects of public policy. In 1994 the unions have decided to retreat from the board of administration of social security institutions where they had been traditionally present (with a relative majority of members). This direct participation in the administration was held too 'compromising' for the unions and for the institutions as well; union representatives have been instead inserted in the surveillance committees which have no direct power of administration but have the task of giving guidelines and of controlling the governing bodies of the institutions: their role has continued, however, to be significant.

557. Beginning in the late 1970s, foreign experiences of co-determination and the EU proposals for a reform of company law, suggesting employee representation on the supervisory board, and for a European statute were taken into consideration. But while the trend towards the involvement of union representatives within public institutions continued (even though somewhat limited), the proposals to adopt some form of workers' institutional participation within the enterprises did not materialise.

558. The reasons for the unions' diffidence have remained the same over time: first the fear of being involved in responsibilities which limit their autonomy more than they give them real powers not only on labour matters but also on the main strategic decisions of the employers. Union diffidence is increased by the traditional difficulties and uncertainties of the Italian economic and political situation: while they justify, also on the side of the employers, pressing requests that the unions become more responsible and moderate, they do not guarantee more balanced economic growth and powers to the unions themselves capable of offsetting the moderation asked of the workers.

A new challenge has come more recently to the unions by management initiative. Participative management is active as never before in promoting 'employee involvement' as a way of greater identification of employees with the enterprise's interest and of increasing productivity outside union channels or possibly against the unions.

Forms of 'direct' participation of employees, often organised in teams, are spreading particularly in sectors and plants of 'intelligent' manufacturing.

The Stability Act for 2016 (n. 208, 28 December 2015, Article 1 co. 182) has introduced specific fiscal incentives to productivity bonuses and profit sharing. These incentives are increased if the employers negotiate forms of employees participation in matters concerning the organisation of work; this type of participation has been recently adopted in quite a few agreements concluded in same large company technologically advanced (*see* below).

559. Different solutions have so far been explored, which take into account the various positions within the trade union movement itself as to the possibility of institutionalising this union control. The most realistic solution so far has been to broaden and reinforce, if necessary by means of legislation, the right of disclosure of information and to negotiate with respect to investment, job security, manpower planning, etc., already recognised in most national agreements (*see* above). A more ambitious proposal, mainly coming from CISL, has concerned the workers' participation in capital formation but has proved short-lived.

On 2 July 1980 the government, following a compromise proposal of the three confederations, approved a decree which set up an investment fund financed by a special contribution imposed on all employees amounting to 0.5% of their regular pay. On the one hand, this initiative responded to the need to reduce the wage push on inflation (in fact it resulted in an immediate reduction of the wage earner's total disposable income). On the other hand, the 0.5% was a temporary forced saving, to be compensated with (average) interest and to be used to finance investment, especially in the depressed areas of the country. In order to guarantee this use of the fund, unions were given qualified representation on the board of directors. The decree was dropped by the government itself following strong political opposition, particularly from the Communist party. Subsequent attempts had no better results.

Some major experiments in concertation and cooperative bargaining have been conducted in some large state-controlled groups (IRI, ENI) and in a few private firms as well (Pirelli, Olivetti, Bassetti, Electrolux-Zanussi). A most comprehensive example was the framework agreement signed in 1986 directly between IRI and the three confederations. Joint committees were set up at national and local levels different from the regular bargaining agents and from factory councils although connected – with the aim of discussing and monitoring the whole group.

A complex network of joint participatory bodies competent in various matters, training, health and safety, equal opportunities, improvement of productive methods, has been set up in Electrolux-Zanussi (1997), in Telecom (1997), and more recently in other large companies and groups like ENI, Finmeccanica, Ducati, Lamborghini.

560. Directive No. 94/45/CEE on European Works Councils has favoured diffusion and intensification of information and consultation rights in large Italian multinationals. Its procedures and content have been transposed in a series of collective agreements, both company-wide and sectoral: *see* e.g., the agreement signed on the 27 November 1996 by Confindustria and Assicredito (the organisation active in the banking sector), on the one side, and CGIL, CISL, UIL, on the other side.

But since collective agreements do not have *erga omnes* effect in Italy, it is necessary to get these agreements confirmed by legislation. This has been done by Decree 74/2002 which transposes Directive 94/45 in the Italian legal system. Following the EU directive the forms of constitution and functioning of the EWC are left to be determined by bargaining between the parties. Lacking agreement some provisions must in any case be respected concerning the members and composition of the EWC. In Italy the rules are stated by interconfederal agreements, lately that of 10 January 2014; their distribution between the various plants in different European countries; the content of information and consultation (including the most important aspects of enterprise life); the basic protection of the members of the EWC; the possibility of being assisted by experts.

561. A further development in this matter follows from the approval of the EU directive on the statute of the European company. The directive has been received with cautious favour by the unions, mainly due to its 'openness', i.e., to the various alternative types of participation proposed, and has not been rejected by the employers. In March 2005 the major union confederations and Confindustria concluded a 'common opinion' which served as a basis for Decree 188/2005 implementing the directive (the usual method followed for the application of EU social directives).

Various Bills, coming from both majority and opposition political parties, have been presented in Parliament aiming at introducing forms of workers participation along the EU guidelines, and also at promoting workers' financial participation (stock option plans and the like). Act 92/2012 has delegated the government to introduce forms of employees' participation along the lines of the European directive; but the government has not made use of this power, mainly due to the opposition of Confindustria.

562. It seems, however, that the issue of worker participation cannot be solved only at the enterprise level. Italian unions, and the major political parties to which they are related, believe that union participation and control at the enterprise level can hardly be successful if it is not connected with the increasing influence of the workers over the major economic decisions which determine also the enterprise policies.

563. It is believed that union participation must be applied both to macro- and microeconomic decisions – which is obviously not an easy task. The prospects are here again not of drastic changes but slow evolution. Collective bargaining, widened in scope and becoming more cooperative, will probably continue to be the main instrument for governing industrial relations. It may be complemented (not substituted) by more or less institutionalised forms of joint consultation and workers' participation.

Contrary to the resistance to employees participation within the enterprises Italian unions have been traditionally favourable to having their representatives within the board of directors or the committee of surveillance of public institutions, such as the boards which administer social security, the regional and provincial committees which supervise public employment services (paragraph 106). Moreover the social parties have set up bilateral entities which have acquired growing importance in the organisation of vocational training (they a financed a contribution on wages), in the administration of various contractual and welfare benefits (pension funds, social assistance and health care) and also the certification of labour contracts (paragraph 347). The development of these forms of bilateral social participation has been promoted by the legislator (since Act 30/2003). Their extension also to other areas of activity is advocated by the agreement of January 2009.

CGIL has been reluctant to use of bilateral bodies in activities such as certification of contracts and employment services on the labour market, because it considers these activities not to be appropriate for the unions or even incompatible with their bargaining role.

The interconfederal agreement of March 2018 signed by Confindustria and CGIL CISL UIL has for the first time overcome the traditional diffidence of the Italian social parties, in particular CGIL but also Confindustria, towards the participation of workers representatives within the enterprises, and has explicitly endorsed the adoption of a contractual way to this participation, whereby the forms and contents and contents of it are to be defined not by legislation but by collective agreements.

Chapter 6. Industrial Conflict

§1. Dimensions and Forms of Industrial Conflict

564. Industrial tensions have been traditionally high in Italy, reflecting the serious social imbalance and political division of the country. Industrial conflict, however, was not as intense as might have been expected until the late 1960s, due, among other factors, to the weakness of organised labour. In 1968 and 1969 a series of industrial stoppages began without precedent for industry or forms of industrial action. The number of hours lost through strikes, which reached an absolute maximum in 1969, remained high also in the 1970s, showing a relatively increased independence from the economic cycle (*see* Table 5). Although dis-aggregated data are not completely satisfying, the table indicates certain significant characters of conflict: the persisting importance of strikes to the renewal of national collective agreements, which cause an increase in lost hours in the years of renewal; an increase in conflicts in plant- and company-wide bargaining, which after 1968 remains at the highest levels in the post-war period; a similar, though more unstable growth in intercategorial strikes. In the latter group, central importance has become attached to strikes for social reforms, which renovate the Italian tradition of political strikes, limited in the past to isolated forms of protest, with a view to acquiring real bargaining significance vis-à-vis political power. Industrial conflict appears more intense in the developed areas of the country than in the depressed areas, while it does not seem to vary according to the dimension of the enterprise (probably further evidence of the extension of union action to medium-to-small firms after 1969).

A few significant changes have taken place in recent years also in the dimension of industrial conflict brought about by modifications in the socioeconomic context and by the general change common to most European countries of attitude of the protagonists of the industrial relations system. The major change is a reduction (since 1979) of all the indicators of industrial conflict (duration, intensity, participation) with a particularly noteworthy reduction of political strikes. This trend has accelerated in the last decade and lately in the economic crisis begun in 2008. An exception is represented by the period 2001—2003 when the tensions with the government, particularly in CGIL, have caused some resurgence of both political and industrial conflict. The average days lost due to industrial action has decreased from 150 per 1,000 employees in the 1990s to eighty days in the first decade of 2000 to 50 in 2009.

On the other hand, there has been, in some periods, a diffusion of 'microconflicts', particularly in public services, that are not controlled by the confederal trade unions. Indeed, the workers involved are either implicitly or explicitly hostile to official union policy, spurred on by groups who contest the representative leadership of the confederal trade unions.

565. As far as forms of the conflict are concerned, it is noteworthy that the organisation of contractual strikes is often decentralised, even when the decision on the total number of hours is taken centrally. The strikes for social reform are more centralised due to the nature of the opponent (most often the state) and to the limited effectiveness of the horizontal structures of the unions below the provincial level. Workers' participation in the strikes, particularly the contractual variety, is usually high even by non-union members following a well-established tradition and goal of Italian unionism. This high rate of participation is favoured by the decentralised net of 'delegates' representing all workers and often by a systematic use of picketing.

566. Wild-cat strikes are rare in Italy: cases of spontaneous action, if not promptly controlled by the unions and their delegates, are normally endorsed and guided by them. Several wild-cat strikes have occurred in the public sector, sometimes endorsed or guided by independent unions. This confirms the growing difficulties of the main confederations in controlling the most troublesome areas of the labour force.

567. The average duration of strikes remains short, again in keeping with Italian tradition; nevertheless, their impact has been sometimes great, due also to the forms of action adopted, which tend to result in loss of production with minimum loss of wages. There was particularly in the 1960s and in the 1970s a frequent resort by Italian unions to intermittent strikes and *grèves tournantes*, called 'rotating strikes' (*scioperi articolati*), affecting successively different units or groups of employees within a firm, often combined and initially used only by small groups of workers. In most serious disputes sit-downs, occupations, work-ins, blockades of goods entering or leaving the firm, etc., have been fairly common, in the late 1960s and 1970s, while go-slows and other forms of passive job actions are also known, although not generally approved by the unions. As a reaction to these forms of industrial action, employers have sometimes resorted to partial lock-outs, or to non-payment of wages during the intervals between intermittent strikes or to workers made idle by others' strikes. In the last decades these forms have been reduced to a minimum.

Table 6 Strike Trends in Italy
(In General, Including Disputes Not Concerning to Employment Relations)

	Number of Strikes	*Number of Workers Participating (000)*	*Hours Lost (000)*	*Average Hours Lost per Striker*
1960	2,471	2,338	46,289	19.80
1970	4,162	3,722	146,212	39.28
1980	2,238	13,825	115,200	8.33
1990	1,094	1,634	36,269	22.20
1995	545	445	6,365	14.30
2000	966	687	6,189	9.01
2001	746	1,125	7,182	6.38
2002	616	5,442	34,027	6.25
2003	710	2,561	13,732	5.36

	Number of Strikes	*Number of Workers Participating (000)*	*Hours Lost (000)*	*Average Hours Lost per Striker*
2004	745	709	4,890	6.89
2005	654	961	6,348	6.61
2006	587	467	3,883	8.32
2007	667	906	6,508	7.18
2008	621	669	5,059	7.56
2009	889	267	2,601	9.76

Source: Istat (the series stops in 2009).

The Commission on strikes in the essential public services publishes yearly data on the conflicts falling under its competence: in 2012, 2,330 strikes have been 'proclaimed', 1,375 have been implemented for a total of 695 days of strikes; 680 have been totally a partially revoked following the intervention of the commission. In 2021, 1527 strikes were proclaimed and 1009 have been implemented; in 2022 1612 were proclaimed and 1127 were implemented.

§2. The Right to Strike

568. The strike, as an extreme form of collective action by the workers, and ultimate guarantee of its effectiveness, has been viewed historically with disfavour by the law; either penalised as such (before 1889 and under the fascist regime) or, when tolerated by criminal law in general, strongly restricted in many of its forms and illegal in civil law as breach of contract. A fundamental change of attitude has been introduced, again, by Article 40 of the Italian Constitution, which guarantees 'the right to strike, within the limits of the laws regulating it'.

569. Article 40 is the basic constitutional provision in the field of collective labour relations, prior even to Article 39 inasmuch as it founds the effectiveness of labour organisation itself. It represents a fundamental innovation with respect to the classical principles of formal equality and democracy, since it recognises the right of the workers alone (there being no right of lock-out) to withdraw their labour in order to promote their own interests. Article 40 is closely linked to Article 3, second paragraph, the right to strike being one of the means granted to workers 'to remove the obstacles which hinder their effective equality and their full participation in the economic social and political life of the country' (thus the Constitutional Court recognises the right to political strike).

570. As the major political parties present at the constitutional assembly of 1947 could not agree on the rules governing, i.e., limiting, the right to strike, they were delegated to ordinary legislation, through a compromise solution taken from the preamble to the French Constitution of 1946. But this same lack of consensus, which prevented any disciplining of the right in 1947, plus the persistent opposition of the trade unions, has rendered impossible any general legislation on this matter. This does not mean, of course, that there are no rules limiting the right to strike. The provisions of the Penal Code (1930) relating to the strike were not explicitly eliminated with the fall of the fascist regime. The expression of Article 40 – 'laws regulating it' – although probably referring to 'future laws', might also be, and in fact has been, interpreted by the courts as including the pre-existing rules of the Penal Code.

571. The provisions of this code, assuming a totally negative attitude towards industrial conflict, differed so clearly from the constitutional approach, however, that it could not be used without profound modifications and adaptations (indeed, certain commentators believe, with good reason, that it should not have been used at all). This work of adaptation has been carried out by the ordinary courts and (since 1958) by the Constitutional Court, giving rise to a huge corpus of precedents. These judicial precedents are the source of the strike law, a source not always fully consistent, which reflects the persistent contrasts of opinion existing in Italian society with respect to industrial conflict.

572. Article 40 sanctions, first of all, the basic freedom to strike vis-à-vis the state. This implies the unconstitutionality of any public act which contradicts it: consequently the Constitutional Court has declared completely unconstitutional (in 1960) Article 502 of the Penal Code, which punished in general the economic strike, and partially unconstitutional some of the later articles of the Penal Code, which punished various forms of strike. Article 40 operates also as a restriction on the employer's anti-strike action: this has been practically recognised only with Article 4 of Act No. 604 of 1966 (for discriminatory dismissals) and most clearly with Articles 15 and 28 of Act No. 300 of 1970, which have greatly strengthened the protection of the right to strike vis-à-vis the employer. A major limit to the employer's freedom of action traditionally derived from the recognition of the right to strike, is that the employer cannot substitute, in a definitive way, other workers recruited from outside to take the place of the strikers. Under Article 28 of the Workers' Statute, even the temporary recruiting of strikebreakers from outside might be considered an illegal anti-union activity: this practice is in fact hardly ever used by Italian employers, also due to the short duration of most strikes.

573. The recognition of the right to strike, finally, implies that the concerted abstention from work does not constitute in principle a breach of contract, but rather a cause of legitimate suspension of the individual employment relationship, and that therefore the employer cannot dismiss the strikers during the strike period. This is true only if the strike remains within the limits established by law or by the courts. The individual employee participating in an 'unlawful' strike violates his obligations under the labour contract and is liable according to the general rules of civil law, i.e., subject to disciplinary action by the employer, up to dismissal, and is in theory also liable for damages. No contractual liability rests on the unions, unless they violate a (lawful) no-strike clause.

574. A consequence of the suspension of the labour relation is that the strikers have no right to remuneration for the period during which they are on strike. This applies to all the elements, also indirect, of remuneration, such as Christmas bonuses and the like (although this consequence has recently been challenged by some lower courts). It is uncertain whether it is also legitimate for the employer to reduce annual vacations proportionately to the strike periods of that year. Employees who report for work at a plant which is on strike must in principle be provided with work and be paid by the employer, unless he can prove that the strike, as a force majeure, made it impossible for him to give work. We will discuss below the matter of how this problem is to be solved in the case of intermittent strikes, 'rotating strikes', etc.

575. It is noteworthy that in Italy there are no funds from which strike benefits can be paid. The traditional poverty of the unions, the lack of a strictly associative tradition, together with the general appeal of unions to the working class as a whole, may account for this situation. Certainly, the traditional pattern of short strikes and the (once) frequent resort to 'rotating' strikes can easily be explained in these circumstances.

576. A part from diverging opinions as to the legality of the right to strike, there is a widespread consensus among Italian commentators and in the courts as to the fact that the beneficiary of the right is the worker as such: the usual formula considers the strike as an individual right of the worker to be exercised collectively. It is a matter of discussion whether non-subordinate workers may also strike, or, rather, how their abstention from work is to be qualified under the law.

577. The main consequence of this is that in order to be lawful a strike does not have to be called or authorised by a union. It is enough that a group of workers decides to strike together or actually go on strike together to defend common interests. It all depends on the types of collective interests being defended by the strikers – they might concern even a very small number of workers (in theory the possibility of a one-person strike cannot be excluded). Of course, union members organising a strike or participating in it against their union's indications are subject to union disciplinary action. The major role of the unions in regulating strike action, has been recognised by Act No. 146 of 1990 modified by Act. 83/2000, in essential services; which, in itself, counterbalances the individual nature of the right (*see* paragraph 518).

§3. Limits to the Right to Strike

578. Limits to the right to strike have been traditionally identified by Italian courts and by commentators with two chief justifications: their derivation from the very *notion* of the strike (the so-called limits inherent in the strike itself) and from the possible contrast between the interest guaranteed by Article 40 and other interests constitutionally recognised (the so-called external limits to the right). The former justification has been widely criticised, with good reason since the notion of the strike is not founded in any source of law, but conventionally and a priori built up by the same commentators. The second line of argument justifies a wide range of limits.

The actual definition of the limits to the right to strike is the product mainly of court decisions.

The judicial activity has been rather intense in the first decades after the constitution but has then been progressively reduced and stabilised also due to the decline of strike action.

Subjects: Public and Essential Services

579. As to the subjects of the right to strike, the right is generally denied to the police and to military personnel, in order not to imperil national safety (Article 52, Constitution), the physical welfare and property of citizens. The same was traditionally held true for public employees in general. In addition to laws providing for administrative sanctions against public employees striking, Article 330 of the Penal Code of 1931 makes it a crime punishable by two or three years of imprisonment for three or more persons to leave their work collectively or to act in any other way so as to disturb the continuity of work if they are either public officials proper or persons charged with a public duty, including private employees exercising public services or employed in public service enterprises or in enterprises essential to public needs. Article 333 also renders individual cessation of work a crime in similar circumstances, and Article 359 refers specifically to attorneys and medical personnel abandoning essential services. The organisers of such strikes are liable to imprisonment for up to five years, or even longer if the strike has a ‘political’ rather than an industrial objective. These articles cover not only public employees but also a good part of the ground dealt with by the ‘emergency’ provisions of other countries’ labour laws.

580. This negative attitude has been changing since the 1950s, a change registered first by the ordinary courts and then by the Constitutional Court, parallel to the narrowing of the differences in status between private and public employees and the recognition by law of collective bargaining as a means of regulating conditions of public employment.

581. In a first decision (of 1962) the Constitutional Court, while refusing to declare Article 330 completely unconstitutional, held that its application was limited to strike action endangering ‘basic general interests recognised as superior’ by the Constitution itself. From this decision derived the situation that certain categories of employees, public or exercising public services, had no right to strike, because their stoppage would endanger such community interests. This conclusion was widely criticised on the grounds that there may well be workers within these categories who can strike without giving rise to such dangers, e.g., groups of office workers employed in public service enterprises or similarly productive workers, provided they guaranteed certain essential services. This interpretation, demanding a case-by-case judgment relating not to the category on strike but to the specific exercise thereof, has in fact been largely followed by ordinary courts and has now been indirectly endorsed by the Constitutional Court itself (Decision No. 222 of 1976 relating to Articles 330 and 340, Penal Code).

582. Meanwhile, in 1969, the Constitutional Court intervened again in the matter of Article 330, Penal Code, declaring it partially unconstitutional, and consequently recognising the right to concerted action of these employees on the same conditions as above (the safeguarding of superior interests) and on the further condition that the strike be for 'socioeconomic' objectives (broadly understood: *see* below paragraphs 518 ff.).

583. A similar problem is posed by Article 1105, Naval Code (1942) which prohibits the crime of mutiny: the Constitution Court (Decision No. 124 of 1962) held that this article applied if serious damages would be incurred by the seamen's strikes with respect to the security and interests of the community, i.e., to all strikes organised during voyages. The same criticisms as those have been addressed to this conclusion and here again some ordinary courts have not denied the right to strike during the voyage, but have held it sufficient for the strikers to guarantee (case by case) the minimum services necessary to protect the vital interests of the ship and of its passengers.

The right to strike has also been recognised to autonomous workers following a decision of the Constitutional Court (n. 25/1975) which declared unconstitutional, as against Article 40 of the Constitution, the norm of the fascist penal code which punished the abstention from work of small merchants (operating without employees). This decision has been followed by ordinary courts which have extended this right to so-called parasubordinate workers (*see* above) and other categories of self-employed.

The right to bargain collectively (and consequently to strike) has been denied by the ECJ (Dec. C-413/13, 4 Dec. 2014) as being against the principle of free competition, recognised by the European treaties. But the European Commission, after wide public consultation, has taken an opposite view and is about to recognize the right to association and collective bargaining to those autonomous employees who are in a condition of weakness in the labour market similar to that of employers and consequently must be allowed to organize and bargain collectively.

584. The extent to which the right to strike is limited in the public service industries has been very unclear since there was no general regulations defining the area of these industries, what supplies and services must be maintained in case of strike (or lock-out) and how these needs should be met (regulations existing, e.g., for hospital personnel are similarly rather vague and insufficient). Interventions by the courts, which have the last word, have been limited and also insufficient. An old provision (Articles 20 and 55 of Act No. 383, 3 March 1934), entitling the prefect and the mayor to issue temporary and urgent injunctions for reasons of public health, safety and policing, has been repeatedly used in the past by these authorities in order to intervene in industrial conflicts and order the measures necessary to guarantee the protection of these vital needs, including the fixing of a minimum number of workers remaining at work. Although much criticised account of the broad discretionary powers it grants to the administration, this provision has been confirmed as being legitimate by the Constitutional Court (Decision No. 41 of 1977), recalling its earlier decision on the limits to the right to strike. This provision has been superseded by the new regulations of Act No. 146 of 1990 and Act 83/2000 (*see* paragraph 517). Restrictive rules have been fixed by law in specific sectors particularly important for the protection of public goods: Decree No. 185 of 1964 and now Decree 230/1995 strictly limit the strike of employees working in nuclear plants (by setting minimum services to be guaranteed). Act No. 242 of 1980 and Act No. 121 of 1981 similarly limit the right to strike air traffic controllers; and, as already mentioned, deny altogether the right to strike to policemen.

585. As a matter of common practice, the form of strike action in essential services – both public and private – has been subject to control by the relevant unions (particularly those affiliated with the major confederations). In fact, the confederation charters traditionally provided that strikes in essential public services must be decided after consultation with the horizontal organs of the organisation (Article 42 of the CISL charter) or must be authorised by the latter (Article 14 of the CGIL charter). The problems arising from these forms of struggle are often handled through informal bargaining between employers and trade unions, especially regarding the activities and the minimum professional services to remain functioning.

586. Traditional attempts to meet the problem have proved less and less satisfactory. They have been particularly inadequate in controlling strikes in public services which have been organised by independent unions without regard for those elementary precautions normally observed by the three confederations in order to reduce consumer inconvenience and danger. This is the case with system of self-regulation adopted already in the 1970s by CGIL, CISL, UIL which required precise conditions in exercising the right to strike:

(a) proclamation of the strike, definition of modalities by the proper union body and notification to the horizontal organisations;
(b) discussion of strike plans between the different vertical unions and the horizontal organisations representing workers at various territorial levels (provincial, regional and national);
(c) in case of divergent opinions by the latter on the opportunity to strike, the vertical union is required to re-examine its decision, yet still remains free to proceed. Following these directives the vertical trade union must develop more precise rules on the matter, particularly regarding the forewarning to consumers, the minimum services to remain functioning, and the gradual implementation of strike decisions (some vertical unions have followed this line).

This initiative on the part of the major unions proved only partially effective, especially since the self-imposed rules do not apply to non-union workers and autonomous unions.

For this reason, the law has intervened to improve the effectiveness of these codes.

Act No. 93 of 1983 (framework law on the public service) provided that the adoption of an adequate code of self-regulation by the unions should be a condition for admittance to the bargaining table by the competent public employers' representative (mostly central or local governments).

But even this rule proved to be insufficient or self-defeating when the independent unions or other groups were so strong as to defy the government decision.

They need to go beyond these partial measures and regulate in a comprehensive way industrial disputes in essential services has been fully recognised by the major confederations themselves. Overcoming a long-standing opposition to legislative intervention, they collaborated to draft a Bill which was approved after a long debate by Parliament (Act No. 146, 14 June 1990). Ten years later, Act 83/2000 was passed aiming at redressing some weaknesses of the previous law, as indicated by practical experience. The amendments are mainly directed to strengthening the powers of the experts commission in charge of monitoring and enforcing the law. Moreover, the main regulations have been made explicitly applicable not only to the strike action of workers, but also to the abstention from work decided by independent workers, professional employees and even small entrepreneurs when they provide essential services: lawyers, entrepreneurs running gas stations, etc.

587. This Act (indeed both) combines the force of law with the principle of self-regulation. First of all, the law puts a general duty of advance notice of ten days for each strike in essential services. Second, it entrusts collective bargaining with the task of establishing the minimum services to be performed by workers (even in case of strike) in a series of sectors which are of general interest and identify as such with an open formula by the Act (from energy to transportation, health services, schools, justice) with the aim of balancing the exercise of the right to strike with fundamental citizen's rights (health, personal safety, education, social assistance, free movement).

The agreements acquire generally binding effects because they have to be implemented by all interested employers in the plant work rules.

A special commission of (nine) experts, designated by Parliament, has the power to evaluate the adequacy of these minimum services and submit a proposal to the parties in case of disagreement. This proposal has been declared to be binding until the parties reach an agreement by Act 83/2000; indeed it has proved to be quite influential. The commission may also arbitrate the issue of minimum services, if asked by the parties but not the merit of the grievance: the award is binding (Article 13(1)).

The Commission activity is mainly focused on promoting agreement among the parties. To this extent it may investigate the case, hear the parties and provide them with opinions and guidelines. Some guidelines of the commission are indeed binding: e.g., the prescriptions which the commission think necessary in order to respect the law, the indications on the timing and duration of the strike, on the measures necessary to reduce damages to the citizens users of the essential services. In case of serious disagreement among the union, or among different groups of employees, on specific rules concerning the minimum services, the commission may organise a referendum among the interested employees.

Until these minima are fixed by agreements the Act of 1990 gave (Article 14) temporary legal effect to the codes of self-regulation but now the codes have lost importance relative to the agreements. The employer is responsible for applying the collective rules on minimum services in order to guarantee the protection of consumers/users (but not in case of lack of agreement).

The enterprises in charge of essential services must inform the consumers of the coming strike and its modalities at least five days in advance. Under Act 146 it frequently happened that strikes already announced were cancelled at the very last minute by the organisers so as to disrupt the service anyhow and frustrate the aim of advance information. Act 83 has reacted to this practice, confirming previous decisions of the commission, and declared illegal the cancellation of the strike after the users had been informed of it, apart from cases in which the cancellation is due to the settlement of the dispute or to a request by the competent public authorities (the prefect, the commission).

If these rules are not obeyed and a danger exists to the interests protected by the law an order can – following a proposal by the commission or even apart from it – be issued by the prefect (for local conflicts) or by the government (in case of national conflicts) ordering the strikers to respect the minimum essential services and, in case of non-compliance, the employer to take the necessary measures to the same effect.

In case of strikes simultaneously affecting various kinds of transportation, the relevant public authorities may order their postponement. This is a solution often adopted by these authorities and also by the commission. In the issuing of the order, the evaluations of the commission on the minimum services are usually followed (even though this is legally not necessary).

588. Non-compliance with the order issued by the prefect or the government is sanctioned with an administrative fine (for each day of strike) to the striking employees and/or the unions and by (public) employers with suspension of their functions. The concept of indispensable services has proved to be the most difficult to evaluate. The commission has issued a considerable body of decisions, evaluating collective agreements and also in substitution of them. In some cases the concept is fixed according to a time dimension. The legal provision is implemented, for instance, by excluding strikes altogether at certain times of the year (e.g., during holiday seasons in the case of the railways and airlines, and during examination periods in the schools) or at certain times of the day (rush hours in urban transport); by stipulating minimum intervals between one strike and the next; by excluding the coincidence of more than one strike within the same sector or in associated sectors (airlines and railways); by imposing a maximum duration for a strike or, inversely, a minimum frequency, even in the event of a strike, at which services must be provided (garbage removal); and by excluding or limiting short strikes (e.g., in the schools they are permitted only at the beginning or at the end of daily teaching sessions).

In other cases the minimum levels of service are fixed according to a quantitative Dimension. Act 82/2000 states that in general the percentage of service to be guaranteed may not on average exceed 50% of the usual and may not involve more than 30% of the employees normally used. But this indication is hardly to be taken literally and the commission evaluation is decisive.

589. The most common form is to fix a percentage of the service (e.g., the number of flights or of trains to be guaranteed). But often the percentage is directly related to the number of employees who must remain at work during the strike: this is the case with most state and local administrations. In both cases the 'quantitative' dimension is combined with 'qualitative' elements. The percentage corresponding to the minimum level of services varies according to sector, ranging from a very high percentage in urban transport to a very low percentage in telecommunications and radio TV, and according to the particular type of service concerned within a given sector: for example, the percentage for flights linking the Italian islands is higher than the percentage for regular flights, and a higher percentage of commuter trains must be guaranteed as compared with that for ordinary trains.

590. Similarly, the percentage of employees required to remain at work varies within the same sector according to their categories and qualifications: e.g., in hospitals, for example, the percentage is much higher for doctors and nurses than for administrative staff. These provisions must be respected by collective agreements in order to be judged positively by the commission. The law itself requires some of them to be inserted into the agreements: e.g., the minimum intervals between strikes (Article 2(2) Act 83/2000).

591. The application of Act 146 has been uneven but has been strengthened by Act 83/2000. A positive effect is that the Acts have contributed to creating significant set of rules and a 'regulation culture' particularly important in a system, like the Italian system, which has been reluctant to institutionalise conflicts. The fact that in most sectors the parties have been able to reach agreements is in itself a positive sign.

A major weakness had to do with the enforcement of the rules. For this reason Act 83 has strengthened the powers of the commission and the sanctions for the violation of the rules.

The violation by the employees is ground for disciplinary measures proportionate to the violation, but short of discharge (Article 4(1) (this limitation has been criticised for reducing the effectiveness of the rules). The sanctions must be applied by the employer of the strikers, following the directives of the commission (Article 4(4)). The violations by the unions of their obligations are sanctioned with the suspension of their rights (time-off work, leaves for union representatives), and possibly with exclusion from the bargaining table. If the unions are not benefiting from these rights they will be sanctioned by an administrative fine imposed on their legal representatives.

The managers in charge of enterprises providing essential services who do not fulfil their obligations (information, adoption of measures necessary to protect consumer's rights) are also sanctioned with administrative fines proportionate to the seriousness of the violation.

The sanctions on both the unions and the managers are decided directly by the commission.

'Substantive rules' have developed considerably – often in a progression which has imposed an increasing number of limits on strike action. The parties have been less capable or willing to agree on procedural rules directed at preventing conflicts and monitoring the application of the agreement in order to control the degree of compliance with the objective stated by the Act.

The greater powers granted to the commission by Act 83 have corrected in part this weakness: the commission binding powers have often prevented illegal conflicts or reduced their negative effects on the consumers.

This imbalance between substantive and procedural rules reflects, however, a general characteristic of Italian industrial relations. The delicate compromise between regulation and consensus pursued by the law would have profited greatly from a strong procedural network directed specifically at preventing strikes and checking, bilaterally, the degree of compliance with the limits of strike action set by the agreements.

Even more important would be to empower the commission to mediate the merit of labour dispute and possibly to arbitrate the most serious cases.

592. Another proposal which has been advanced is to give to the commission the power to order a referendum among all the interested workers prior to strike action. This would be particularly important in order to prevent microconflicts organised by small groups of employees, often against the decision of the major unions and capable of causing serious disruption of the services due to the key role played by these groups (e.g., train conductors, air traffic controllers). Both these proposals have met with strong opposition because the resort to arbitration and to referendum are considered as excessive limitation to the individual right to strike.

In any case procedural improvements may not be per se sufficient to guarantee a good control of strike action in public services. A major difficulty to achieve such a control derives from the weakness of the social parties, namely from the fragmentation of the employers' side and, in particular, of union representation in most sectors, and consequently from inadequate social, rather than institutional, legitimation. It is significant that the effectiveness of the law in controlling strike action has been particularly low in the transport sector where unions and employers fragmentation is more acute.

Counteracting this situation and filling the deficit of legitimation is the primary responsibility of the actors themselves, particularly of the unions; the law can support the process and create favourable preconditions. In Italy some preconditions are particularly urgent: first of all, a clearer definition and reinforcement of the criteria that the various organisations must meet in order to be recognised as representative unions and, consequently, as legitimate actors of the bargaining process. A possible intervention of the law in this sphere would, however, raise other fundamental problems: selection of the criteria for representativeness (majority principle as in the USA, or proportional representation as in most European unions) and definition of the constituent areas over which to measure representativeness. The scope defined for these areas, particularly in the complex sectors of the services and the new professions, is decisive in determining not only the outcome of union representativeness but also its political and social orientation; for example, too narrow a scope for the constituent areas would give to small groups of skilled/professional employees an almost unlimited power not only of self-determination but also embodying a high conflictual deterrent, difficult to reconcile with broader policies of solidarity.

Objectives and Forms of Strikes

593. A major distinction, traditional in Italy as in most countries, is that between the 'economic' and the 'political' strike; the latter has traditionally been held unlawful, because it does not fall within the conventional notion of the strike (abstention from work to further common economic interests). The original definition of the 'economic' strike was (indirectly) based on the target of the concerted pressure: i.e., the subject matter had to be something which could be dealt with by the employer and form the substance of a collective agreement with him. A political strike, that is aimed not at the employer but at the state or at a public institution, would be illegal under civil law (legitimating the employers to discipline the strikers and, theoretically, to recover damages from them) and, in principle, also under criminal law, under Articles 503, 504, 505 (but *see* below).

594. This restrictive notion of the economic strike has been progressively abandoned, following a series of decisions of the Constitutional Court. The two abovementioned decisions (1962 and 1969), and Decision No. 1 of 1974, considered the term 'economic' in a broader sense, as had already been suggested by certain legal commentators, whereby all strikes designed to defend the workers' interests mentioned in Chapter 3 of the Constitution (a very extensive list, including social security, health, public employment policy, public education, etc.) were legitimised. This implied the validity of strike action for basic social reforms, fairly common in recent Italian union practice, directed against the government (central and local), as the only authority capable of satisfying those constitutional interests. A 'pure' political strike, still deemed illegal, would be that undertaken against the government as such or against its general political orientation.

595. After these decisions, an objective distinction between a 'socioeconomic' and 'purely political' strike still exists, but becomes very subtle. According to various commentators such a broadening of the notion of economic strike has indeed confirmed that the objective distinction is untenable, much in the same way as in the present state of our society it is impossible to separate economic and political decisions, since there is in fact no area of economic activity, and consequently of workers' interests, not affected by politics and vice versa.

596. A further step in this direction has been taken with another decision (No. 290 of December 1974) of the Constitutional Court. The court has almost completely eliminated Article 503 of the Penal Code, which incriminates the political strike, holding that even though not protected as a right (under civil law), such a strike still remains penally legitimate as a means of promoting workers' social dignity and full equality in society (Article 3, 2nd paragraph). This conclusion, and the explicit connection with Article 3, 2nd paragraph, are important because they imply the recognition by the supreme constitutional authority that social equality and the full participation of the workers in the social and political life of the country (envisaged by Article 3, 2nd paragraph) are not fully pursued by the duly constituted political machinery, and therefore that the workers and their organisations can legitimately exert direct pressure on them towards those ends (*see also* Decision No. 165 of 1983 on strike to put pressure on public powers).

597. The only limits beyond which Article 503 can still be applied are that the strike should not be designed to 'subvert the constitutional order' or go beyond a legitimate form of pressure', or hinder the free exercise of those rights and institutions in which the people's sovereignty is directly or indirectly expressed. While the first limit is clear (it refers to the extreme case of a revolutionary strike), the second is very uncertain. The strikes for social reforms in the past years have been called precisely in order to put pressure on the duly constituted political and institutional machinery of the state, and yet cannot be held illegal (no one would claim so any longer). Consequently, certain commentators believe that this pressure goes beyond legitimacy so as to hinder the 'free' exercise of this machinery, again only in extreme cases (material occupation of public institutions, pre-revolutionary strikes, etc.), and can be considered a crime under Article 503 only if a specific intention to hinder the institutions in question is proven. The final decision is left to the ordinary courts, but there are so far no decisions.

598. A decision of the Constitutional Court, No. 123 of 1962, according to the latter's basic assumption that the strike could lawfully pursue objectives not obtainable by the direct employer, recognised the legitimacy of sympathetic 'solidarity' strikers, on one condition, namely that there was sufficient community of interest between the two groups of workers concerned, i.e., where, without the two groups joining forces in the struggle, the needs of workers concerned would not be met. This condition is widely criticised because leaving it to the judiciary, and not to the workers themselves, to judge the existence of common interests among them, infringes the constitutional principle of 'collective autonomy' and self-determination of the workers. The Supreme Court considered to be legitimate a strike in solidarity with a union representative who had been dismissed (No. 5053/1979).

599. A set of limits concerning the forms of strike action has been traditionally justified by the so-called doctrine of unreasonable damage, according to which a strike is lawful insofar as the damage caused by it is proportionate to that which would be caused by a straightforward stoppage, i.e., balanced by the non-payment of wages. This doctrine, established since the early 1950s by the Supreme Court, has led to the condemnation on the grounds of illegality under civil law, of the intermittent strike, the *grèves tournantes* or 'rotating strikes', and strikes without notice, whose consequences alter that balance, e.g., causing disorganisation of production, bottlenecks in production, the impossibility of resuming work immediately after the end of the strike and, sometimes, physical damage to equipment and loss of raw materials. The consequences of the civil unlawfulness of these strikes rest on the individual employees as usual. Attempts by some employers to sue the unions for damages, apparently in tort, but on uncertain grounds, have been rejected by the courts.

600. The doctrine of unreasonable damages has been criticised by legal commentators, and more recently by the lower courts, particularly the *pretori*, judging claims under Article 28 of the Workers' Statute. The main reason for this criticism is that no principle of Italian law requires equality of damages for employers and strikers, nor the principles of good faith and diligence in the execution of the labour contract, since they do not operate during a stoppage, which suspends just this execution. On the other hand, the damage is inherent in strike action and therefore constitutionally recognised by Article 40, and it can hardly be expected that the workers, without explicit legal provisions to this effect, use their concerted pressure so as to reduce it. According to these writers and lower courts, the lawfulness of such forms of strike must be judged according to the same basic principles laid down by the Constitutional Court in other respects, i.e., it must be recognised until the stoppages cause serious material damages, threats to safety and deprivation of goods essential to the community protected by the Constitution itself. This criticism has influenced the attitudes of the judiciary, of the superior courts as well, causing them to be cautious and to judge case by case whether or not rotating strikes disrupt production so seriously as to be deemed illegal. The Court of Cassation itself stopped ruling these strikes illegal per se, deciding that the employer can refuse to accept the employees' work and to pay them (whether or not they participate in the conflict) when the continuation of production has become impracticable due to the strike: impracticable in the given circumstances and conditions of production, which the employer is not obliged to change in case of strike.

According to the court, the strike remains illegal when it endangers basic constitutional interests at the same level as the right to strike. The court includes among them not the production but the 'productivity' of the enterprise, which could imply (but this remains to be seen) the illegality of a strike (whatever the form) which seriously imperils the survival of the enterprise in a given economic situation.

§4. Other Forms of Industrial Action

601. Sit-down strikes and occupation of factories (sit-ins) have become quite rare in recent years. They have in common the fact that the strikers remain at the workplace. The first form, however, generally coincides with short stoppages and does not prevent management from running the firm, whereas the second is a much harsher form of action, which brings the entire activity of the firm to a halt, or on occasion continues it against the management's will. Occupation with a sit-in has sometime been adopted as a last resort by the workers, faced with the threatened closure of the enterprise, mainly as a means of backing up their opinion that the enterprise is economically viable. The courts often hold that a sit-down strike becomes an occupation when the workers refuse to obey the employer's order to abandon the premises.

602. Sit-downs and occupations are considered illegal under civil law; the remedy is a possessory action (most clearly in the case of the occupation), which may be enforced by the police, forcing the strikers out of the firm's premises. Under criminal law, occupation, but not the simple sit-in, might be punishable under

Article 508 of the Penal Code, specifically concerning the occupation of land and factory. This provision has been confirmed as constitutional, in spite of its origin, by the Constitutional Court (Decision No. 220 of 1975). Ordinary courts, however, have almost always avoided implementing it, most often interpreting in a narrow sense the condition required by Article 508, and emphasised by the Constitutional Court, that the occupation had the *single* and specific intent of blocking production.

603. It is doubtful whether Article 633 of the Penal Code (trespass of land or building) can apply in these cases, because the norm requires that the trespass aims at profit, which is not the case here. Article 614 of the Penal Code has also been used only rarely in the past; the assumption that the firm's premises be considered the domicile of the employer is contradicted by the Workers' Statute, particularly Article 20, which legitimates the workers' meeting within the firm, even in company time.

604. Slowdowns and non-cooperation (refusal to perform any duties not strictly related to a worker's job) tend to be regarded as illegal by the courts insofar as they represent a partial failure to fulfil in good faith the obligations of the labour contract. It may not always be easy, however, to distinguish this partial failure from behaviour whereby the workers legitimately carry out only the minimum required. The same is true of 'working to rule', and of the collective refusal to work overtime whose legality is controversial. Courts decisions tend however to consider them legitimate. Piece-work strikes, which consist of producing a quantity necessary to earn basic pay, but not enough to earn any incentive pay, have been held lawful by some *judges*, because the workers fulfil their minimum contractual obligations, but has been declared illegal by the Supreme Court, apparently because workers on piece-work are paid more than other workers and are thus required to exercise greater diligence in the performance of their job.

605. The boycott is almost unknown in Italy. A 1969 decision (No. 84) of the Constitutional Court held that Article 507 of the Penal Code, making punishable the crime of boycotting (defined as concerted action to induce others not to conclude labour contracts or to supply materials necessary for work or to buy industrial or agricultural products) is still partially in force, because it protects goods (basically, economic private initiative) protected by the Constitution itself. Article 507 is repealed only insofar as it prohibits boycotts limited to mere propaganda, which are therefore lawful unless they bring excessive pressure to bear (a very unclear restriction indeed).

606. Picketing in Italy is lawful, provided it is peaceful. Non-peaceful picketing is illegal as a violation of the freedom to work, or as amounting to private violence. More passive resistance, even though plainly designed, and effectively so, to prevent persons from entering a plant on strike, such as the formation of a 'human wall', has been held not to be criminal. Italian courts, here again, are in fact somewhat reluctant to apply criminal statutes to this type of action, closely connected with the strike; in the most serious cases it may be sufficient to have the police intervene de facto on other grounds, e.g., disturbance of possessions. A possessory action has been granted to the employer in a few cases, including the physical prevention of goods from entering or being taken out of a plant on strike by peaceful obstruction of the plant's gates.

§5. Lock-Out

607. The Italian Constitution does not mention the lock-out. This silence has always been interpreted as a clear indication that such a form of individual action by the employer is not considered a legal counterpart of the strike, i.e., it is not protected as a right. Here again the Constitution attributes legal significance to the different positions of the employer and the workers in labour and social relations, recognising only the latter's privilege of legally refraining from fulfilling their contractual obligations for reasons of industrial conflict. Such a privilege on the part of the employer could not be recognised by the ordinary legislature because it would contradict the clear indication of the Constitution. Consequently, the legal status of the lock-out under civil law must be derived from the general principles governing the individual labour contract: generally speaking it constitutes a failure on the part of the employer to perform his contract, and more precisely it is *mora accipiendi* on his part. The employer must accordingly reimburse his workers for the time they have lost, paying them their regular wages.

608. The lock-out is also treated differently from the strike under criminal law. The Constitutional Court (in 1960) declared unconstitutional Article 502 of the Penal Code, which prohibited as a crime the bargaining lock-out (like the strike). This conclusion was inferred from Article 39, Constitution (freedom of organisation) on the grounds that such a provision implies the penal freedom (not the right) of industrial action as well. In 1967, however, the same Constitutional Court held that a lock-out in solidarity with other employers or in protest against the government was still a crime under Article 505 of the Penal Code. The decision is consistent with its assumption that the freedom of lock-out descends from Article 39, i.e., a freedom strictly related to labour relations. Accordingly, the same conclusion should hold true also for the lock-out for political reasons (sanctioned by Article 504 of the Penal Code).

609. The legal status of the lock-out has been changed by Article 28 of the Workers' Statute. Several times the courts have held the lock-out not justified by defensive reasons, to be in violation of Article 28, as an anti-strike activity, and have accordingly ordered the employer to reopen the factory and to pay the wages for the period of the closure. In this way a criminal prohibition of the lock-out has been indirectly introduced, because the refusal to obey the order of the judge under Article 28 is a criminal offence (prohibited according to Article 650 of the Penal Code).

610. For these reasons, the bargaining lock-out or offensive lock-outs in general, are hardly ever used by Italian employers. More frequent is the so-called retaliatory lock-out, decided by the individual employer as a counter to an illegal strike, most frequently a 'rotating strike'. Such a form of lock-out has traditionally been regarded as legal by the Italian courts, also under civil law (i.e., legitimating the non-payment of wages), being a reaction to a contractual violation by the employees (by application of the *exceptio inadimpleti contractus*) or a refusal to accept irregular work.

611. This opinion has been questioned by certain commentators, and particularly after 1970, by many lower courts, on different grounds. Most frequently they have denied the basic assumption that 'rotating' strikes and the like are unlawful as such, but have also pointed out that the lock-out is not a proper reaction even to an unlawful strike action, insofar as it denies the possibility of working to all workers, irrespective of their actual desire to participate in the strike. The legitimacy of the lock-out under civil law is recognised in the case of the objective impossibility of continuing work (e.g., a rotating or partial strike forcing groups of non-strikers to be idle for lack of supplies; serious incidents of violence in the course of the strike inducing the employer to shut down the entire plant). In this respect, however, it is not really a lock-out but, rather, the inability to continue operation which is relevant, but the borderline between impossibility and mere difficulty of continuing is not always easy to define. In fact, the distinction has been rendered basically irrelevant by a Superior Court's opinion (*see* paragraph 526) which allows the employers to refuse to continue working whenever it is made impracticable by the strike of the same or of other employees.

612. The employers, too, have begun to follow this direction, i.e., to react to 'rotating' strikes not by a lock-out, but by declaring the inability to use the services of all the workers of the plant whose production is affected by that of the strikers (and thus the non-obligation to pay them). This course of action is generally coupled with the request by the employer of wage integration for time lost by his workers, to the competent social security institution (*see* above paragraphs 203 ff.: this helps generally to reduce the tension deriving from non-payment of wages by the employer). Of course the judgment of the employer concerning his inability to continue operation can be tested before the courts. Indeed this is the most frequent way in which the question of the lawfulness of both 'irregular' strikes and defensive action by the employer is put before the judiciary; but less and less frequently in the last years, given the reduction of strikes in general.

Chapter 7. Prevention and Settlement of Industrial Conflicts

613. The case law produced by the Italian courts on strikes and lock-outs is another indicator of the low level of institutionalisation of industrial conflict in this country. A certain degree of institutionalisation is reached by rules of behaviour, either set unilaterally by the unions or, less often, bargained with the employers, which tend to guarantee some control on the forms of strike action, e.g., an advance notice, the proclamation of the strike, although not recognised law, and the preservation of essential services (*see* above paragraph 517).

614. The conciliation procedures provided for in most national collective agreements are generally effective in settling the majority of conflicts arising out of the application of the agreements themselves and also of the laws governing the individual labour relation. Some improvement and increased formalisation of grievance procedure have been provided for in a few national agreements: but short of arbitration. Arbitration, although recognised and regulated by law as a means of settling disputes of right, is hardly ever provided for in collective agreements and used by the parties (*see* above paragraph 277). One significant example of grievance procedure was that laid down by the IRI protocol (1986) which has been adopted in a few national collective agreements. In each dispute concerning major technological and organisational innovations, the parties promise to suspend any form of direct action (strikes by the trade unions and modifications in the status quo on the part of the employers) until the conciliation procedures laid down in the agreement have been tried out. The agreement also provided for a 'quasi-arbitration' entrusted to a group of experts (three appointed by the trade unions, three by the IRI management) to whom the parties may resort regarding any dispute concerning the protocol. If a state of deadlock is reached among the experts it is then possible to resort to a committee of three 'super-experts' (all ex-presidents of the Constitutional Court). The decision of the experts is only binding within the sphere of the system set up by the protocol itself and is not therefore justiciable in courts. This reflects the caution of this attempt at entrusting a third party with the task of composing a dispute. The formula adopted has proved to be effective on the few occasions in which it has been used; the experts all voted unanimously and their decision was accepted by the parties concerned, thus making it unnecessary to resort to the three super-experts. But no other examples can be found in subsequent agreements.

615. An important role has been played in the past decades by public conciliation and mediation in order to settle both disputes of right (under Act No. 533 of 1973) and conflicts of interest, i.e., to renew collective bargaining. Only the mediation and arbitration activity of labour offices in disputes of right has been recently regulated by law. The intervention of the Ministry of Labour, provincial and regional labour offices, in disputes of interest, rests merely on the vague provision of Act No. 520 of 1955, giving these public officials a general task of conciliation in industrial disputes. Mediation and conciliation by prefects and members of regional government lack any legal basis and rest on the sheer political or personal authority of the mediator. Experts and politicians have recognised the need to reform the system by introducing a more exact definition of the mediators' tasks, by giving greater mediatory powers to the regional councils and, above all, by setting up a specialised body for conciliation and arbitration autonomous and run by a professional staff. So far, none of these proposals has been taken up: but an efficient mediatory apparatus would be one of the major priorities in order to modernise the Italian industrial relations system. One significant step in this direction has been made in the already mentioned Act 146/1990 as modified by Act 83/2000 on strikes in public services. The Act has set up a national evaluation commission on industrial relations composed of experts and entrusted with the task of monitoring the behaviour of the parties during industrial disputes, giving advice over the formulation of codes of conduct, and mediating the more serious disputes. In cases where there is disagreement over the minimum services to be guaranteed during strikes, the parties must ask for the commission's opinion: but the opinion is binding only on the issue of minimum services, not on the merit of the dispute. This limitation has indeed proved to be a factor of weakness.

616. Accepting public conciliation does not imply any duty on the part of the parties involved to refrain from industrial conflict, and does not always interrupt strike action. Similarly, the proposals made by the public mediator, either at the parties' request or at his own initiative, have no binding power on the parties. In the case of disputes of interest such an effect could not, in all probability, be provided for even under ordinary law, being against the constitutionally – recognised collective autonomy of trade unions and employers' associations (Article 39). In practice, refusing these proposals may be very unpopular for the trade unions and/or employers' associations, according to the circumstances, e.g., in the 'hot autumn' of 1969, the industrial employers' association was 'forced' to accept the proposals of the Ministry of Labour for concluding the metalworkers' national collective agreement, although very near to the union's initial requests. Similar 'compelling' proposals have been advanced to solve difficult negotiations impasses on various occasions by the Minister of Labour and sometime also by the Premier office. In these cases the proposal may amount to a sort of informal politically binding arbitration.

617. In Italy there are no emergency laws governing industrial action as such. Some questions dealt with by these laws in other countries are regulated in Italy by provisions and case law concerning strike action in 'essential public services' (*see above*). A similar function can be attributed to certain provisions that relate to emergencies with reference to the social situation rather than to the status of the workers or to the form of industrial action. It has already been mentioned how the powers of prefects and mayors in matters connected with public health and police affairs have been used to order strikers back to work in order to preserve vital needs and goods. The general power of the government to use military forces for public purposes has also been (rarely) used, in order to continue work brought to a halt by strikes, e.g., the running of buses and other transport.

Selected Bibliography

Legislation

Codice del lavoro, G. Fava, P.A. Varesi, IPSOA, 2022.
Codice del lavoro, P. Pucci, F. Toffoletto, IlSole24Ore, Pirola, 2022.
Commentario breve alle leggi sul lavoro, R. De Luca Tamajo, O. Mazzotta, Cedam, Padova, 2022.
Codice del Lavoro, M.T. Carinci, Giuffrè, Milano, 2022.

Law Reports (General)

Foro Italiano (Foro It.) and Repertorio Foro Italiano, Bologna – Rome, 1876ff. Giurisprudenza Italiana (Giur. It.) and Repertorio Giurisprudenza Italiana, Torino, 1862ff.

Special Periodicals (Also Reporting Cases)

Giornale di Diritto del Lavoro e delle Relazioni Industriali, Angeli, Milan, 1978ff.; Diritto delle Relazioni Industriali (Dir. Rel. Ind.), Giuffrè, Milan, 1991ff.; Il Diritto del Lavoro (Dir. Lav.), Rome, 1927ff.; Lavoro e Diritto (Lav. Dir.), il Mulino, Bologna, 1986ff.; Massimario di Giurisprudenza del Lavoro (Mass. Giur. Lav.), Rome, 1928ff.; Orientamenti di Giurisprudenza del Lavoro (Orient. Giur. Lav.), Milan, 1951ff. Rivista di diritto del lavoro (Riv. Dir. Lav.), Giuffrè, Milan, 1948ff.; since 1982. Rivista Italiana di Diritto del Lavoro (Riv. It. Dir. Lav.);. Rivista Giuridica del Lavoro e della Previdenza Sociale (Riv. Giur. Lav.), Rome, 1948ff.

General Periodicals, but of Great Importance to Labour Law

Le nuove leggi civili commentate (N.L.C.C.), Cedam, Padua, 1977ff. Rivista trimestrale di diritto e procedura civile (Riv. Trim. Dir. Proc. Civ.), Giuffrè, Milan, 1947ff.

General Books

Ballestrero M.V., De Simone G., *Diritto del lavoro*, Giappichelli, Torino, 2022.
Candian A., Squeglia M., Tursi A., *Manuale della previdenza complementare*, Giappichelli, Torino, 2022.
Carinci F., De Luca Tamajo R., Tosi P., Treu T., *Diritto Sindacale*, UTET, Turin, 2018 (8th ed.).

Selected Bibliography

Carinci F., De Luca Tamajo R., Tosi P., Treu T., *Il rapporto di lavoro*, UTET, Turin, 2022 (11th ed.).

Cella G.P., Treu T., *Relazioni industriali e contrattazione collettiva*, Mulino, Bologna, 2009.

Cinelli M., *Diritto della previdenza sociale*, Giappichellli, Torino, 2022.

Del Punta R., *Diritto del lavoro*, Giuffrè, 2022 (14th ed.).

Magnani M., *Diritto del lavoro*, Giappichelli, Torino, 2021.

Magnani M., *Diritto sindacale*, Giappichelli, Torino, 2021.

Mazzotta O., *Diritto del Lavoro*, Giuffrè, Milano, 2022.

Persiani M., D'Onghia M., *Diritto della sicurezza sociale*, Giappichelli, Torino, 2022.

Vallebona A., *Istituzioni di diritto del lavoro*, II, *Il rapporto di lavoro*, Cedam, Padua, 2021.

Index

The numbers here refer to paragraph numbers.